Classroom Discourse

Classroom Discourse

The Language of Teaching and Learning

Courtney B. Cazden
Harvard Graduate School of Education

Heinemann
Portsmouth, NH

Heinemann Educational Books, Inc.
70 Court Street   Portsmouth, NH 03801

LONDON   EDINBURGH   MELBOURNE   AUCKLAND
SINGAPORE   NEW DELHI   IBADAN   NAIROBI
JOHANNESBURG   KINGSTON   PORT OF SPAIN

The following have generously given permission to use quotations from copyrighted works:

Chapter 2: From C. B. Cazden, "What is sharing time for?", *Language Arts* 62 (1985), pp. 182–88. Reprinted by permission of the publisher.

Figure 2–1: "Puppy–2" from J. P. Gee, "The narrativization of experience in the oral style," *Journal of Education* 167 (1985), pp. 34–35. Reprinted by permission of the publisher.

Figure 3–1: Transcription of birthplaces from initiation 5 through initiation 34. Reprinted by permission of Hugh Mehan.

Figures 3–2 and 3–3: From H. Mehan, *Learning Lessons* (Cambridge, MA: Harvard University Press, 1979), Figures 2.1 and 2.2, pp. 73–74. Reprinted by permission of the publisher.

Figure 3–4: From J. McH. Sinclair and R. M. Coulthard, *Towards an Analysis of Discourse: The English Used by Teachers and Pupils* (London: Oxford University Press, 1975), p. 31. Reprinted by permission of the publisher.

Chapter 4: Excerpt from transcript of history class in J. T. Dillon, *Teaching and the Art of Questioning* (Bloomington, IN: Phi Delta Kappa Educational Foundation, 1983), pp. 18–19. Reprinted by permission of the publisher.

Chapter 4: Quotation from S. B. Heath, "Questioning at home and at school," in G. Spindler (ed.), *Doing the Ethnography of Schooling* (New York: Holt, Rinehart & Winston, 1982), pp. 124–25. Reprinted by permission of the publisher.

Chapter 4: Quotation from Paul Naso, journal entry for March 4, 1985. Reprinted by permission of the author.

Table 5–1: From R. L. Allington, "Teacher interruption behaviors during primary grade oral reading," *Journal of Educational Psychology* 72 (1980), pp. 371–77 (Table 2–4). Copyright 1980 by the American Psychological Association. Reprinted by permission of the author.

Figure 6–1: From D. P. Pearson and M. C. Gallagher, "The instruction of reading comprehension," *Contemporary Educational Psychology* 8 (1983), p. 337. Reprinted by permission.
(Acknowledgments continue on p. 219.)

Library of Congress Cataloging-in-Publication Data

Cazden, Courtney B.
    Classroom discourse.

    Bibliography: p.
    Includes index.
    1. Communication in education.   2. Interaction analysis in education.   3. Verbal behavior.   4. Teacher-student relationships.   I. Title.
LB1033.C34   1988   371.1'022   87-11874
ISBN 0-435-08445-3

Designed by Marie McAdam.
Printed in the United States of America.
10   9   8   7   6   5   4   3   2   1

For my grandchildren:
Hannah, David, and Sarah
and
For colleagues around the world
who are working to improve the quality of
life and education for all children

Contents

Chapter 1

Introduction

My interest in the study of classroom discourse comes from my experience as a primary-school teacher as well as a university researcher. Before becoming a graduate student and then a university professor, I had been a primary teacher for nine years in the 1940s and 1950s. Then, in the fall of 1974, I took leave from my job at the Harvard Graduate School of Education to become again, for one year, a fully certified, full-time public-school teacher of young children. After thirteen years in a university, it was time to go back to children, to try to put into practice some of the ideas about child language and education that I had been teaching and writing about,[1] and to rethink questions for future research.

I left Cambridge to teach in San Diego in order to make possible a collaboration with sociologist Hugh ("Bud") Mehan. Bud and I had met in Berkeley in 1968, when we were both participants in an interdisciplinary summer-long seminar, "Language, Society, and the Child." We kept in touch, and when I decided to go back to a primary classroom and wanted someone there looking over my shoulder, I knew Bud would be the ideal observer. A couple of years and many negotiations later, that collaboration came to pass.

I taught in a section of San Diego that was one of the lowest in the city in income and school achievement, a community that was then about evenly divided between black and Chicano families. I had twenty-five black and Mexican-American children in a combined first, second, and third grade. They will appear in this book—Prenda, Caroline, Wallace, Greg, Veronica, and others.[2]

. Also in 1974, just as I was setting off for San Diego, the National Institute of Education assembled a set of panels to suggest an agenda for research on teaching. One panel, which I chaired, was on teaching as a linguistic process in a cultural setting. British researcher Douglas Barnes wrote a paper for that conference (though at the last moment he was unable to attend). It said in part:

> The study of linguistic phenomena in school settings should seek to answer educational questions. We are interested in linguistic forms only insofar as through them we can gain insight into the social events of the classroom and thereby into the understandings which students achieve. Our interest is in the social contexts of cognition: speech unites the cognitive and the social. The actual (as opposed to the intended) curriculum consists in the meanings enacted or realized by a particular teacher and class. In order to learn, students must use what they already know so as to give meaning to what the teacher presents to them. Speech makes available to reflection the processes by which they relate new knowledge to old. But this possibility depends on the social relationships, the communication system, which the teacher sets up.[3]

The study of classroom discourse is the study of that communication system.

Any social institution can be considered a communication system. In the words of one linguist, Michael Halliday, "Its very existence implies that communication takes place within it; there will be sharing of experience, expression of social solidarity, decision-making and planning, and, if it is a hierarchical institution, forms of verbal control, transmission of orders, and the like."[4] But while other institutions such as hospitals serve their clients in nonlinguistic ways, the basic purpose of school is achieved through communication.

Several features of educational institutions make communication so central. First, spoken language is the medium by which much teaching takes place, and in which students demonstrate to teachers much of what they have learned. As the quotation from Barnes says so profoundly, through the actual curriculum as enacted between teacher and students, "speech unites the cognitive and the social."

Second, classrooms are among the most crowded human environments. Few adults spend as many hours per day in such crowded conditions. Classrooms are similar in this respect to restaurants and buses or subways. But in such places simultaneous autonomous conversations are normal, whereas in classrooms one person, the teacher, is responsible for controlling all the talk that occurs while class is officially in session—controlling not just negatively, as a traffic policeman does to avoid collisions, but also positively, to enhance the purposes of education.

3) Third, and perhaps least obviously, spoken language is an important part of the identities of all the participants. Variation in ways of speaking is a universal fact of social life. Schools are the first large institution to which children come from their families and home neighborhoods and in which they are expected to participate individually and publicly (in contrast, for example, to simply sitting and standing at appropriate times and joining in prayers and hymns at church). Especially in this period of school consolidation and desegregation, and continuing migration across state and national borders, classrooms usually include people—adults and children—from different linguistic backgrounds. Differences in how something is said, and even when, can be matters of only temporary adjustment, or they can seriously impair effective teaching and accurate evaluation. For all these reasons, it is essential to consider the classroom communication system as a problematic medium that cannot be ignored as transparent by anyone interested in teaching and learning.

Readers familiar with linguistics will recognize in these three features of classroom life—the language of curriculum, the language of control, and the language of personal identity—the tripartite core of all categorizations of language functions:

- The communication of propositional information (also termed the referential, cognitive, or ideational function).
- The establishment and maintenance of social relationships.
- The expression of the speaker's identity and attitudes.

We can call these the propositional, social, and expressive functions, for short.

More will be said throughout this book about all three functions. But it is important to note at the outset that they are functions of language, not functions of separate utterances. Any one utterance can be, and usually is, multifunctional. In each and every utterance, speech truly unites the cognitive and the social.

The study of classroom discourse is thus a kind of applied linguistics—the study of situated language use in one social setting. I hope that this study will answer important educational questions. Three questions in particular will be prominent in the chapters that follow:

- How do patterns of language use affect what counts as "knowledge," and what occurs as learning?
- How do these patterns affect the equality, or inequality, of students' educational opportunities?

- What communicative competence do these patterns presume and/or foster?

This book discusses research—my own and others'—that attempts to answer these questions. Because my own teaching experience has been in the primary grades, my research has focused there too. The book begins, in chapters 2 and 3, with the talk of primary-school children and their teachers. But in later chapters, examples are drawn from classrooms at other levels, from preschool through postsecondary education. Most of the research describes classrooms in the United States and England, but wherever possible I have included examples and commentary from other countries.[5]

I have tried to write both for people who see themselves primarily as teachers (or teacher educators and supervisors) and for those who see themselves primarily as researchers. Notes at the end of each chapter give references, and sometimes additional comments (addressed mostly to researchers). The entire book can be read without referring to the notes at all.

The task for both teachers and researchers is to make the usually transparent medium of classroom discourse the object of focal attention. Because of the importance of language to the goals of schools, some aspects of language in education are subject to explicit language planning—such as decisions about whether to have some kind of bilingual education, which language tests to administer, and which language competencies to require for professional employment.

But other aspects of language in education are the result of nondeliberate, usually nonconscious choice at the moment of use. It is these nonconscious aspects of language use in the classroom that this book is about.

NOTES

[1]Cazden 1972; and Cazden, John, and Hymes 1972.
[2]Mehan 1979 reports his analyses; Cazden 1976 is my personal account.
[3]National Institute of Education 1974, 1.
[4]Halliday 1978, 230–231.
[5]Cazden 1986 details the recent history of research on classroom discourse; and Cazden (in press b) discusses assumptions of various research perspectives. In my own research, I am grateful for past support from the Ford Foundation, Carnegie Foundation, Spencer Foundation, and the National Institute of Education. And to Sarah Michaels, special thanks for detailed comments on these chapters, and for colleagueship during the past six years.

Section I

Talk with the Teacher

Chapter 2

Sharing Time

A classroom day divides easily into events with familiar labels: math lesson, reading group, and so on. I start with one such event, sharing time—sometimes called show and tell, or news—often the first "official" event of the day in kindergarten and first-grade classrooms.

Sharing time is organized to answer the teacher's seemingly ordinary question: "Who has something to tell us this morning?" The question, in whatever version, is an invitation to the children, a request to them to "share" a narrative of personal experience about their out-of-school lives. To the children, and even to a casual observer, it may sound like questions heard often at home.

Here is one first grader's story and the reaction of his teacher (T):

Paper Boat

Jerry: Ummmm. [Pause] Two days ago, ummm, my father and my father's friend were doin' somethin' over the other side and my sister wanted, uhhh, my father's friend to make her a little boat outta paper 'n' the paper was too little. He used his dollar and, umm, my sister un-doed it and we, ah, bought my father and my mother Christmas presents.

T: A man made a boat out of a dollar bill for you?!! Wow! That's pretty expensive paper to use![1]

The participation structure of sharing time varies from classroom to classroom, but only in minor details. Someone, usually the teacher, calls on children to speak; sharers usually come to the front of the room, often standing at the teacher's side; the teacher comments at the end, as Jerry's teacher did, and sometimes also interpolates questions into the child's narration; sometimes other children are invited to comment or question. In some classrooms, there are limitations on possible topics: no retelling the plot of movies or TV programs, for example; and describing an object such as a birthday present or pair of new shoes may be allowed only on certain days. Sharing time is thus a true speech event in the technical sense: recurring, bounded with a clear beginning and end, with consistent rules for participation in each classroom.

Sharing time is of special interest for several reasons. First, it may be the only opportunity during official classroom air time for children to create their own oral texts: to give more than a short answer to the teacher's questions, and to speak on a self-chosen topic that does not have to meet criteria of relevance to previous discourse. Second, one purpose of sharing time is to allow a sharing of out-of-school experiences, and it is often the only time when they are considered relevant in school. Otherwise, talking to the teacher about personal experiences may be restricted to transition moments such as before school or while waiting in line; in fact, a teacher shift from listening to not listening to such stories is a clear marker that school has officially begun: "I can't listen now, Sarah, we have to get started." (That is, we have to enter a different discourse world in which what you're talking about, no matter how important to you, is out of bounds.) Third, in addition to sharing time's unique features in expected length and topic of children's speech, it is of interest as a context for the production of narratives of personal experience—perhaps the most universal kind of text.

Given these features of what might seem a routine and unimportant part of the school day, important questions can be raised. What kind of narratives do children tell, and are there differences in the texts that seem related to different home backgrounds? How do teachers respond and why? In a series of studies begun by Sarah Michaels in California, and which we have continued together in the Boston area, we have tried to answer these questions.[2]

CHILDREN'S NARRATIVES

Formulaic features of the children's narratives indicate that sharing time is a unique event not only for researchers but also for the children themselves. Typically, the narratives begin with information about time, such as "two days ago" in "Paper Boat"; next, the place is explained if it is somewhere other than home. Then the key agent is introduced and the action begins. Here are some typical opening lines:

- "At Thanksgiving, when I went to my grandma and grandpa's, we . . ."
- "Yesterday, me and my father went out for a sundae, and then we came home and we . . ."
- "Last Christmas, my mom . . ."
- "When I slept over my mother's, the cat—in the middle of the night—she . . ."
- "When we went down the Cape once, my mother . . ."
- "Last Friday, my mother and grandmother went out, and they . . ."
- "Yesterday, I was walking and this man was walking beside me, and we . . ."

Another marker of sharing-time narratives is a rising intonation that will be familiar to primary-school teachers. This "sharing intonation" (henceforth SI) occurs in no other classroom activity. In its most pronounced form, SI consists of a high, rising tone with an elongated vowel, stretching over the last word or two of a tone group (an unbroken intonational phrase). Shuy suggests that while this intonation pattern is "unnatural for mature narration . . . it seems to provide evidence that the speaker is aware of potential interruption and that by keeping the intonation contours rising he will prevent interruption."[3]

Here are two examples, with SI marked by a rising arrow:[4]

Well / last night

my father

he was at work /

Well when I slep' over my mother's /

the cat /

in the middle of the night she w— /

she went under the covers /

There are differences among the stories too. Most striking is the difference between what we have come to call topic-centered and episodic narratives. "Paper Boat" is topic centered. The next two narratives are also topic centered, each focused on a single object or event. (The titles for all narratives are ours, for easier reference.)

Transcription conventions vary from researcher to researcher, depending on the focus of the research. Michaels uses a single slash (/) to represent the oral equivalent of a comma, signaling more to come, and a double slash (//) to represent the equivalent of a period, a full stop. To get a richer sense of the narratives as spoken, try reading the transcriptions out loud.[5]

Stamp Pad

Evan: Last Christmas /
   my mom / she / I was telling my mom /
   that I want a stamp pad /
   and so / on Christmas / I mean on my birthday /
   she got / a stamp pad / and a stamp for me / /
T: OK let's try it out / /

A Hundred Dollars

Carl: Well / last night / my father was at work /
   he / every Thursday night they have this thing /
   that everybody has this dollar /
   and it makes up to a hundred dollars /
   and my / and you've gotta pick this name out /
   and my father's name got picked /
   so he won a thousand dollars / / a hundred dollars / /
T: Tell us what he's gonna do with it / /
Child leader: Donald [*Calling on next child*]
T: Wait a minute / / He's gonna tell us what he's /
   what his father's gonna do with it / /
Carl: He's gonna pay bills / /

Episodic stories are usually longer and always include shifting scenes. Here is the first part of Leona's long story about her puppy, until T's first question, with scene changes indicated by paragraph spacing after lines 5, 12, 17, and 21. The vertical bracket joining lines 30 and 31 indicates simultaneous speech.

My Puppy

Leona: Last / last / yesterday / when / my father / in the morning /	1
and he / there was a hook / on the top of the stairway /	2
and my father was pickin' me up / and I got stuck on the hook /	3
up there / and I hadn't had breakfast /	4
he wouldn't take me down until I finished all my breakfast	5
'cause I didn't like oatmeal either / /	
and then my puppy came / he was asleep / and he was— he was /	6
he tried to get up / and he ripped my pants / and he dropped the	7
oatmeal all over him /	

and / and my father came / and he said "did you eat all the   8
oatmeal?"
he said "where's the bowl?" / /   9
he said "I think the do—" / I said "I think the dog took it" / /   10
"well / I think I'll have to make another can" / /   11
and so I didn't leave till seven / and I took the bus/ /   12

and / my puppy / he always be followin' me /   13
and he said / my father said / "he—you can't go" / /   14
and he followed me all the way to the bus stop /   15
and I hadda go all the way back / by that time it was seven   16
thirty / /
and then he kept followin' me back and forth and I hadda keep   17
comin' back / /

and he always be following' me when I go everywhere / /   18
he wants to go to the store / and only he could not go to places /   19
where / we could go like / to / like / t' the stores /   20
he could go but he have to be chained up / /   21

and we took him to the emergency / and see what was wrong   22
with him /
and he got a shot and then he was cryin' /   23
and la—last yesterday / and / now / they put him asleep /   24
and / he's still in the hospital / and th—the doctor said that   25
he hasta /
he got a shot because he / he was / he was nervous /   26
about my home that I had / and he / and he could still stay but /   27
he thought he wasn't gonna to a—/ he thought he wasn't gonna be   28
able to let him go / /
    ⌈ he's—   29

T: ⌊ Who's in the hospital Leona?   30

Michaels, in her original research in California, found that white
children were more apt to tell topic-centered narratives, while black
children—especially black girls—were more apt to tell episodic narratives, and we found that difference again in the Boston area. In one
classroom, for example, topic-centered stories included 96 percent of the
white children's narratives but only 34 percent of the black children's
narratives, and an even smaller percentage—27 percent—of those told
by black girls. This difference in thematic structure is accompanied by
differences in frequency and use of the formulaic features. The topic-
centered stories have only one temporal marker, whereas the episodic
stories have from three to nine. In the topic-centered stories, 60 to 80
percent of the tonal groups end with SI, whereas only 37 percent of the
tonal groups in the episodic stories do. Functionally, SI seems to mark

continuity within the single episode of the topic-centered stories, but it is more apt to mark shifts in time and place in the episodic stories.

We have no explanation for these differences in narrative style, and are not even sure of the ethnic labels. We originally identified them as black-white differences simply because that aspect of the speaker's identity was obvious, and we could find no descriptions of sharing-time narratives of children from other ethnic groups—Hispanic, Native American, white Appalachian, and so on. We have since found related descriptions of black rhetorical style. For example, Afro-American scholar Gineva Smitherman speaks of black adult narrative style as "concrete narrative . . . [whose] meandering away from the 'point' takes the listener on episodic journeys."[6]

Since this research was completed, I have read a similar description of Native American writing by Gail Martin, a student at the Bread Loaf School of English, writing about her work as teacher-researcher with Arapaho students in Wyoming:

> One of our major concerns was that many of the stories children wrote didn't seem to "go anywhere." The stories just ambled along with no definite start or finish, no climaxes or conclusions. I decided to ask Pius Moss [the school elder] about these stories, since he is a master Arapaho storyteller himself. I learned about a distinctive difference between Arapaho stories and stories I was accustomed to hearing, reading, and telling. Pius Moss explained that Arapaho stories are not written down, they're told in what we might call serial form, continued night after night. A "good" story is one that lasts seven nights. . . .
>
> When I asked Pius Moss why Arapaho stories never seem to have an "ending," he answered that there is no ending to life, and stories are about Arapaho life, so there is no need for a conclusion. My colleagues and I talked about what Pius had said, and we decided that we would encourage our students to choose whichever type of story they wished to write: we would try to listen and read in appropriate ways.[7]

In classrooms, as in American life generally, ethnicity is confounded with social class and with experience with what is loosely referred to as oral versus literate cultures. But what seems similar about black and Arapaho stories is probably only their contrast with the topic-centered stories told primarily by white, middle-class children. With detailed analyses of stories by children from diverse cultures, I am sure the category now labeled "episodic" will become more finely differentiated.[8]

THE TEACHER'S RESPONSE

In informal conversation, storytelling places special obligations on the audience. As one linguist puts it:

> We waive our right to preempt the floor until the storyteller himself offers to give it up (with his narrative coda). . . . We can, of course, interrupt to request clarification or details, but we do not thereby put an end to the storyteller's turn. More than nearly any other speech act, I believe, narratives, once begun, are immune to control by other participants in a conversation.[9]

But in school, sharing-time narratives—although about out-of-school experiences and unrelated to the curriculum—are not immune to control by another participant.

Most teachers make some response to each narrative. Many of the responses we observed can be placed along a dimension of the extent to which teacher and child share a sense of appropriate topic and appropriate way to tell about it. At one end is Jerry's teacher's enthusiastic appreciation of "Paper Boat": "A man made a boat out of a dollar bill for you? Wow! That's pretty expensive paper to use!"

At the other end is another teacher's negative reaction to "Deena's Day." In this transcription, vertical brackets indicate simultaneous speech.

Deena's Day

Deena: I went to the beach Sunday /
and / to McDonalds / and to the park /
and I got this for my / birthday / / [*holds up purse*]
my mother bought it for me /
and I had two dollars for my birthday /
and I put it in here /
and I went to where my friend / named Gigi /
I went over to my grandmother's house with her /
and she was on my back /
and I / and we was walking around / by my house /
and she was HEAVY / /
she ⌈was in the sixth or seventh grade / /
T: ⌊OK I'm going to stop you / / I want you to talk about things that
are really really very important / / that's important to you but can you
tell us things that are sort of different / / can you do that? / / . . .

Jerry's teacher expresses a similar evaluation to one of Jerry's classmates: "If you have something that was special for you, that you would like to share with us, but we don't want to hear about TV shows and regular things that happened."

Between these extremes are responses that can be grouped into four categories. First are cases where the teacher has clearly understood the story and simply comments or asks a question for further information. After "Stamp Pad," the teacher suggests, "OK, let's try it out"; and after "A Hundred Dollars," the teacher asks Carl to "tell us what he's gonna do with it."

A second kind of response leads to an extended collaboration between questioning teacher and reporting child that results in a more complete story about an object or event than the child would have produced alone. Here is a teacher-student dialogue, "Making Candles":

Making Candles

Mindy: When I was in day camp / we made these candles / /

T: You made them?

Mindy: And I—I tried it with different colors / with both of them but
/ one just came out / this one just came out blue /
and I don't know / what this color is / /

T: That's neat-o / / Tell the kids how you do it from the very start
Pretend we don't know a thing about candles / /
OK / / What did you do first? / / What did you use? / /
Flour? / /

Mindy: There's some hot wax / some real hot wax /
that you / just take a string / and tie a knot in it / /
and dip the string in the wax / /

T: What makes it have a shape? / /

Mindy: You just shape it / /

T: Oh you shaped it with your hand / / mm / /

Mindy: But you have / first you have to stick it into the wax /
and then water / and then keep doing that until it gets to the
size you want it / /

T: OK / / who knows what the string is for? / / . . .

When Mindy's teacher says, "Tell the kids how you do it from the very start. Pretend we don't know a thing about candles," she seems to be speaking from an implicit model of literate discourse. With the help of questions asked by the teacher (or in some classrooms by other children), sharers are often encouraged to be clear and precise, and put more and more information into words, rather than relying on shared background knowledge (here, about candle making) or contextual cues (here, the candles that Mindy is holding) to communicate part of the intended message. If teachers see sharing time as an opportunity for young children not only to share out-of-school experiences with the whole class, but also to construct an oral text that is as similar as possible to a written composition, then sharing time can be, as Michaels calls it, an "oral preparation for literacy."

A third response is a question that expresses the teacher's perplexity, her inability to keep track of the thread of the story as the child tells it. An example is the teacher's question about Leona's puppy, "Who's in the hospital, Leona?" One day, we asked Leona's teacher about her problems in understanding sharing-time stories. She answered from her experiences as a mother as well as a teacher:

> It's confusing when you listen, because their time frame is not the same as ours. When my son was six, he would suddenly talk about something from months earlier, and I could understand because I'd been there; I could make the connection. It's different in class. It's hard to make the connection with so many different individuals.

A fourth and last kind of response is a question by the teacher that shifts the topic to one the teacher either understands better or values more highly. After the teacher's request for information about who's in the hospital, Leona explains that her puppy is there because he's "vicious." This leads to a discussion of the meaning of "vicious" and then a retelling by Leona of the hospital episode, ending with, "I'll tell you Monday what happened." (She was telling the story on a Friday.) The teacher, perhaps still not understanding that Leona's concern for her puppy is literally a matter of life or death, ends with a comment on dogs' need for house training.

Similarly, Deena's teacher follows her interruption of "Deena's Day" with a question about the scene of Deena's first sentence, the beach:

T: That's important to you but tell us things that are sort of
different / /
Can you do that? / / and tell us what beach you went to over the
weekend / /

Deena: I went to um—

T: Alameda Beach?

Deena: Yeah / /

T: That's ⌈nice there huh? / /
Deena:　　⌊I went there two times / /

T: That's very nice / / I like it there / / thank you Deena / /

This topical shift to the beach could have two motivations that, in this case, converge. The beach is the scene mentioned in Deena's first sentence and thus might be considered by the teacher as the one that should have been sustained throughout; alternatively, going to the beach may represent the kind of familiar scenario that the teacher finds either more appropriate or just more comprehensible than activities among family or friends—such as picking up an older and larger child—that, no matter how important to the child, seem to the teacher more ordinary or even trivial.

Here is another teacher's attempt to change the focus of the child's narrative, not because of any lack of comprehension but because of a conflict between child and teacher about what constitutes the highlights of a family outing:

Old Ironsides

Nancy: I went to Old Ironsides at the ocean.

[*Led by a series of teacher questions, Nancy explains that Old Ironsides is a boat and that it's old. The teacher herself offers the real name,* The Constitution. *Then Nancy tries to shift the focus of her story.*]

Nancy: We also spent our dollars and we went to another big shop.

T: Mm. 'N' what did you learn about Old Ironsides? [*Led by teacher questions, Nancy supplies more information about the furnishings inside and the costumes of the guides, and then tries to shift focus again.*]

Nancy: I also went to a fancy restaurant.

T: Haha! Very good!

Nancy: And I had a hamburger, french fries, lettuce and a—

T: OK. All right, what's—Arthur's been waiting and then Paula, OK?[10]

Teacher responses can also be categorized according to their relevance to the child's story. As Karen Tracy points out, a conversational maxim to "be relevant" "does not inform us what 'relevant' means. Is a relevant remark one that responds to anything in the immediately prior discourse or is it limited in some way? What criteria are used for judging relevancy?"[11] In a series of experiments, Tracy presented conversational stories to adult subjects and asked them to evaluate, or to produce, responses. She found that if the story was comprehensible, the preferred response was to the main idea, the point of the story. In the sharing-time stories, T's responses to "Paper Boat," "Stamp Pad," and "A Hundred Dollars" can be put in this category. But when stories were harder to understand, Tracy found that listeners were more apt to respond, with a query or comment about some detail of a narrated event, as T did to "Leona's Puppy," or with some vague remark or no response at all.

Not present in Tracy's protocols were responses that focused on vocabulary, such as "vicious"; or that asked questions about details even when the point was clear, as in "Making Candles"; or that rejected the child's story altogether, as in "Deena's Day" or "Old Ironsides." Such responses distinguish classroom discourse from conversation, and make obvious one objective of education in many classrooms: to inculcate in learners at the beginning of their school career some new criteria for appropriate ways of talking in school, and even appropriate topics for that talk as well.

In both the California and Boston-area classrooms, the teacher's lack of comprehension and appreciation was especially marked for the episodic stories told by black children. We wondered if this could be due to a cultural mismatch between the narrative themes and styles of the children and the knowledge and expectations of their white teachers. We could not answer this question from our observational studies alone, because in the natural situation, each child was responded to by only one teacher. Even if we had observed a black teacher, we could never have observed both a black and a white teacher responding to the same child.

In order to explore further a possible ethnic basis for the teachers' responses, we conducted a small experiment in which mimicked versions of children's topic-centered and episodic narratives were played to five black and seven white adult informants, all students at the Harvard Graduate School of Education. The mimicked versions, all recorded by a single speaker, maintained the child's rhythm and intonation contours, while changing black dialect grammatical features to Standard English, and possible social-class indicators (such as "down the Cape") to more neutral ones (such as "at the beach"). The adult informants were asked to comment on the well-formedness of the story, and make evaluative comments as to the probable academic success of the child narrator.[12]

The number of black informants was small, but the responses of the two groups were strikingly different. White adults were much more likely to find the episodic stories hard to follow, and they were much more likely to infer that the narrator was a low-achieving student. Black adults were more likely to evaluate positively both topic-centered and episodic stories, noticing differences but appreciating both.

To show their contrasting responses in more detail, here is the story, also told by Leona, that elicited the most divergent responses, followed first by Michaels's analysis and then by a summary of the informants' responses. In line 11, "were" has been substituted for the original "was," and spaces have been inserted to separate the three episodes.

At Grandmother's

Leona: On George Washington's birthday /	1
I'm goin' / ice / my grandmother /	2
we never / haven't seen her since a long time /	3
and / and she lives right near us /	4
and / she's / and she's gonna /	5
I'm gonna spend the night over her house /	6
and / every weekend / she comes to take me /	7
like on Saturdays and Sundays / away / from home	8
and I spend the night over her house /	9

and one day I spoiled her dinner /	10
and we were having / we were /	11
she paid ten dollars /	12
and I got eggs / and stuff /	13
and I didn't even eat anything / /	14

Leona begins with a temporal indicator and a future-tense orientation, using SI (sharing intonation) contours. She marks the end of this segment with increased tempo in line 6, "I'm gonna spend the night over her house." The second segment begins with a shift in temporal perspective, from the future, "on George Washington's birthday," to the iterative "and every weekend," with a resumption of SI contours. This segment ends with increased tempo in line 9, a lexical and prosodic repetition of line 6. Played side by side, these two phrases are indistinguishable, an implicit signal of the association across these segments. What they have in common is the fact that on both the holiday and the weekend, Leona spends the night at her grandmother's. The third segment shifts to a particular occasion, a dinner one day, and a particular event in the relationship with the grandmother. The closing is marked by staccato rhythm and falling tones.

In responding to the mimicked version of this story, white adults were uniformly negative, with comments such as "terrible story, incoherent." "Not a story at all in the sense of describing something that happened." "This kid hops from one thing to the next." When asked to make a judgment about this child's probable academic standing, they without exception rated her below children who told topic-centered accounts, saying, for example, "This child might have trouble reading if she doesn't understand what constitutes a story." Some referred to "language problems" that affect school achievement, and others suggested that "family problems" or "emotional problems" might hold this child back.

The black adults reacted very differently, finding this story well formed, easy to understand, and interesting, "with lots of detail and description." Three selected it as the best story of the five they had heard. All five commented on the "shifts" and "associations," or the "nonlinear" quality of the story, but none appeared to be disoriented by them. Two expanded on what the child meant, explaining that the holiday is just like the weekend because it's an occasion when she gets to visit her grandmother, who is an important figure in her life. One informant commented that if you didn't make this inference, you missed the entire point of the story (which was the case with the white adults). In addition, all but one of the black adults rated the child as highly verbal, very bright, and/or successful in school.

A few months after we conducted this experiment, I spent several months in New Zealand and played the experimental tape to three groups of white ("Pakeha") teachers, graduate students, and speech therapists. The responses were very similar to those of the white informants at Harvard; again, "At Grandmother's" was considered very hard to follow. One New Zealand teacher, however, evaluated it as our black U.S. informants had done. In her words, it was "the best in terms of rich description of grandparent as well as a twist of humor." She had not had as much multicultural teaching experience as others in the New Zealand group, and certainly none with American black children; so her unusual response seemed more due to her general sensitivity to the underlying meanings the child was trying to express.

POSSIBLE EXPLANATIONS OF THE ADULT RESPONSES

How can we explain these responses of both the classroom teachers and our white adult informants? Aspects of form and topic may be important, as well as cultural differences in both.

Aspects of Form

Episodic stories are, almost by definition, longer than topic-centered ones. Sheer length alone can create problems for the classroom teacher, whose attention is inevitably divided between listening to the child who is speaking and thinking (even worrying) about the rest of the class: Is their attention being maintained? How many more children will want a turn? What time is it getting to be anyway?

Also by definition, episodic stories have shifting scenes and often a larger cast of characters. Both of these features pose increased problems for their young narrators in making time relationships and pronoun reference clear. For example, "My Puppy" has three same-sex characters—father, puppy, and doctor—and we know from other research that this poses problems for young writers throughout the elementary-school years.[13] Moreover, the increased cognitive load caused by these complex tasks may cause a greater incidence of false starts, repeated or corrected words, and other disfluencies that in turn increase the comprehension problems of the listener.

The one explanation of the comprehension problems the episodic narratives presented to the white teachers that we have been able to eliminate is an explanation of egocentricity on the part of the child narrators. Both white and black children, including our prototypical episodic narrators—Deena in California and Leona in the Boston area

—include in their stories spontaneous corrections that demonstrate both their syntactic competence and their metalinguistic concern for their listeners.

Structurally, the repairs are of two kinds. One kind consists of lexical replacements. For example:

- From an inaccurate noun to a more accurate nominalization: in re-telling the movie *ET*, Joe—evidently not knowing the word *ramp*—spontaneously corrects "ship" to "thing that you walk on up."
- From an ambiguous anaphoric pronoun to an unambiguous noun: in line 13 of "My Puppy," Leona pronominalizes "puppy" to "he"; then, in line 14 (presumably realizing that she faces the problem of two same-sex characters), she repairs the next "he" to the full nom-inal, "my father."
- From indirect (*he*) to direct (quoted) discourse (*you*): as in line 15 of "My Puppy," "My father said / um / he—'You can't go.' "

A second kind of repair, not previously noticed in children's speech, we call "bracketing": the insertion of explanatory material, as if in brack-ets or parentheses, in the middle of an otherwise intact sentence. In the beginning of "My Puppy," lines 2–3, Leona interrupts the first sentence, in which her father is the agent of the action, to explain about the hook. Here are those two lines with the words immediately preceding and following the bracketed material italicized:

and *he* / there was a hook / on the top of the stairway /
and my father was pickin' me up / and I got stuck on the hook

The stories of our other prototypical episodic narrator, Deena, also include bracketing. Here's the first episode of her story about her tooth. Again, the words just before and after the bracketing are italicized:

Tooth Story
Deena: Today I gon' put my tooth under my pillow /
   and and I been putting my tooth under my pillow every night /
   and I st—and I was getting money /
   and still / have my tooth / /
T: You still have your tooth? / / well maybe the fairy will come get
   it tonight / stick it under there / / . . .

Although putting teeth under the pillow is a familiar script, the teacher misses the child's intended meaning. While the child's implicit evalu-ation is of a magically wonderful tooth that keeps producing money, the teacher infers a disappointment that the tooth hasn't disappeared as it should. The teacher's lack of comprehension may be caused by the story's novel ending, but we infer from the bracketing that the narrator was trying to be clear.

"A Hundred Dollars" contains a more complicated bracketing structure, with one bracket inserted within another:

A Hundred Dollars

Well / last night / my . . . father / . . . was at work /
⎡ *he* / . . . every Thursday night / they have this thing /
⎢ that . . . everybody has this dollar /
⎣ and it makes up to a hundred dollars /
⎡ and . . . *my* / and . . . you've gotta pick this name out /
⎣ and *my father's* name got picked /
⎣ so *he* won a thousand dollars / / a hundred dollars

Carl wants to tell the class that last night his father won a hundred dollars. But to explain where the money came from, he inserts a description of a lottery. Embedded within this bracketing is another insertion about the process of picking out a name.

In these bracketings, the children, black and white, are not just replacing one word with another within a sentence or solving a problem of anaphoric pronoun reference across adjacent sentence boundaries. They are making repairs for the listener at the level of the thematic content of the narrative as a whole. They are thinking about the information the listener needs in order to understand part of the story not yet told, and making a midstream repair to provide needed orientation. In this way, these children are showing their ability to do more than retrospectively monitor what has already been said, and more than provide local repairs if something doesn't come out quite right; they are thinking ahead and monitoring against an internal criterion of information needed by their audience. This criterion can be called metalinguistic—or, more specifically, metapragmatic—awareness.

The most dramatic contrast between what listeners hear and what an analyst can reveal is in "My Puppy." Listeners almost always find this story incoherent, and some jump to inferences about the child's ability. One remedial teacher in a group to whom we played a tape of Leona's own rendition said immediately, "She has no time sense, a very slow child." Psycholinguist James Gee became interested in Leona's narratives and has done an independent analysis of several of them. His analysis of "My Puppy" is too long to report here in full. But his version of the story itself reveals a complex, even elegant structure:

> If we remove obvious false starts and repairs from the text and collapse the few subject nouns or noun phrases that are idea units by themselves into

the clauses they belong to, we get an ideal realization of the text, which is given in Puppy-2 [Figure 2–1]. . . . Once we have gotten to the basic clauses or "lines" that L [Leona] is aiming at, it becomes apparent that L groups her lines together into series of lines—often four lines long—that have parallel structure and match each other either in content or topic. I will call these groups of lines "stanzas." Furthermore, prosodically, these lines sound as if they go together, both by tending to be said at the same rate and by having little hesitation between lines. . . . They are separated by space in Puppy–2.[14]

In another paper about two of Leona's stories—"My Puppy" and "Birthday Cakes" (about making cakes for her grandmother)—Gee points out that the disfluencies eliminated in Puppy–2 are themselves informative. They can be indications of increased cognitive load for the child at those points:

An increase in false starts, hesitations, and nonclausal units coincides with major boundaries in the narrative. That is, when L has finished a major segment of the narrative and must move on to [plan] the next one she displays these sorts of phenomena, perhaps because of cognitive load at these points or because her attention is shifting from content back to audience (or both).[15]

Topic

When a teacher tries to "make connections," story topics can make a big difference. Some stories, such as "Stamp Pad" and "A Hundred Dollars," are about widely shared experiences with publicly familiar scripts. Requesting and getting Christmas presents constitutes such a widely shared script in this culture, and we know that those actions can be sequenced in only one way. Carl's explanation about lotteries has extensive problems of vague words: "this thing," "this dollar," "it make up to," "this name." But adult listeners would get enough clues to some kind of lottery to clarify the vagueness on their own. Other stories, more often the episodic ones, are about the idiosyncratic events of family living—such as the adventures of Leona's puppy, or when and why she sleeps at her grandmother's—and it is much harder for the listening teacher to make connections and clarify relationships among actions from extratext knowledge.

Leona's teacher commented on an important difference between being a parent and being a teacher: because of their participation in the child's world, it is much easier for parents to "make connections." This difference in familiarity is important for teacher-student interaction in general, not just at sharing time. British psychologists Barbara Tizard and Martin Hughes have compared conversations between four-year-

Part 1: INTRODUCTION
  Part 1A: SETTING

Last yesterday in the morning	1
there was a hook on the top of the stairway	2
an' my father was pickin' me up	3
an I got stuck on the hook up there	4
an' I hadn't had breakfast	5
he wouldn't take me down	6
until I finished all my breakfast	7
cause I didn't like oatmeal either / /	8

  Part 1B: CATALYST

an' then my puppy came	9
he was asleep	10
he tried to get up	11
an' he ripped my pants	12
an' he dropped the oatmeal all over him	13
an' my father came	14
an he said "did you eat all the oatmeal?"	15
he said "where's the bowl?" / /	16
I said "I think the dog took it" / /	17
"Well I think I'll have t'make another bowl" / /	18

Part 2: CRISIS
  Part 2A: COMPLICATING ACTIONS

an' so I didn't leave till seven	19
an' I took the bus	20
an' my puppy he always be following me	21
my father said "he—you can't go" / /	22
an' he followed me all the way to the bus stop	23
an' I hadda go all the way back	24
(by that time it was seven-thirty) / /	25
an' then he kept followin' me back and forth	26
an' I hadda keep comin' back / /	27

  Part 2B: NONNARRATIVE SECTION (EVALUATION)

an' he always be followin' me when I go anywhere	28
he wants me to go to the store	29
an' only he could not go to places where we could go	30
like to the stores he could go but he have to be chained up	31

Part 3: RESOLUTION
  Part 3A: CONCLUDING EPISODES

an' we took him to the emergency	32
an' see what was wrong with him	33
an' he got a shot	34
an' then he was crying	35
an' last yesterday, an' now they put him asleep	36
an' he's still in the hospital	37
(an' the doctor said . . .) he got a shot because	38
he was nervous about my home that I had	39

  Part 3B: CODA

an' he could stay but	41
he thought he wasn't gonna be able to let him go / /	42

FIGURE 2–1 Puppy-2 (from Gee 1985)

olds at home and at school. Tizard reflects on this research in a pamphlet for practitioners:

> Familiarity helps adults to interpret little children's meanings, and their communications. It also enables them to help children connect together different aspects of their experience. In my study of four year olds at home and school I was able to show how the mother's familiarity with her child allowed her to relate the child's present experiences to past and future events, and in this way give added meaning to them. In contrast, the nursery staff, who were relatively unfamiliar with the children, and knew little or nothing about their homes and families or their past, often had difficulty in communicating effectively with them.
>
> Familiarity thus facilitates not only attachment, but responsiveness . . . [and] responsiveness also plays an important part in learning—it is essential if an interactive sequence is to be sustained and if a high level of social skills is to be developed. . . . Aspects of children's intellectual functioning thus seem to be intimately related to the social relationships in which they are embedded.[16]

This problem of familiarity is undoubtedly especially acute in preschool and the primary grades. Older students can take more responsibility for describing their worlds to the teacher. But the teacher, on her part, has to convey genuine interest, and a willingness to learn.

Cultural Differences

Narratives are a universal meaning-making strategy, but there is no one way of transforming experience into a story. In the words of British educator Harold Rosen, narratives are

> first and foremost a product of the disposition of the human mind to nar-ratize experience and to transform it into findings which as social beings we may share and compare with those of others.

But while "the story is always out there,"

> the important step has still to be taken. The unremitting flow of events must first be selectively attended to, interpreted as holding relationships, causes, motives, feelings, consequences—in a word, meanings. To give order to this otherwise unmanageable flux we must take another step and invent, yes, invent, beginnings and ends, for out there are no such things. . . . This is the axiomatic element of narrative: it is the outcome of a mental process which enables us to excise from our experience a meaningful se-quence, to place it within boundaries, to set around it the frontiers of the story, to make it resonate in the contrived silences with which we may precede and end it. . . . The narrative edits ruthlessly the raw tape.

Our potential and disposition to construct narratives is similar to our potential and disposition to acquire language:

> If we are programmed to learn a language, we must still be exposed to a language in order to learn it and its socially constituted use. In the same way, however universal our human bent for narratizing experience we encounter our own society's modes for doing this. There is no one way of telling stories; we learn the story grammars of our society, our culture. [17]

We mustn't forget that our black informants did not have the problems understanding episodic stories that their white colleagues did. So some of the lack of comprehension and appreciation must be caused, or at least exaggerated, by cultural differences—by the different contexts in the mind, the expectations about form and topic, that black and white listeners bring to the listening task. Are the black children using systematic intonational and rhythmic cues that white listeners either misinterpret or simply do not hear? Are the black children's story themes, such as staying at grandmother's or the novel twist at the end of "At Grandmother's" or "Tooth Story," more immediately familiar to adults from the same cultural background? Do black adults have greater appreciation for a good oral story, regardless of how well or poorly it would communicate in written form?

THE SIGNIFICANCE OF SHARING TIME

In subsequent chapters, we shall return to many of the issues raised here. With respect to sharing time itself, I realize that researchers' appreciation of these narratives comes from time-consuming analyses of tapes and transcripts. To teachers who have to respond in real time, the experience is understandably very different. I hope that this close look at some children's texts and teachers' responses will raise anew the question of what sharing time is for and make it more likely that, when children fail to meet a teacher's expectations, the cause will be sought in the complexities of the child's task, or cultural differences in our expectations, rather than in deficiencies in the children themselves.

Consider again the teacher's interaction with Mindy about making candles. Here there is no negative evaluation and no evidence of teacher interruption. As Michaels pointed out in her analysis,

> most of Mrs. Jones's questions occur when Mindy pauses after a low falling tone. Such pauses indicate some kind of closure. Hence Mrs. Jones's questions occur at the end of a complete unit and are not seen as interruptions. Furthermore, her questions descend from general to specific, until a level

is reached at which Mindy can and does respond appropriately. Lastly, the teacher's responses and clarifications build on Mindy's contributions.[18]

This dialogue can be interpreted positively as a kind of interactional "scaffold" by which the teacher helps Mindy put into words a more explicit and precise description of making candles, a description that is more "literate" in assuming (in the teacher's words) "that we don't know a thing about candles."

But another interpretation is possible. When I presented Mindy's sharing-time turn to a group of teachers at a National Council of Teachers of English conference, several felt that the teacher had "appropriated" the child's text for her own teaching purposes, and forced the development of the narrative in particular ways. Mindy started talking about colors, they pointed out. But the teacher shifted the talk to materials. Later, language educator Dennis Searle asked, "Who is in control of the language?" with specific reference to my presentation of sharing-time turns such as Mindy's as examples of scaffolding. Searle acknowledges the usefulness of the scaffolding metaphor, but asks the question at the heart of all teaching dilemmas: "Who's building whose building?"[19]

Sharing time occurs only in primary classrooms. But writing conferences, which are different in some ways and similar in others, occur throughout elementary and high school and beyond. In the conference, the teacher can reread the text before responding, and talk with the writer out of public view. But in both, there is a student text and a teacher who must somehow resolve the dilemma of an appropriate response. With the aid of a stationary microphone on the teacher's desk, or a portable cassette recorder that the teacher wears as she circulates around the room, writing conferences can be analyzed too.

In both sharing time and school writing, there is the all-important question of audience. Who is the child supposed to be speaking to and writing for? In sharing time, the peer audience is obvious, and the event could be justified as much for its contribution to a sense of community among children as for the opportunity for oral-language development. The fact of the dual audience may itself add to the rhetorical problems faced by the child speakers, just because teacher and peers may hear stories very differently. The same ambiguity about audience applies to writing. In both situations, it is the teacher who always responds, and often in an evaluative way. More generally, in all school speaking and writing assignments, no matter who the ostensible audience may be, it is usually the teacher's response that counts.[20]

Teachers, like physicians and social workers, are in the business of helping others. But as a prerequisite to giving help, we have to take in and understand. Piagetian psychologist Eleanor Duckworth speaks of the importance of teachers "understanding learners' understandings."[21] And British sociologist Basil Bernstein puts the same idea in different words:

> If the culture of the teacher is to become part of the consciousness of the child, then the culture of the child must first be in the consciousness of the teacher.[22]

Important elements of that consciousness are our expectations about text structure and our familiarity with the events the texts are about. I call that consciousness our "context in the mind." We usually think of the importance of these contexts in the mind when children are learning to read; but they are just as important when the texts are childrens', oral or written, and when the interpreter is the listening or reading teacher.

NOTES

[1] From Dorr-Bremme 1982.

[2] Michaels 1981; Michaels and Cazden 1986; Cazden, Michaels and Tabor 1985. Unless otherwise indicated, the narratives in this chapter are from our research. There are a few earlier studies. Hahn 1948 compares ST stories with the same children's performance in an interview. Lazarus and Homer 1981 report one teacher's attempt to change ST into a group discussion. Dorr-Bremme 1982 compares ST in two years in the same teacher's classroom. Wilcox 1982 compares sharing time in a middle-class and working-class school.

[3] Shuy 1981, 172.

[4] Michaels 1983.

[5] See discussion in Ochs 1979b of "Transcription as Theory."

[6] Smitherman 1977. See also Heath's description of the stories of black children in another U.S. community (1983, 299–308), especially Nellie's story (Table 8–3), which, like Leona's, is about her puppy.

[7] Martin 1987, 166–67.

[8] In an important review of research in infrequently cited disciplines relevant to the activity of writing, Purves and Purves 1986 call for inquiry "in the emerging field of contrastive rhetoric."

[9] Pratt 1977, pp. 103–104.

[10] Dorr-Bremme 1982. Another remarkably similar example comes from a Danish study reported (with translated excerpts) by Chaudron 1980. According to Chaudron, the Danish researchers found that when "pupils are asked to contribute their own experiences . . . the teacher responds to some aspect of a student's experience that seems somehow important to an adult" (167). For example, when a third grader relates an experience with a blackbird nest in a discussion about birds, the teacher asks a series of questions about the nest's height.

[11] Tracy 1984.

[12]This "matched guise" technique has been used in research on language attitudes in bilingual communities. See, for example, Lambert, Hodgson, Gardner and Fillenbaum 1960.

[13]Bartlett and Scribner 1981.

[14]Gee 1985, 14, with some transcription marks deleted.

[15]Gee 1986, 396.

[16]Tizard 1986, 29–30. The book-length version is Tizard and Hughes 1984.

[17]Rosen 1984, 12–14.

[18]Michaels 1981, 433.

[19]Searle 1984.

[20]In a study of "news time" in England, which shows great similarity to sharing time in the United States, Dinsmore 1986 mentions the interesting contrast between official "news time" and unofficial conversations that take place as children arrive at school, when some of the same events may be reported. A comparison of the same story told intraconversationally to teacher or peer and then told again as a sharing-time monologue could yield important information on how young children shift between the two contexts, and on their perceptions of the kind of language that sharing time requires.

[21]Duckworth 1981.

[22]Bernstein, 1972, 149.

Chapter 3

The Structure of Lessons

The sharing-time sequences discussed in chapter 2 all have the same basic structure:

1. The teacher initiates the sequence by calling on a child to share.
2. The nominated child responds by telling a narrative.
3. The teacher comments on the narrative before calling on the next child.

Some narrative sequences, such as "Paper Boat," have only this basic structure. Others, such as "Making Candles" and "Old Ironsides," are extended by additional teacher questions and child responses before the teacher's final comment and next nomination.

The three-part sequence of teacher initiation, student response, teacher evaluation (IRE) is the most common pattern of classroom discourse at all grade levels. Usually the initiation is in question form. (In sharing time, the questions—such as, "Who has something to share?"—may be asked only of the first child and remain unspoken but understood thereafter.) All analyses of teacher-led classroom discourse find examples of this pattern, and anyone hearing it recognizes it as classroom talk and not just informal conversation:

Conversation	Classroom Talk
What time is it, Sarah?	What time is it, Sarah?
Half-past two.	Half-past two.
Thanks.	Right.

The classroom-speech event in which this IRE pattern is most obvious is the teacher-led lesson, or recitation, in which the teacher controls both the development of a topic (and what counts as relevant to it) and who gets a turn to talk. Most analyses of classroom discourse are analyses of this one speech event.

The focus on lessons in classroom-interaction research, old and new, may have been influenced by their greater audibility to human observers or overhead microphones. During lessons, teachers and children speak up, and they talk (pretty much) one at a time. Without some kind of wireless microphones (for which small cassette recorders are an inexpensive substitute), talk in small student groups, or between the teacher and individual students at her desk or theirs, is as hard to overhear as talk at tables in a restaurant or on a bus.

But the justification for attention to lessons goes beyond the artifact of recording constraints. Seemingly invulnerable to repeated criticisms, the recitation-type lesson has had a long and hardy life through many decades of formal, Western-type schooling.[1]

Of the recent detailed analyses of lesson structure, this chapter will be based primarily on Mehan's analysis of nine videotaped lessons from my classroom in San Diego. In part, this choice is a matter of personal knowledge: since I was the teacher and know the children, richer commentary is possible. But, in addition, Mehan's analysis is especially valuable in four ways: because he works from videotapes, he has nonverbal as well as verbal evidence for inferences about lesson structure; he presents a formal statement of that structure, which facilitates comparison with other events; he reports the frequency with which all the talk in the nine lessons fits this structure and gives careful attention to all the anomalous exceptions; and he traces changes in children's participation over the course of a school year. After presenting an excerpt from one lesson, I'll discuss these aspects of his analysis, with additional comments from other research.[2]

EXAMPLE OF A LESSON: BIRTHPLACES

The lesson that Mehan refers to as "Birthplaces" occurred in mid-November. It was part of a social-studies unit that had two objectives. One was making and understanding maps. The children had made individual maps of the classroom and a group map of the school. Now we were locating where individual children and their parents were born on a commercial wall map of the United States and northern Mexico. The second purpose was to lessen the psychological distance between myself as a visiting teacher from New England and the California children by displaying on the map the shared experience—via parents or grandparents—of geographical mobility; we or our families had all come to San Diego from somewhere else.[3]

Here is the teacher's introduction of the lesson, after the children were assembled on chairs facing the map:

> Some people did some good homework last night in finding out where they were, were born or where your family, your parents came from. And Miguel has a little box of colored paper here, and what we're going to do is—if you know where you were born, we are going to put your name up with orange paper. If you know where your parents came from, we're going to put their name up with green paper and pin them right on the map [*demonstrating*]. Now some people were already telling me as soon as they came into school this morning that they had some, that they had some, they knew some things to put on the, to put on the map.

Prenda was the first child called on. Figure 3–1 is a transcript of the segment of the lesson concerning Prenda's family. The assignment of turns to three IRE columns was done by Mehan. The comments in the fourth column on the right are my addition, combining Mehan's ideas with my own.

According to Mehan's analysis, in this lesson the basic sequence (which may include more than one IRE) includes "determining each student's (or family member's) birthplace, locating that place on the map, and placing that information on the map." Discussion of Prenda's birthplace (5–7) has only that basic sequence. But discussion of where Prenda's mother and father were born extends beyond the basic sequence to conditional sequences about the basis of student knowledge (12–17) or the relative distance between cities (31–34). Mehan calls the combination of basic plus (optional) conditional sequence(s) a Topically Related Set (TRS).[4]

Mehan was originally motivated by some nagging problems to look for an intermediate unit of discourse structure between the IRE sequence

INITIATION	RESPONSE	EVALUATION	COMMENTS
5 *Teacher:* Uh, Prenda, ah, let's see if we can find, here's your name. Where were you born, Prenda?	*Prenda:* San Diego.	*Teacher:* You were born in San Diego, all right	5. Individual nomination of Prenda.
6 *Teacher:* Um, can you come up and find San Diego on the map?	*Prenda: (goes to board and points)*	*Teacher:* Right there okay.	6. Teacher acknowledges answers, even to questions for which only Prenda knows the answer.
7 *Teacher:* So, we will put you right there *(pins paper on map).*			
8 *Teacher:* Now, where, where did, where was your mother born, where did your mother come from?	*Wallace: (raises hand)* *Prenda:* Oh, Arkansas.	*Teacher:* Okay.	8. Wallace bids nonverbally at end of basic sequence but does not get the floor. Instead Prenda's turn continues.
9 *Teacher:* Prenda's mother *(writes on paper).*			
10 *Teacher:* Um, now we *(pause)* I did point out Arkansas on the map yesterday.	*Prenda:* I know where Arkansas is.		10. A two-part IR sequence.
11 *Teacher:* Can you, do you know where it is, Prenda?	*Wallace: (points from his seat toward Arkansas on the map).* *Prenda: (goes to board and points).*	*Teacher:* Yeah, good for you.	

32

#			
12	Teacher: How did, how did, how did you come, how did you know that?	[Prenda: Cause I— [Carolyn: —this morning.	12. A metaprocess question that asks child to reflect on the basis of knowledge. The teacher's evaluation is simultaneously a negative sanction of Caroline for interrupting, and a request to Prenda to repeat, though neither is explicit in the words of her utterance.
		Teacher: Wait a minute, wait a minute. I didn't, couldn't hear what Prenda said.	
13	Teacher: What?	Prenda: (turns head away)	
14	Teacher: Who told you? Who told you?	Prenda: Carolyn did she told me where it was, where Arkansas was.	
15	Teacher: And, Carolyn, how did you remember where it was? It's kind of in the middle of the country and hard to find out.	Carolyn: Uh, cuz, cuz, cuz, all three of the grandmothers (pause) cuz, cuz, Miss Coles told us to find it and she said it started with an A and I said there (pointing) and it was right there.	
16	Prenda: Little Rock.	Teacher: Uh hum.	
		Teacher: Yes, and I thought maybe you remembered, because, Carolyn, you mentioned Little Rock yesterday.	
17	Teacher: Okay, well so this is green for your mother or your father, and we'll put that (pins card to map).	Prenda: My father wasn't born in there.	17. Prenda's evaluation also functions to initiate sequence of talk about father, the logical next topic.

FIGURE 3–1 Transcript of Segment of Lesson Concerning Prenda's Family

(continued)

	INITIATION	RESPONSE	EVALUATION	COMMENTS
18	*Teacher:* Well, that says mother.			
19	*Teacher:* Do you know where your father was born?	*Prenda:* (nods yes)		
20	*Teacher:* Where was he born?	*Prenda:* Baltimore, Maryland.	*Teacher:* Really, oh good!	
21	*Carolyn:* Where's that at?		*Teacher:* Now, where's that at? That's a good question, Carolyn.	21. Carolyn's question is both well slotted in timing and appropriate in content and receives a meta evaluation (on talk itself) from teacher.
22	*Teacher:* I don't, I wonder if anybody knows.			
23	*Carolyn:* It's on there with a B, huh?	*Teacher:* Um, well yes, it is on here with a B.		
24	*Teacher:* Uh, Prenda's father (*writing on paper*).			
25	*Carolyn:* I see it—			
26	*Teacher:* I think I'll have to tell you that because I don't think there's any way that you would know. It's way over . . . here. *Carolyn:* Here.			
27	*Teacher:* Maryland is MD, and there's Baltimore.			

28	*Teacher:* Can you see it from where you are with a B?	*Many:* Yeah. *Carolyn:* There it is right there. *Many:* [Noise]	
29	*Teacher:* [Beckons Prenda to map]	*Prenda:* [Goes to map, locates Baltimore]	*Teacher:* Baltimore and that circle.
30	*Teacher:* Now, now let's . . .		
31	*Wallace:* That's ten times farther than . . .		31. Wallace initiates verbally at a reasonable place—preceding sequence is completed and teacher's *now* indicates a new beginning. The content of his comment is unexpected in contrast to Carolyn's (21) but relevant.
32	_____: Can I do it?		
33	*Teacher:* And now, now let's what were somebody was saying something about ten times or something what?	*Wallace:* That's ten times, and that, far from, ah, San Diego.	*Teacher:* Yes, it is, it is far from San Diego.
34	*Teacher:* Uh, Prenda, who came, who came from a, who came farther: your mother from Arkansas to San Diego or your father from Baltimore to San Diego?	*Prenda:* My father.	*Teacher:* Yes, he came ah, he came a long, a long way.

FIGURE 3–1 *(continued)*

and the lesson as a whole. If IREs were the only structural component of a lesson, one could assemble them in any order; it is clear that, in terms of topic (or propositional content), that wasn't so. Moreover, we couldn't understand why the evaluation component was sometimes present and sometimes not; that is, some sequences were not full IRE but just IR (as in 10 and 14). Mehan's construct of Topically Related Sets solved both these problems. The basic and conditional sequences are ordered within each set, and evaluations always occur at the end of sets, but not necessarily after each student response within them.

Anyone reading this transcription may speculate about alternative assignment of utterances to columns. For example, the following alternative coding of sequences 22–25 seems plausible:

Initiation	Response	Evaluation
T: I don't I wonder if anybody knows . . .	C: It's on there with a B, huh?	T: Um, well, yes, it is on here with a B.
T: Uh, Prenda's father [*Writing on paper*].	C: I see it—	

And I would consider Prenda's utterance "Little Rock" in 16 an additional Response to T's Initiation in 15 rather than a student Initiation. But such small changes do not diminish the value of the overall structural description.

NONVERBAL CUES TO LESSON STRUCTURE

Discovery of the TRSs was prompted by questions about features of the talk. But because Mehan worked from videotapes, he found additional evidence of their psychological reality in nonverbal aspects of the teacher's behavior. The beginning of each set "is signaled by a unique combination of verbal, paralinguistic, and kinesic behavior." Kinesically, the beginning is "marked by the teacher's [postural] orientation toward the instructional materials to be used"—in the above example, the map or the colored papers to be pinned to it. Verbally, the TRSs are initiated by a small set of markers such as "now" (as in 8 and 30). Paralinguistically, "these verbal markers were often produced in a sharp staccato tone. The cadence of the teacher's voice quickened as she initiated a new topical set."[5]

Nonverbally, the basic and conditional sequences form a single interactional unit, with the seams between them unmarked. Then, at the end of the TRS:

> The closings of topically related sets are marked in ways that are similar to their openings. A finite set of verbal markers, which includes "all right" and "that's right," often with the correct reply repeated, appears only at the final juncture of TRSs. The cadence of the teacher's presentation slows as she pronounces these words. Certain postural shifts occur simultaneously with verbal and paralinguistic boundary markers. She lowers presented materials, removes her hand from indicated material.[6]

It's hard to convey in words the sights and sounds available to students or observers that mark the end of TRSs as qualitatively different junctures from the end of IRs or even IREs within them. Perhaps a metaphor will help. The transition of one TRS to the next is like a music box winding down, and then being started up again by the teacher, or occasionally by a child.

Lessons, and the TRSs within them, are activities constituted primarily of and by talk. Here, nonverbal actions supplement words as cues to speech-event structure. Other observers have noted how nonverbal actions can play a more direct role in communication. During work time, for example, when students are occupied in small groups at a variety of tasks around the room, the teacher may use deliberate nonverbal signals such as flicking the light switch off and on as a signal for the children to stop and listen, or positioning herself in a particular space in the room as a signal that she is or is not available for help. And when she is working with individual children, her posture may indicate—perhaps without her own awareness—the degree of her involvement and therefore of her willingness to be interrupted by others. Given the complexities of use of the verbal channel of communication in a crowded classroom, it is not surprising that the nonverbal channel should be used to fulfill part of the needs of the entire classroom communication economy.[7]

FORMAL STATEMENTS OF LESSON STRUCTURE

The structure of many human events has two dimensions. Consider the structure of a typical American restaurant menu—what all menus have in common regardless of variations in the food served. There is a set of categories (with names like "appetizer" or "dessert") in a particular order. The appetizer is never at the end nor dessert at the beginning, and permissible variations are rare. Only the beverage (and sometimes salad) can be moved about in the sequence to suit individual taste. That's the sequential (syntagmatic or horizontal) dimension. Then, within each slot in the sequential structure, there are options within each category —choices of appetizers, main courses, and so on. That's the selectional (paradigmatic or vertical) dimension of the same structure.

A cultural product even closer to the horizontal dimension of English is the rubber stamp on which month, day, and year can be inserted. The sequential dimension is the horizontal series of these three slots; the selectional dimension requires the selection of particular numbers at any one time, with the set of alternatives visualized as a vertical list from which a selection is made. Readers who have filled out immigration forms outside the United States may have realized that there are cultural differences in the conventional sequence: month-day-year in the United States, but day-month-year in England and many other countries.

So it is with lessons.

Sequential Dimension

The next page gives Mehan's description of the sequential dimension of lesson structure in two forms. The chart in Figure 3–2 becomes transformed in Figure 3–3 into an even more economical set of statements about how the smallest units (starting with I, R, and E at bottom left) are combined to constitute the successively larger units, up to the lesson itself.

One feature of this lesson structure is important in Mehan's analysis, although not apparent in these formal statements: the relationships that tie together parts of the sequences in Figure 3–3 can hold across a considerable stretch of discourse, not just immediately consecutive utterances. For example, in "Birthplaces" the metaprocess question "How did you know that?" which initiates sequence 12 is not answered and evaluated until ten turns of talk later, at sequence 16; and Carolyn's question about the location of Baltimore in 21 isn't finally answered until 27–29. Here is the IRE structure, stripped of verbal content, for sequence 12–16:

12. I R
    R E (negative sanction)
13. I R   (R nonverbal only)
14. I R
15. I R E (acknowledgment but not evaluation)
16.   R E

As Mehan points out, this means that "teacher-student interaction does not appear to be under immediate stimulus control."[8] It also means that

Event	Lesson							
Phase	Opening		Instructional				Closing	
Type of sequence	Directive	Informative	Topical sets		Topical sets		Informative	Directive
			Elicit	Elicit	Elicit	Elicit		
Organization of sequences	I-R-E	I-R(E_0)	I-R-E	I-R-E	I-R-E	I-R-E	I-R(E_0)	I-R-E
Participants	T-S-T	T-S-T	T-S-T	T-S-T	T-S-T	T-S-T	T-S-T	T-S-T

← Hierarchical organization

Sequential organization →

Key: T = teacher; S = student; I-R-E = initiation-reply-evaluation sequence; (E_0) = evaluation optional in informative sequence

FIGURE 3–2 The Structure of Classroom Lessons (from Mehan 1979, 73–74)

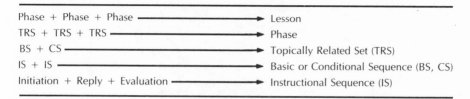

FIGURE 3–3   The Hierarchical Arrangements of Lessons (From Mehan 1979, 73–74)

criteria of "relevance" at any moment are more complex than if governed only by the immediately preceding utterance.

Formal statements such as Figure 3–2 and 3–3 sharpen our understanding of event structure. As Hymes says, "A considerable clarification of what one understood to be the structure has been demanded. The form of the events is disengaged . . . from the verbal foliage obligatory in prose sentences, and can be more readily seen." When the words in which the pattern has been enacted in any one instance have been stripped away, it is much easier not only to understand classroom lessons but also to consider similarities and differences between this speech event and others. Similarities to sharing time have been noted already; similarities to homework collection in another classroom will be discussed in chapter 5.[9]

Moreover, similarities don't end at the classroom door. Mehan's analysis also helps us to see what may be important similarities to one speech event common in many homes: book-reading sessions between parents and young children. In the family observed by Ninio and Bruner, for example, picture-book reading early in the child's second year had a four-part event structure:

1. An attentive vocative, such as "Look."
2. A query, such as "What's that?"
3. An answer, usually a label, such as "It's an X."
4. A feedback utterance, such as "Yes, that's an X" (if the child has provided the label).

With the mother's attentional vocative replacing the teacher's turn-allocation procedures, the remaining parts of the book-reading dialogue fit the IRE sequence of lessons. Moreover, the initiations in both events are typically questions to which the adult asker knows the answer.

In studies of the antecedents of school success, many researchers have found a high correlation between being read to at home and succeeding in school, and have remarked on the special linguistic features of written texts or of the conversation interpolated into the text-reading event.[10] The structural similarities suggest that picture-book reading may, in addition to its substantive contribution, provide preparation for participation in the discourse of classroom lessons several years later.

Selectional Dimension

Structural descriptions should consider both sequential and selectional dimensions, but the relative degree of attention to each will vary from one researcher to another. Mehan analyzes the sequential organization of lesson sequences in detail, but comments only briefly on alternative selectional realizations: for example, that initiations can be questions ("Where were you born, Prenda?"), directives ("Can you come up and find San Diego on the map?"), or declarative statements ("I did point out Arkansas on the map yesterday"). By contrast, John Sinclair and Malcolm Coulthard, two British linguists interested in speech-act theory, focus much of their analysis of classroom discourse on form-function relationships: for example, how the syntactic question "Can you come up and find San Diego on the map?" is understood immediately and unequivocally not as a yes/no question (which syntactically it is) but as a command to act (which Prenda follows). Their answer is diagrammed in Figure 3–4, with the conditions applicable in this example circled:

- The subject of the sentence, *you*, is the addressee, Prenda.
- The action, finding a city on the map, is not proscribed.
- The utterance contains a modal *can*.
- The form is a polar (yes/no) question.
- The question refers to an action feasible at the moment (and, one could add, obviously appropriate to the lesson as just introduced).

Thus the interpretation of the teacher's intended meaning as a directive or command.[11]

As Sinclair and Coulthard point out, preconditions for the interpretation of such indirect directives that are stipulated in abstract speech-act theory—"B [addressee] has the ability to do X" and "A [speaker] has the right to tell B to do X" can, in lessons, be derived from the general rights and obligations of classroom participants and do not need to be invoked separately for the interpretation of a particular utterance. The indirect directive in sequence 12 would require a more complex analysis, because neither of the requested actions (Carolyn keeping quiet or Prenda repeating what she just said) is verbalized in the actual words of the utterance.

Conventions of language use give speakers many ways of requesting actions from another person in addition to bald imperatives, and teachers take advantage of these options in complex ways. In "Birthplaces," the

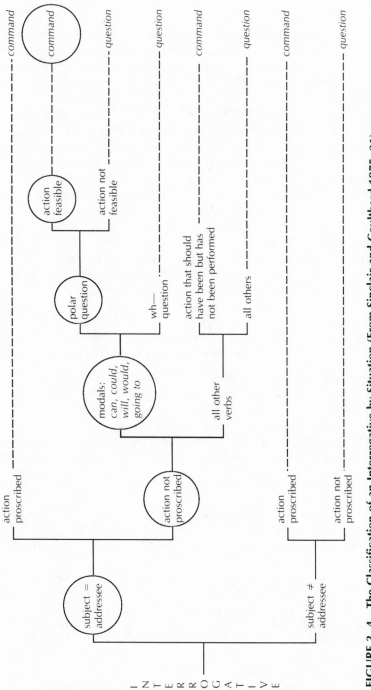

FIGURE 3–4 The Classification of an Interrogative by Situation (From Sinclair and Coulthard 1975, 31).

42

teacher's evaluation in sequence 12 consists of a repeated imperative, "Wait a minute," plus a declarative statement, "I didn't, couldn't hear what Prenda said." Functionally these utterances told Carolyn to stop speaking out of turn and requested Prenda to repeat what she had just said.

In secondary science lessons, Lemke found other examples of such complex forms. "I can't hear you, Ian," spoken after the nominated student Ian's turn is overlapped by another student, Rosie, "functions both as a request for repeat and as an admonition to Rosie." And "C'mon. I mean I was looking at you when you did it. Be a little subtle," said to a student who had just thrown a paper wad, invokes not only the norm against throwing things but also the "deeply implicit convention that violations done 'while teacher is looking' may be presumed deliberate challenges to teacher's authority, acts of defiance, and not just lapses from rules."[12]

These indirect directives exemplify two features of all discourse: the lack of one-to-one correspondence between syntactic form and interactional function, and the expression of social meaning in the choice of any particular formal alternative. In chapter 9, we will consider the social meaning of many instances of indirect directives in teachers' talk.

STRUCTURE AND IMPROVISATION

Descriptions of human behavior require both searching for repeated patterns and acknowledging, even with admiration, the inevitable improvisation. The repeated patterns—which we call the "structure" of the event, or the "rules" that the participants seem to be tacitly following—can be formally represented. But that is only part of the story. If we were trying to describe the competence of jazz musicians, for example, we would have to attend both to their knowledge of a musical system (a set of notes constituting a scale, and rules for combining them both sequentially and simultaneously), and to their ability to use that knowledge in creative ways at particular moments. The same is true of speakers; they act on more than the general rules. In the words of two classroom researchers, Peg Griffin and Mehan, classroom discourse can be characterized as "negotiated conventions—spontaneous improvisations on basic patterns of interaction."[13]

Consider alternative ways in which teachers control discourse traffic and nominate students to speak. Mehan found three variations in the San Diego lessons, of which two appear in the excerpt from "Birthplaces":

- Individual nomination: of Prenda in 5 and Carolyn in 15.
- Invitation to reply: "I wonder if anybody knows—" in 22 (to which

Carolyn responds); and "Can you see it from where you are with a B?" in 28 (which many answer).

In "Birthplaces," the child whose family is being discussed—Prenda in the excerpt—is understood to be the addressee unless another child is specifically designated (Carolyn in 15 and "somebody," who turns out to be Wallace, in 33). The third variation, Invitation to Bid ("Raise your hand if you know . . . ") takes two IR sequences: first a request for bids, followed ideally by student nonverbal responses of raising hands, and then the nomination of one bidder to answer. (The third variation was relatively rare in this classroom—less than 10 percent, in contrast to about 45 percent for each of the other two.[14]

In all nine lessons, there are 480 nominations. The three normal forms occur 423 times (88.1 percent); and there are 28 violations (5.8 percent), as in sequence 12, where a student speaks out of turn and receives a negative teacher sanction. That leaves 29 anomalous cases (6.1 percent) that don't fit the structural description: unsanctioned violations (where students speak out of turn but are not reprimanded) and unwarranted sanctions (where children behave according to the rules but are reprimanded nevertheless). Mehan considers these 29 cases "flags to warn us that the analysis is not yet complete"[15] and discusses them in qualitative detail (a productive combination of qualitative and quantitative work). He complements the analysis of structure with categorizations of "improvisational strategies" that he calls Doing Nothing, Getting Through, Accepting the Unexpected, and Opening the Floor. The particular names, even the particular strategies, are less important than the recognition of improvisation as a necessary part of teacher competence.

Here I want to speak from my experience as the teacher. In a funny way, the more elegant the analysis, the more unreal it can seem to the participant. Where the researcher sees order, I often felt impending chaos. As Mehan points out, whereas utterances are psychological phenomena produced by a single person, speech events such as lessons are social events accomplished by the collaborative work of two or more people. In metaphorical terms, "school" is always a performance that must be constituted through the participation of a group of actors. But only one of them—the teacher—knows (or thinks she knows) how it is supposed to be played, and so she assumes the dual roles of stage director and principal actor. She is the only native speaker in the classroom culture; yet she has to depend on her "immigrant" students for help in enacting a culturally defined activity.

In the San Diego classroom, even that one actor felt pretty rusty as a primary-school teacher. So to me, the psychologically most compelling part of Mehan's analysis is his story of the 29 anomalous cases, the sequences of talk that don't fit the descriptive system, the times when the children talk out of turn or no one answers at all. Even his names for the improvisational strategies ring true, especially Getting Through. That's what teaching is: the hard core, the bottom line—whatever else happens, one somehow has to Get Through.

Frederick Erickson, an anthropologist who is also an accomplished musician, makes improvisation more than a metaphor in his rhythmic analysis in musical notation of variations on a theme (rule) in a math lesson in another primary classroom. At the end, he comments:

> From examination of a number of instances of the performance of a small lesson sequence, an underlying ideal model [canonical form] was inferred. . . . Looking closely at the performance of an instance of the lesson sequence, however, one sees that it is usually discrepant in some features of specific organization from the general, inferred model. If one is not simply to regard these discrepancies as random error (free variation), one has at least two options: to elaborate the formalization of the model by stating an embedded system of optional rules; or to assume that what is happening is adaptive variation, specific to the immediate circumstances of practical action in the moment of enactment.[16]

In his analysis of lesson structure, Mehan (like Erickson) has chosen the second alternative.

Acknowledging the existence of improvisation is not simply the observer's way of accounting for behavior that does not fit a single, prototypical pattern in every detail. More positively, it attributes to the participants—here the teacher—the competence to adapt tacitly known schemata to inevitable moment-to-moment variations in a complex environment.[17] But whereas musicians, whose image the metaphor invokes, depend on shared schemata in their collective performance, the teacher may feel less sure of her coparticipants, less sure of their understanding of how the lesson should precede, and of their commitment to getting through it in a trouble-free way.

COMMUNICATIVE COMPETENCE

A formal statement of speech-event structure not only sharpens our understanding of the event but also constitutes a claim about communicative competence, about "what it is a member of society knows in knowing how to participate."[18] In the case of lessons, it is therefore a claim, or hypothesis, about the communicative competence of both teacher and students.

For the teacher, we can assume that the lesson structure is a psychological reality from the beginning. In its canonical form, it exists as an idealized schema in the teacher's head, to be realized more or less adequately in any particular instance.[19]

But not so for the children. Their communicative competence develops more gradually. Just as a description of a language (a grammar) asserts hypotheses about what the speaker of a language must learn, so a description of a lesson asserts hypotheses about what children must learn in order to participate fully and be judged as competent students. Mehan tracked their progress over the year as they responded more appropriately (in timing and form) as well as correctly (in content) to the teacher's initiations and as they became more successful in initiating sequences of interaction themselves. That is, they learned to speak within the structure he describes, for their own purposes as well as the teacher's.

The "Birthplaces" excerpt includes two successful student initiations, where "successful" means not only not being reprimanded but positively "getting the floor" and affecting the subsequent discourse topic.[20] Carolyn's initiation in "Birthplaces" 21 and Wallace's in 31 are both timed exactly right. Carolyn's question, "Where's that at?" anticipates what almost certainly would have been the teacher's next question within the basic sequence of the TRS about Prenda's father. (Her close monitoring of the teacher is seen even more dramatically in 24, where she shadows T's utterance with the word *here*, which is appropriate for T, who is physically close to the map, but would not be appropriate if Carolyn were simply speaking for herself from some distance away.) Wallace's statement, "That's ten times farther than—" is even more impressive. It is spoken exactly as the teacher has completed the TRSs about Prenda's family and indicates by the marker "now" that she is about to initiate the next TRS. And it introduces the new—and to the teacher related and interesting—conditional sequence of relative distance. (Later in the "Birthplaces" lesson, Wallace successfully initiates a new TRS by asking T where she was born.)

Over the year, Mehan found that student initiations were less often negatively sanctioned or ignored and more often incorporated into the lesson content. "Significantly, those that disrupt the course of the lesson occur within the boundaries of a TRS, while those that influence the course of the lesson occur at the junctures between topical sets."[21]

In considering the implications of these developments for the children's communicative competence, it is important to say "learned to speak within the structure" rather than "learned the structure," because the children may be learning the meaning of local cues rather than the structure of the event as a whole. Consider a church service in which the congregation stands, sits, kneels, sings, and prays aloud at appropriate times. This does not mean that the sequential structure of the service is part of each member's communicative competence. It must be known by the minister. But members of the congregation have available to them many local cues. Some cues are verbally explicit, as in "Let us pray." Others may be visual, such as where the minister is standing, which direction he or she is facing, and what he or she is holding. So too in the lesson. The kinesic, verbal, and paralinguistic markers that Mehan discovered at the beginning and end of TRSs are also available to the children as cues to slots in the lesson structure where their initiations are most apt to get the floor.

The children's communicative competence is demonstrated implicitly by their appropriate responses and initiations, and also explicitly by their overt sanctions of peers who speak out of turn. In "Birthplaces," the next child to be called on for family information is Martha. When T asks her, "Where were you born, Martha?" and Edward responds, "Hawaii," Prenda provides a negative evaluation, "How do you know? You don't know where she was born." In this instance, Prenda's negative evaluation seems to be based on the content of Edward's utterance rather than form. In another instance later in the same lesson, Roberto is nominated and again Edward responds, "San Diego." (Edward is one of the six first-grade children in the class, while Prenda and Wallace are third graders, and Carolyn a very capable second grader.) This time Carolyn and Prenda both offer negative sanctions solely on the basis of who has the right to speak: "Why don't you guys shut up." "Let him talk, you guys talked already." "It's his turn now."[22]

Only a small part of the lesson structure is ever verbalized by the teacher, and even then the actual constitutive rules must be inferred. In Mehan's terms, "Students hear statements that only index the existence of classroom rules."[23] Negative sanctions like "Wait a minute" have to be interpreted retrospectively in relation to the already completed actions of another student. And even if "Raise your hand" has a prospective reference, the children have to figure out each time how long this admonition remains in effect. The critical question of when there are junctures or seams in which student initiations can be successful is never made explicit, and could not have been. It was part of the teacher's tacit competence, brought to light by the researcher. Thus the children had to learn what they needed to know as they learn language, without explicit tuition. As with language, they learned more than anyone could have explicitly taught.

THE SIGNIFICANCE OF LESSONS

One benefit of a clear and consistent event structure is that it allows participants to attend to content rather than procedure. The well-known children's TV program *Sesame Street* offers an analogous example. Some

Sesame Street shows include a categorization game, "One of these things is not like the other." It is always played on the same visual format (a two-by-two matrix) and always introduced by the same music. The visual and auditory "contextualization cues" tell frequent listeners quickly and without further introduction what game is going to be played and what mental task needs to be performed. Moreover, once the format is familiar to viewers, a wide variety of content—categorizations by color, shape, number, species, function, and so on—can be inserted into it without further directions.

So too with lessons. To the extent that a lesson structure is consistently enacted by the teacher (with flexibility for improvisations, as we have seen) and learnable by her particular students, it can become sufficiently familiar and predictable to offer clear cues to the shifting contexts, and to the talk that is appropriate within them. Management problems will thereby be minimized, and teacher and students can all give more attention to the academic focus of the lesson.[24]

But some caution is necessary in working toward this ideal. First, some discourse patterns can be learned by students too well. Consider the following teacher-student sequence:

T: What's four times three?

S: Eigh—

T: What is two times four?

S: Eight.

T: Mm, three times four?

S: Nine, ten, eleven, twelve.

T: So what's three times four?

S: Twelve.

T may hope that, from such a sequence, students will learn something about the relationship of addition to multiplication. But they may only learn the pattern of a verbal sequence in which "so" introduces a question that has the same answer as the preceding question. This pattern, complete with the particular connector, "so," seems to be common at all grade levels. It gets the right answer into the air and thus helps T "get through." But as Swedish researcher Lundgren points out, "The language used establishes a pattern of communication which gives the illusion that learning is actually occurring."[25]

The important task for the teacher is to listen for evidence that learning of more than the pattern itself has taken place. Here's another example from a preschool classroom observed by preschool educator Kathryn McGeorge:

S: There's a fly in here [in the classroom].

T: Why did the fly come inside?

S: I don't know.

T: Why did the mice [in the story that we just read] come inside?

S: Because it was cold.

T: So why do you think the *fly* might have come inside?

S: Because *he* was cold.[26]

In this case, the child's emphasis on *he*, tying it to *fly* in the preceding teacher's utterance, seems to indicate understanding of the substantive relationship between the two animals that the teacher was hoping to suggest.

The second potential problem is for the teacher's control, not for children's learning. If, from repeated experience, children learn the sequential structure of a stretch of classroom discourse, they may express their tacit knowledge by anticipating, out loud, what will happen next. Teachers vary in their response to such initiative.

In a comparison of two first-grade teachers on a Canadian Indian reservation, Erickson and Mohatt found a marked difference between them on this point. In the classroom of a teacher who was herself Native American and had taught on the reservation for twenty years, the children anticipated a series of questions about the calendar at the beginning of the morning: not only did the teacher initiate activity without waiting for the students, but the students did so without waiting for the teacher. Interaction was organized so that the teacher and the children could initiate and follow without either holding up the other.[27]

In the second classroom, a teacher new to teaching Native American children was less tolerant of such student initiatives:

> After the teacher's first focusing move ["OK guys/let's look at the words/ /"] children in various parts of the room begin to read aloud the columns of words. They have done this for two of the columns by the time the teacher gets the activity of the total group focused [and turns to face the class. Before then], however, according to the teacher's agenda the children's reading aloud was "off the record." It only becomes "on the record" after the teacher directs that ["Okay/ I'm sure everybody knows these easy words]." In the context of the teacher's ways of organizing, the children's initiations are "too soon." Notice the teacher's comment, "SH/wait for me now."[28]

Do we accept such anticipations as welcome indications that children have learned our scripts and are paying careful attention to them, or do we criticize them for not listening to directions and usurping our role?

Consider now the lesson structure as a whole. What can we say about its educational significance? Jay Lemke, a physicist and science educator who has analyzed high school science lessons, suggests that "as a mode of thematic development the triad structure [IRE] can be understood as a teacher-monolog in which some key T Inform has been transformed into a T Question/S Answer pair, with T Evaluation required to confirm their equivalence to the 'underlying' T Inform."[29] TRSs are then analogous to major divisions in the lesson outline, and the markers such as "now" at the beginning are exactly like such markers as "Right, well, let me move forward to . . . " at major topical junctures in a real lecture. At first thought, Lemke's suggestion seems to fit best those lessons in which the teacher asks only questions to which she knows the answer. In those cases, the entire lesson can be seen as an interactional transformation of a lecture she could have given herself but preferred to transform into IRE sequences, with slots for student responses in order to keep their attention or test their knowledge.

What about "Birthplaces"? Here the teacher did not know the answers in advance. The particular set of places that would be marked on the map could not be known in advance. So this lesson is not a transformation of a preplanned lecture. But the topical outline, the themes to be repeated for one child after another, are set; and particular locations are easily substitutable within them. Lemke's suggestion even helps to explain one otherwise strange-sounding evaluation in sequence 20. When Prenda reports that her father was born in Baltimore, Maryland, T answers, "Really, oh good!" Observers watching the videotape often laugh at that line and wonder what is so special about Baltimore. One possibility is that because Baltimore is so far from San Diego, discussion of its location will enhance the overall scope of the lesson. The positive evaluation is not so much for what Prenda knows as for what her report will contribute to the lesson as a whole. Similarly, T's appreciation of Carolyn's and Wallace's initiatives—expressed in "That's a good question, Carolyn" in 21, and the return to Wallace's interrupted comment in 33—also may indicate their double value: as indications of individual children's attentiveness and thought, plus their contribution to the always fragile success of the whole activity.

Any one event structure is suitable for only some educational purposes. Rather than argue about the general value of lessons as a kind of classroom discourse, we should consider which purposes they fit well and which they don't. In "Birthplaces," the lesson structure is appropriate for assembling factual information about places and distances that can be provided in short answers. It would not fit a discussion about the reasons families move (as when a Hispanic mother visited the classroom to describe her family's move from Mexico to San Diego).

Stodolsky and her colleagues discuss the fit between discourse form and pedagogical function at the end of their research on the distribution of math and social-studies lessons, which they call "recitations" (in contrast to "discussions"), in school systems serving children of three levels of socioeconomic status (SES). They found more recitations for mathematics than for social studies, and more in the lower-SES schools, and conclude:

> Pedagogues have long asserted that the recitation format is a poor instructional device. The criticisms arise from the assumption that recitations emphasize lower mental processes, are teacher-dominated and "boring." While our data do not by any means eliminate these criticisms, we believe that some thought should be given to the possible positive aspects of recitation. . . . Children's attention is relatively high during recitations and a number of teacher purposes can be served in a recitation format. Particularly in a skill-oriented subject like fifth-grade mathematics, public practice, review, and checking work may facilitate learning as well as or better than, for example, seat-work sessions in which the teacher can only interact with a limited number of children. . . . [It may serve particularly] for topics which are algorithmic and factual.[30]

If we acknowledge the importance of fit between discourse structure and educational purposes, we have to ask why the lesson-recitation form is more common in some schools than others, and we have to be alert to the danger that too much of the curriculum—especially for some children—is being reduced to the "algorithmic and the factual."

NOTES

[1] For discussions of the persistence of lessons, see Hoetker and Ahlbrand 1969; White 1974; and Cuban 1984. For analyses of lesson structure at various grade levels, see Dunkin and Biddle 1974; Sinclair and Coulthard 1975; Mehan 1979; Lemke 1982, 1986; and Malcolm 1979, 1982.

[2] Mehan 1979. Some of the transcripts are from his unpublished work.

[3] All the San Diego examples used in this book are reported as discourse, none are advocated as pedagogy. Reflecting on this particular lesson, I regret that the children were not encouraged to write their own birthplace markers and place them on the map.

[4] Mehan 1979, 65–71.

[5] Ibid., p. 66.

[6] Ibid., p. 68.

[7] These examples come from Shultz and Florio 1979 and Shultz 1979. For reviews of nonverbal communication in the classroom, see Woolfolk and Brooks 1983, 1985.

[8] Mehan 1979, 76. Evidence of dependencies across nonadjacent units has been important in cognitive critiques of behaviorist explanations of learning. See, for example, Lashley 1961 and N. Chomsky 1957.

[9]Hymes 1972b, 661.

[10]See Ninio and Bruner 1978 on picture-book reading. Also, see C. Chomsky 1972 about important features of texts; Snow 1977; Snow and Goldfield 1982; Cochran-Smith, 1983, 1986; Wells 1986; Heath 1982a; and Miller, Nemoianu, and DeJong 1986 about the interaction. Lemish and Rice 1986 compare adult-child conversation while watching television with book reading.

[11]Sinclair and Coulthard 1975.

[12]Lemke 1982, 96, 81.

[13]Griffin and Mehan 1981, 205. In this book, I use the term *structure* to refer to the patterns analyzed by researchers. The terms *rules*, *scripts*, and *schemata*, by contrast, refer to the mental representations of those patterns that we assume must be present in the minds of at least some of the participants. While further differentiation could be made among these mental terms, I have used them interchangeably.

[14]Mehan 1979, 96.

[15]Ibid., p. 106.

[16]Erickson 1982b, 178.

[17]Schön 1983 discusses professional practice of all kinds in these terms.

[18]Hymes 1972b, 66.

[19]For discussions of the concept of "canonical form" with this meaning, see Erickson's 1982b musical metaphor; Malcolm's 1982 descriptions of variations on that form in classrooms of Australian Aboriginal students; Willes's 1983 study of young children learning to be pupils; and Cazden's (in press b) review.

[20]The phrase "getting the floor" is from Philips 1983.

[21]Mehan 1979, 80.

[22]Ibid., p. 111.

[23]Ibid., p. 161.

[24]A related category of classroom formats are "routines"—sequences of behavior that are repeated with little variation and thereby automatized, such as passing out paper—that save valuable classroom time and mental attention. See, for example, Leinhardt, Weidman, and Hammond (in press), a study of routines in elementary-school math lessons.

[25]Lundgren 1977, 202, from which the example is adapted.

[26]McGeorge, personal communication, 1984.

[27]Erickson and Mohatt 1982, 161.

[28]Ibid., p. 164.

[29]Lemke 1982, 46.

[30]Stodolsky, Ferguson, and Wimpelberg 1981, 129; also Graybeal and Stodolsky 1985.

Chapter 4

Variations
in Lesson
Structure

The three-part IRE sequence is the most common sequence in teacher-led speech events. In linguistic terms, it is the "unmarked" pattern. A more informative label comes from computer terminology: IRE is the "default" pattern—what happens unless deliberate action is taken to achieve some alternative.

For example, the word-processing software with which this book was written will print everything in double-spaced lines unless I change one number in a list of printing-format features. Each time I turn the computer off, the memory of that change is lost, and the program goes back to its double spaces. Double space is the default option—doing what comes naturally. So, in the classroom, by the nature of school as an institution, the default pattern of classroom discourse—doing what comes naturally, at least to teachers—is IRE.

But other, more marked, nondefault patterns of teacher-student interaction do occur; and even small changes can have considerable cognitive or social significance.

The purpose of this chapter is to raise awareness of alternatives and suggest ways of thinking about them. We shall explore variations that reflect differences in educational purposes for talk; number of participants (teacher and one student instead of a group); medium of interaction (electronic mail instead of oral); and cultural differences among students. Surprising as it may seem, there is little research on differences in talk that occur along with differences in student age or grade.

THE PURPOSES OF TALK

Classrooms are complex social systems for many reasons, not the least of which are the many different purposes of talk. Even if we limit attention to talk that is part of official classroom air time (ignoring unofficial chat during cracks or seams in the daily schedule), and limit it also to talk that is instructional (ignoring, even if teachers can't, the talk that is managerial and procedural), there are still multiple agendas within any single classroom—shifting from hour to hour and even minute to minute.

One important shift is from recitation to something closer to a "real discussion" in order to treat topics that do not fit the lesson structure. It is easy to imagine talk in which ideas are explored rather than answers to teachers' test questions provided and evaluated; in which teachers talk less than the usual two-thirds of the time and students talk correspondingly more; in which students themselves decide when to speak rather than waiting to be called on by the teacher; and in which students address each other directly. Easy to imagine, but not easy to do. Observers have a hard time finding such discussions, and teachers sometimes have a hard time creating them even when they want to.

Fortunately, a few examples have been reported—enough to see what discussions sound like, and to explore why they seem to be so rare. These analyses show changes in three discourse features: speaking rights, the teacher's role, and speech style.[1]

Speaking Rights

In typical classrooms, the most important asymmetry in the rights and obligations of teacher and students is over control of the right to speak. To describe the difference in the bluntest terms, teachers have the right to speak at any time and to any person; they can fill any silence or interrupt any speaker; they can speak to a student anywhere in the room and in any volume or tone of voice. And no one has any right to object. But not all teachers assume such rights or live by such rules all the time.

The procedures for teacher nomination described by Mehan are typical of lessons. One important feature of discussions is the shift to more self-selection by students, from preallocation of turns by the teacher to more local management of turn taking at the moment of speaking. With this shift, classroom talk becomes more like informal conversation—not the same as conversation, because there is still the large group of potential speakers and the educational necessity to stick to an agenda, but closer to it.[2]

Here's one example from Vivian Paley's kindergarten classroom, introduced and reported by the teacher:

> [*Lisa is telling us the story of "Tico and the Golden Wings" by Leo Lionni. The children and I do not agree about Tico; I applaud him as a nonconformist while they see him as a threat to the community. . . .*]

Teacher: I don't think it's fair that Tico has to give up his golden wings.

Lisa: It is fair. See, he was nicer when he didn't have any wings. They didn't like him when he had gold.

Wally: He thinks he's better if he has golden wings.

Eddie: He is better.

Jill: But he's not supposed to be better. The wishing bird was wrong to give him those wings.

Deanna: She has to give him his wish. He's the one who shouldn't have asked for golden wings.

Wally: He could put black wings on top of the golden wings and try to trick them.

Deanna: They'd sneak up and see the gold. He should just give every bird one golden feather and keep one for himself.

Teacher: Why can't he decide for himself what kind of wings he wants?

Wally: He has to decide to have black wings.[3]

Here's another example, this time from a high school history class. The topic is Louis XIV's treatment of Huguenot dissenters:

T: The treatment that Louis XIV gave to the Huguenots is anything but acceptable, and yet some people say that he was justified in his treatment of the Huguenots, in respect to the point that he was trying to take care of his country. Do you feel that Louis was justified in his treatment of the Huguenots?

S1: I think, you know, they had their rebellion and stuff like that. I don't think he should have gone as far as totally kicking them out of the country and giving them, like, social disgrace, you know, like taking their jobs away from them. If they wouldn't interfere with his way of ruling, and their religion, why should he interfere with them?

S2: He's partially right in what he did, but I don't feel he should've kicked them out, like she said. 'Cause who is he to say how they can . . .

you know? Even though it's all Catholics, he gave 'em, like, religious freedom.

S3: I feel that he had hardly any justification at all. He wound up at the end, as Lydia said, having to almost be persuaded by all the people around him that were saying, "Well, look at the Huguenots." You know, "Why don't you do something about the Huguenots? We don't like the Huguenots". . . . It was one of the last places that he had to conquer, so he figured he'd just go out and then kill them. I think it was totally unfair.

T: OK, I can see where you're coming from, but I don't know if I can totally agree with that. Is there anyone who disagrees with what these people are saying? Marty?

Marty: I don't really disagree, but you know, we know the story, how everything worked out. . . . They wanted to get rid of the Huguenots. And just like that, you know, us here, we don't like somebody, like, you know, Italians and Nazis—sorta the same thing, something like that, in their eyes. I don't think he was justified himself.

S4: OK, in those days the church and state were like the same thing and everything, and so I think, well, like Louis—well, it isn't like today, when you can be a member of a country, just a member of a country. In those days, the church and the country meant the same thing, and when he saw people breaking away from the church, then he thought that they were breaking away from him. And he wanted to stop it. That was about the only thing he could do.

T: So you feel that he was justified in what he was doing, as far as he was concerned—he could justify it to himself.[4]

In both examples, turn taking does not follow the usual lesson sequence. Instead of the teacher regaining the floor after every student turn, there are sequences of turns in which students follow each other without nomination. In the kindergarten, the sequence is

T-S-S-S-S-S-S-S-T-S-

In the history class, it is

T-S-S-S-T-S-S-T and continues S-T-S-S-T-S-S-T

The history class may not look like a big change, but it is a significant one. And for students who are used to lesson procedures, it will feel very different too.

The shift away from teacher nomination eliminates the need for students to raise their hands. In the high school discussion, at the end of the second utterance by T, he nominates one student (Marty) by name, presumably because Marty (and maybe others as well) raised hands in response to T's question "Is there anyone who disagrees . . . ?" It is not easy for students or teacher to refrain from well-learned habits.

I remember a small seminar at Harvard that had been meeting for several months discussing Marxist writings on education. I played a relatively minor role, intellectually as well as managerially; and student self-selection was the norm. But once, when I did take a turn to speak, the next student momentarily lost his sense of this particular discussion context and, much to everyone else's amusement, started to raise his hand.

Related to the change to more self-selection of turns, but not following from it automatically, is a change in how speakers refer to each other and to the teacher. In most lessons, the teacher is the addressee for all student utterances, and references to other students' talk are rare. In the history excerpt, note S2's phrase "as Lydia said." Later, another student begins, "I think Marty is wrong." Students refer to each other, but in the third person, and T is still the direct addressee.

Still closer to conversation among equals and harder to find in schools is students addressing each other directly. Lemke calls this "cross-discussion" and looked for it in his study of high school science classrooms:

> Cross-Discussion is dialog between students in which teacher is not a constant intermediary. Such dialogue is rare as part of the public discourse of the science classroom. . . . Public cross-discussion is signalled when one student addresses another publicly rather than addressing teacher. . . . When one hears a student say, "I think you forgot . . . ," in place of (to teacher) "I think she forgot . . . " cross-discussion is taking place. Similarly if teacher is referred to in the third person.[5]

Such cross-discussion, with students addressing each other directly, occurred often in a class of fifteen-year-olds in a London comprehensive school, perhaps not only because the teacher encouraged it but also because he taught an integrated English and social-studies course to the same group of students for five years. The school is in Hackney Downs, then one of the poorest districts in London. The class included students from Africa and the Caribbean as well as white working-class families. English educator Alex McLeod recorded one discussion on the place of Afro-Caribbean culture in the school curriculum. The teacher, John Hardcastle, started with a question:

> Really what I'm working around to is asking a big question, that is, is all this business about racism something that's only of interest to black people, or is it something that's got to be important for everybody?

At one point, discussion goes back and forth between David (whose family came from Trinidad) and Ricky (who is white). Note the use of *you* and the addressee's first name (in the turns marked with an arrow in the left margin):

> *David:* It goes back to the days of slavery. . . .
>
> → *Ricky:* David, how can white people accept the full of what their ancestors done?
>
> *David:* They can recognize that it's not them.
>
> → *Ricky:* Don't you reckon that black people know that? Don't you think that black people are using that as an excuse, sort of, to ask for more sympathy?
>
> → *David:* Don't you think that some white people don't even know about the history of black people? . . .[6]

Not evident in these transcripts, and hard to determine even on videotape, is eye gaze, particularly of student speakers. In the typical lesson, students look at the teacher while speaking. She is the only official addressee. Philips describes the usual pattern:

> While the teacher is speaking, the students look at the teacher much more often than elsewhere. And when a student is speaking, the student designates the teacher as the addressed recipient of the speech by looking at [her]. Peers, in turn, do not gaze at the speaker's face nearly as often as the teacher does. They look more often at the teacher listening than they look at the student who is speaking. As often as not, while one student is speaking, the other students do not look at anyone, but gaze off in the distance or downward.
>
> This pattern of gaze direction supports an impression conveyed by the system for regulating talk that students are not supposed to play a role in regulating the talk of their peers. A child's claim to the floor is validated by the teacher, both verbally and visually, or not at all, in the official structure of talk.[7]

One primary teacher, who valued real discussion but admitted difficulty in getting it to happen, told me that she tried to avoid looking at the child who was speaking. Rude as this might seem, she felt it encouraged the speaker to make eye contact with peers, and made it more likely that another child would self-select to be the next speaker.

These changes cannot happen unless students can see one another. Discussion is almost impossible—for anyone, not just students—when seats are in rows. One experimental study compared the behavior of three fifth-grade classes brainstorming ideas for writing assignments. Each class was observed three times—while the students were seated in rows, clusters, and a circle. The circle arrangement produced the least hand raising, the most on-task comments not in response to teacher nominations, and the fewest indications of student withdrawal from the class activity. The authors concluded with a simple recommendation: "Teachers who wish to facilitate pupil interaction during discussion sessions would be wise to consider arranging desks in circles."[8]

Moving chairs can seem a nuisance in classrooms, especially with young children who have to learn how to carry them in safe ways. But, in addition to the particular value of a circle for discussion, it may be generally helpful, especially for young children, to have different physical arrangements for events where different discourse norms prevail. Just as learning a second language is facilitated by the separation of languages by setting, learning to shift ways of speaking should be helped by such visual signals as well.[9]

The Teacher's Role

In a series of studies, J. T. Dillon—from whose research the history-class example is taken—has been trying to understand why discussion is so hard to achieve. His conclusion is that what "foils" discussion, surprising as it may seem, is teacher questions, and with them the fast pace of lesson interactions.[10]

Teacher Questions. In lessons, the teacher asks questions to which she almost invariably knows the answer (often called test questions) and evaluates student answers. In discussions, her role not only is reduced in quantity but has to be changed in function as well.

Consider again the three examples just cited. The kindergarten teacher makes one comment, asks one sincere (nontest) question, and does no evaluating. The history teacher asks two sincere questions, makes one comment, and expresses one disagreement. The London teacher starts off with "a big question," intervenes to probe further ("Sunday"—from Nigeria—"what would you say if you took a white middle-class teacher that was going to come and work in an area like this . . . and says 'Why should I bring in black materials, because all it's going to do is divide kids?' ") and makes space for someone to be heard ("Go on, David, then Kevin speak.")[11]

For the teacher, this change away from a series of questions is more than a change in surface verbal behavior. At the heart of the shift from lesson to discussion is a different conception of knowledge and teaching. At the end of chapter 3, I suggested that the lesson is an interactional format that fits knowledge that is factual and can be evaluated as right or wrong, and can be subdivided into short units for demonstration in short student answers. As Stodolsky and her colleagues point out, some school content is like that—arithmetic facts and geographical information, for example. But kindergarten children's conception of fairness, and high school students' understanding of the treatment of dissenters or the question of who should learn about racism, are different kinds of knowledge that require a different kind of discourse structure.

Unfortunately, a change of teacher intent is not sufficient. Teachers and students alike are well practiced in lesson behavior, and talking in another way doesn't come easily. I suggested earlier some specific ways of encouraging a shift in turn taking. Dillon has some suggestions for alternatives to the usual teacher questions:

1. Declarative statements—as in the kindergarten T's opening.
2. Reflective restatements—as in the history T's last comment.
3. Invitations to elaborate—as in the London teacher's question to Sunday.
4. And (hardest of all) silence.[12]

Pace. Most research on classroom discourse is not done with a stopwatch. While great care may be taken to transcribe talk of one speaker that overlaps that of another, attention is not usually given to the absence of talk, to the placement and duration of silence.

One science educator, Mary Budd Rowe, has made this the major focus of her research for the past twenty years. In a recent summary of all this work—in classrooms from elementary school to college, from special-education teachers to museum guides—Rowe confirms her earlier findings that "when teachers ask questions of students, they typically wait 1 second or less for the students to start a reply; after the student stops speaking they begin their reaction or proffer the next question in less than 1 second." And, by contrast, when teachers wait for three seconds or more, especially after a student response, "there are pronounced changes in student use of language and logic as well as in student and teacher attitudes and expectations."[13]

Rowe describes the "pronounced changes" of increased wait time:

1. Teachers' responses exhibit greater flexibility, indicated by the occurrence of fewer discourse errors and greater continuity in the development of ideas.
2. Teachers ask fewer questions, and more of them are cognitively complex.
3. Teachers become more adept at using student responses—possibly because they, too, are benefiting from the opportunity afforded by the increased time to listen to what students say.
4. Expectations for the performances of certain students seem to improve, and some previously invisible people become visible.
5. Students are no longer restricted to responding to teacher questions

and get to practice all four of the moves. (Rowe adds "structuring" to the three-part sequence of soliciting, responding, and reacting.[14])

So many significant changes from a seemingly small change in pace! Like the shift away from teacher questions, the shift to a slower interactional pace may seem like a change only in superficial behavior. But here too there is an important relationship to implicit conceptions of knowledge. In Rowe's words:

> A complex thought system requires a great deal of shared experience and conversation. It is in talking about what we have done and observed, and in arguing about what we make of our experiences, that ideas multiply, become refined, and finally produce new questions and further explorations.[15]

Increasing wait time is easier to describe than to do. Rowe reports the kind of in-service supervision and support it requires, particularly if it is to be sustained and incorporated into the teacher's routine enactment of her role. In Rowe's words, "There are role and norm transformations taking place," and the teachers need a chance to talk about their experience of this change.[16]

In addition to the educational benefits that result from Rowe's interventions, her work yields an important insight into the nature of classroom discourse: the features found in any classroom are part of a complex system, and a change in any one will inevitably entail changes in others.

Speech Style

Changes in speaking rights and in the functions of the teacher's own utterances are aspects of classroom discourse to which the teacher has to give focal attention. Another feature of discussions that differentiates them from lessons is more derivative: a shift in speech style. In the words of British educator Douglas Barnes, it will be more "exploratory" and less "final draft." In the words of linguist Elinor Ochs, it will be more "unplanned" than "planned," as ideas are thought out in the course of their expression.[17]

Here is an example from Kuhn's analysis of discussions in undergraduate college classes, this one in the history of science. The topic is scientific intuition, and the teacher has asked whether it's just ordinary thought speeded up, or something qualitatively different. A student thinks aloud (in this transcription, P represents a one-second pause):

> It's probably different because it is the former that's uhh you know quick rationalization or explanation of observations and it's uhmm P P that it's P

highly highly usual because P P P because you know you you haven't gone through the whole process. [*Pace quickens*][18]

We see here some of the indicators of exploratory talk suggested by Barnes: hesitations, rephrasings, and false starts; expressions of tentativeness; and a fairly low level of explicitness. Barnes comments:

> The distinction between exploratory talk and final draft is essentially a distinction between different ways in which speech can function in the rehearsing of knowledge. . . . Both uses of language have their place in education.[19]

When Discussions Happen

So far, we might assume that a particular speech event, a particular occasion in which teacher and students gather for talk, is either one or the other—lesson or discussion. But purposes can change more quickly than that, not just from hour to hour but from minute to minute as well. And interactions that have some of the features of discussions may erupt briefly within other events.

In high school science classrooms, Lemke found that cross-discussion occurred briefly as well as rarely. In undergraduate college classes across several departments, Kuhn found that only short segments of the 50-minute periods could be characterized as true discussions, never the whole class. And temporary eruptions of discussions with younger children have been documented by Erickson and his colleagues. For example, Erickson and Catherine Pelissier discovered brief segments of discussion that are a "fine line between order and chaos" and that are—to both teacher and observers—the intellectual high point of the lesson.[20]

These observations point to the importance of infrequent events, ways of talking that have special value at specific moments, ways that would be lost from notice in analyses that combine frequencies for the lesson as a whole.

THE NUMBER OF PARTICIPANTS

Teachers talk with students individually, one to one, as well as in groups. A typology of classrooms according to kinds of discourse would show considerable variability in the amount of teacher time spent with individuals or groups. Sharing time is one context for one-to-one talk (though it takes place in front of the rest of the class). Other contexts that occur in most classrooms include moments when students request help, either from the stationary teacher at her desk or the circulating teacher making her rounds, and more formally scheduled conferences about academic work, especially writing.

Asking for Help

Many times in a school day, students need to ask the teacher for help. But whereas the teacher has the right to speak to any student at any time, students have much more limited conversational access to the teacher, especially when she is already otherwise engaged. How they manage to get the teacher's attention is usually overlooked as just a side sequence to the teacher's main focus of attention, or hidden from consideration altogether because it is outside the range that an observer can hear or record.

Sociolinguist Marilyn Merritt calls the moments when students try to get the teacher's attention "service-like events," to suggest similarities with what happens when customers act to get a clerk's attention in banks or stores. She analyzed successful and unsuccessful requests for help in ten nursery and primary classrooms, and the skills of dual processing required of both teacher and students. Here, for example, is one rule for success:

> The initiating child is most likely to be positively attended to if s/he makes a "nonverbal only" approach to where the teacher is "posted". . . . [perhaps because] a nonverbal initiation by the child allows the teacher to "start the talk." This prerogative means that the teacher can be "more in control" of the service-like event talk. It also means that the teacher can wait to start the service-like event talk until there is a spot in the teacher activity that can "most easily" be slotted out of.[21]

Because Merritt worked from videotapes that spanned five school years from prekindergarten through third grade, she had looked for differences in discourse as the children got older. For example, when the nursery-school teacher's attention was requested for a competing activity, she would often "draw the soliciting child into the teacher activity (T: 'That's very interesting, Johnny, but right now Scott has something he very much wants to tell *us* about.') But the third grade teacher was more apt to ask the soliciting child not to join in but to wait. . . . (T: 'Is this an emergency?')."[22]

Writing Conferences

Because of current interest in the teaching of writing, there is a growing number of studies of writing conferences between teachers and individual students. Research by basic writing teacher Terry Meier includes a rare account of changes in the structure and content of conferences during a six-week summer program for adults in a two-year college. The conferences were two to six minutes long. The teacher, Charlie, commented first on organizational elements in the student's paper and then switched to any grammatical problems.[23]

In one analysis, Meier compared ten randomly selected conferences from the first and second halves of the six-week course. She found striking differences. During the first half, the interaction fit the IRE or IR sequences typical of group lessons. "Charlie exerted most of the conversational control over the introduction of topics . . . , students seldom made 'initiation moves,' either by redirecting the conversation or by interrupting Charlie."

Here's a segment of a typical early conference:

Charlie: I think what, isn't what, you're getting at, ah, that you have to be confident enough to tell someone, you know, this, this isn't any good?

Jeff: Yeah.

Charlie: You have to do it, is that what you mean?

Jeff: Yeah.

Charlie: OK, then just give a little example like that. You know, say, you have to have a strong sense of yourself to tell someone who's older or more experienced or bigger or whatever it is that, no, you didn't do this job right so you're not intimidated.

Jeff: Yeah.

Charlie: You see what I mean?

Jeff: Yeah.

(Friday, week one)[24]

Moreover, even though Charlie made well-intentioned checks on the students' understanding of his comments on their work, they "invariably responded with 'mm,' 'yeah,' or 'OK,' even when they didn't really understand what Charlie was talking about, something which seven of the ten students in the study 'admitted' [in conferences with Meier] to having done on at least several occasions." Meier comments on these "yes" answers:

> Saying no—particularly when yes is the expected or preferred response . . . is a speech act which involves more self-assertion than simply assenting or agreeing. . . . To have indicated lack of understanding in the conferences would have meant taking the risk of "looking dumb," potentially losing face. . . . [It] also implicitly calls into question the adequacy of the questioner as well—i.e., was he not being clear? . . . In addition, the status relationship between Charlie and the students as well as the way in which the conferences were structured—their brevity, Charlie's obvious instructional agen-

da—tended to favor simple, unelaborated assent to whatever Charlie said, whether understood or not.[25]

In the second half of the program, the conferences changed. Students started checking their understanding by restating Charlie's point, or even by saying explicitly that they did not understand: "So what do you mean by run-on?" They also began to take the initiative in introducing issues of their own: "But where's my main idea?"

A change that would usually be overlooked is a shift in the placement, and therefore the meaning, of "mm." Whereas, in the early conferences, "mm's" were responses to a teacher initiation, in the later conferences, they were more often uttered as part of extended exchanges, and functioned as back-channeling devices for keeping speaker and listener in conversational touch with each other. For example:

Charlie: . . . So what do you, what have you described here?

Barbara: My feelings as I'm trying to write something and I get stuck for what I want to put on the paper, and what I do when I get stuck.

Charlie: OK. Is there a conflict in your mind between your, your self-image as a writer—

Barbara: Mm . . .

Charlie: —and the problems you have actually starting a story in writing?

Barbara: Yeah, because when I try to write something you see, like I don't know what I'm, I don't know how to write it, but I know that I have the stories in my head, and I, I should be able to put 'em on paper.

Charlie: OK the reason I raise that—

Barbara: Mm . . .

Charlie: —is that I think there's something underneath this.

Barbara: Right, there is.

(Wednesday, week six)[26]

Meier suggests that Barbara's first "mm" means she is following Charlie's train of thought, shown by her extended response to his question. Her second "mm" seems to indicate interest in what he's saying, which she confirms by her subsequent interruption, "Right, there is." Meier comments on the significance of these changes:

Despite its sometimes ritualistic use, especially in casual conversation, I would argue that students' increased use of backchanneling behavior in the later conferences is highly significant for two reasons.

Frequent backchanneling is not a characteristic feature of classroom discourse, a communicative situation in which students typically speak only when a response has been directly elicited by the teacher. . . . By the end of the course students had begun to interact with Charlie in a way that is more characteristic of genuine discussion or dialogue. . . .

Students' increased use of backchanneling behavior also suggests that students came to see themselves in more equal relationship to Charlie than they did at the beginning. . . . These are metacommunicative utterances—they comment on the discourse itself, and in so doing, they are implicitly evaluative. To backchannel another's utterances requires that one perceive oneself as entitled to make a metalinguistic "comment" on how well the conversation is proceeding.[27]

Meier's explanation of these changes extends beyond the conferences themselves to the students' entire experience in the six-week course. As they "developed more control and mastery over the writing process, they also began to participate more actively in the conference. . . . Broadly speaking, then, the change in conference dynamics can be seen as a movement in the direction of teacher-student co-membership in the academic community."[28]

The observations by Merritt and Meier suggest that changing the size of the student group, and individualizing teacher-student interaction, does not in itself change the structure of classroom discourse. This is also the conclusion of the study by British researchers Edwards and Furlong of an individualized, "resource-based" social studies curriculum based on "Man: A Course of Study" (MACOS) in a mixed-ability school for 11-13-year-olds: "Increased control by pupils over the pacing of their work was not accompanied by a marked relaxation in the teacher's control over what was to count as knowledge."[29] Only when the purpose of talk shifted away from transmitting to the student "the teacher's meaning system" did the structure of the talk depart from the IRE sequence.

THE MEDIUM OF INTERACTION

Until recently, all research on classroom discourse has described communication in the medium of face-to-face interaction. Now we have classes taught via electronic mail. One semester, Mehan taught a college class (on "classroom interaction"!) via two media: to one group of students in a regular classroom setting, and to another group who participated only via an electronic message system.[30]

Some features of the discourse of the class taught by computers are predictable. For instance, there was a difference in the temporal relationship between initiations and responses—a lag time of hours or even days on the computer, rather than seconds or less in the classroom.

More interesting, Mehan and his colleagues also found significant differences in the discourse itself. Topically, in contrast to the regular classroom, discussions via electronic mail pursued "multiple threads" rather than only one at a time. In other words, the criterion of relevance shifted to the class discussion as a whole, not just the immediately preceding talk. Structurally, the three-part IRE sequence was also changed. Students gave longer and more thoughtful answers to questions; teacher evaluations were almost totally absent; and students received more comments from their peers.

This comparison is important not only because it offers a glimpse of what may become a more common medium of instruction, but also because it highlights contrasting features of the more familiar classroom.

CULTURAL DIFFERENCES AMONG STUDENTS

More than ten years ago, an exhibit of Native American children's art was shown around the United States. Among the beautiful drawings and paintings, a few pieces of writing were also displayed. One, by an Apache child in Arizona, speaks for many children:

> Have you ever hurt about baskets?
> I have, seeing my grandmother weaving
>   for a long time.
> Have you ever hurt about work?
> I have, because my father works too hard
>   and he tells how he works.
> Have you ever hurt about cattle?
> I have, because my grandfather has been working
>   on the cattle for a long time.
> Have you ever hurt about school?
> I have, because I learned a lot of words
>   from school,
> And they are not my words.

One of the most important influences on all talk (some say *the* most important influence) is the participants themselves—their expectations about interactions and their perceptions of each other. We shall consider here the variation in classroom discourse that does, or should, co-occur with differences in students' home culture.

All human behavior is culturally based. Ways of talking that seem so natural to one group are experienced as culturally strange to another. Just as all speech has an accent, even though we are not made aware of our own until we travel somewhere where there is a different norm, so patterns of teacher-student interactions in typical classroom lessons are cultural phenomena, not "natural" in any sense either.

In some of its aspects, the demands of classroom discourse are new to all children. In the classroom, the group is larger than even the largest family gathered at meals, and so getting a turn to talk is much harder. When one does get a turn, acceptable topics for talk are more restricted and more predetermined by someone else. And many of the criteria by which teachers evaluate the acceptability of pupil talk are new as well.

But beyond these commonalities, some children may be at a special disadvantage. For some children, there will be greater cultural discontinuity, greater sociolinguistic interference, between home and school. Erickson states the problem in its most general terms:

> Without some considerable capacity of the teacher and learner to take adaptive action together in the mutual construction of learning environments, the species would not have survived and developed. . . . In institutions of schooling [that adaptive action] seems to occur only between some pupils and the teacher. . . . [This is] the major policy issue for schooling in modern societies.[31]

In the symbolism of the new logo for the International Student Office at Harvard University:

YIELD
Cultures
Crossing

During the past twenty years, considerable attention has been focused on cultural differences in patterns of interaction and their possible influence on students' engagement with their teacher and with academic tasks. The first influential description of such differences was anthropologist Susan Philips's study of the interaction patterns of Native American children on a reservation in Oregon.[32]

From a comparison of interaction patterns, which she called "participant structures," in non-Indian classrooms and in the Indian community, she was able to explain the Indian students' silence and nonparticipation in classroom lessons:

> Indian children fail to participate verbally in classroom interaction because the social conditions for participation to which they have become accustomed in the Indian community are lacking. In reviewing the comparison of Indian and non-Indian students' verbal participation under different social conditions, two features of the Warm Spring children's behavior stand out. First of all, they show relatively less willingness to perform or participate verbally when they must speak alone in front of other students. Second, they are relatively less eager to speak when the point at which speech occurs is dictated by the teacher.[33]

Philips called these patterns of expected and appropriate language use the "invisible culture." Anthropological linguist Dell Hymes wrote about work such as hers as examples of "ethnographic monitoring":

> Schools have long been aware of cultural differences, and in recent years have attempted to address them, rather than punish them. Too often the differences of which the school is aware, of which even the community is aware, are only the most visible, "high" culture symbols and the most stereotyped conventions. What may be slighted is the "invisible" culture (to use Philips's title), the culture of everyday etiquette and interaction, and its expression of rights and duties, values and aspirations, through norms of communication. Classrooms may respect religious beliefs and national custom, yet profane an implicit ceremonial order having to do with relations between persons. One can honor cultural pride on the walls of a room yet inhibit learning within them.[34]

Philips's work has stimulated descriptions of cultural influences on interaction, and of problems in classroom discourse that may be due to sociolinguistic interference, in other schools and communities. But neither Philips nor many of the other observers were in a position to influence classroom change. Philips's research was done with the approval, even the encouragement, of the Warm Springs Inter-Tribal Council. But neither she nor they had influence in the schools at that time. And for various reasons, most of the other ethnographies have also been reports only of the status quo.[35]

There are two well-documented exceptions to this limitation, two situations in which ethnographers have not only described problems but also stayed for a decade or more to collaborate with teachers in designs for change. One is anthropologist Shirley Brice Heath's work in the southeastern United States (Appalachia); the other is the work of an interdisciplinary team at the Kamehameha Early Education Program (KEEP) in Hawaii.

Heath's Work in Appalachia

For nine years, Heath was an ethnographer in rural black and white Appalachian communities, working at the request of parents who wanted to understand why their children were having problems in school, and simultaneously a professor in a local college giving in-service courses for teachers. When white teachers in newly desegregated "Trackton" schools complained that black children did not participate in lessons, she helped them understand what she had learned from her previous field work.

For example, the children were not used to known-answer questions about the labels and attributes of objects and events. As one third-grade boy complained, "Ain't nobody can talk about things being about their-selves." She encouraged teachers to observe the questions they asked in their own homes and at school, and then helped them design and try out new patterns of interaction in their own classrooms.[36]

Some of the changes followed this sequence:

1. Start with familiar content and familiar kinds of talk about that content.
2. Go on to new kinds of talk, still about familiar content, and provide peer models, available for repeated hearings on audiocassettes.
3. Provide opportunities for the Trackton children to practice the new kinds of talk, first out of the public arena and also on tape, and then in actual lessons.
4. Finally, talk with the children about talk itself.

Because Heath's collaboration with the Trackton teachers is unusual, I quote her description at some length:

> For some portions of the curriculum, teachers adapted some teaching materials and techniques in accordance with what they had learned about questions in Trackton. For example, in early units on social studies, which taught about "our community," teachers began to use photographs of sections of different local communities, public buildings of the town, and scenes from the nearby countryside. Teachers then asked not for the identification of specific objects or attributes of the objects in these photographs, but questions [more familiar to the Trackton children] such as:
>
> What's happening here?
>
> Have you even been here?
>
> Tell me what you did when you were there.
>
> What's this like? (pointing to a scene, or item in a scene)
>
> Responses of children were far different than those given in usual social studies lessons. Trackton children talked, actively and aggressively became involved in the lesson, and offered useful information about their past experiences. For specific lessons, responses of children were taped; after class, teachers then added to the tapes specific questions and statements identifying objects, attributes, etc. Answers to these questions were provided by children adept at responding to these types of questions. Class members then used these tapes in learning centers. Trackton students were particularly drawn to these, presumably because they could hear themselves in responses similar in type to those used in their own community. In addition, they benefited from hearing the kinds of questions and answers teachers used when talking about things. On the tapes, they heard appropriate classroom discourse strategies. Learning these strategies from tapes

was less threatening than acquiring them in actual classroom activities where the facility of other students with recall questions enabled them to dominate teacher-student interactions. Gradually, teachers asked specific Trackton students to work with them in preparing recall questions and answers to add to the tapes. Trackton students then began to hear *themselves* in successful classroom responses to questions such as "What is that?" "What kind of community helper works there?"

In addition to using the tapes, teachers openly discussed different types of questions with students, and the class talked about the kinds of answers called for by certain questions. For example, *who, when,* and *what* questions could often be answered orally by single words; other kinds of questions were often answered with many words which made up sentences and paragraphs when put into writing.[37]

KEEP in Hawaii

The full story of KEEP's continuing efforts to improve the education of children of Polynesian descent, Hawaii's indigenous minority, is long and complex. Relevant here are the changes in teacher-student interaction during small-group instruction in reading.[38]

One of the many changes was a shift to "direct instruction of comprehension" through the discussion of stories. This shift was a deliberate decision, made when behavior-modification techniques combined with a heavily phonics-based reading program produced attentive, industrious children but little growth in reading. The new teacher-student discussion focused first on children's experience with the ideas the teacher knew the text would be about, followed by silent reading of the text to find answers to specific questions, and finally discussion of relationships between experience and text.

Evidently, this change in lesson content brought with it a serendipitous change in discourse form. When comprehension was stressed in small-group discussions of the stories to be read, these discussions gradually took on an overlapping-turn structure similar to the overlapping speech that is common in ordinary Polynesian conversations, and especially in the stylized speech event called "talk-story."[39] Here, a story is co-narrated by more than one person, and the speech of the narrators is also overlapped by audience responses. The KEEP children were familiar with this pattern in their lives outside of school, and evidently gradually introduced it into the story discussions at school when the change in lesson content, and a teacher who was willing to relax her turn-taking control, made it possible. The teacher addressed many of her questions to the group rather than to named individuals, and the children volunteered answers, often chiming in and overlapping one another's answers.

Later, these lively reading-group interactions were analyzed by KEEP researchers as a bicultural hybrid of indigenous conversational style and teacher-guided content—what Hawaiian anthropologist Stephen Boggs calls "talking story with a book"—and they became an essential feature of the KEEP program. The most detailed analysis of the reading groups is by Au:

> We will argue that there must be a balance between the speaking and turn-taking rights of the teacher and children, if a participation structure or a lesson is to be related to higher levels of productive student behavior. We will refer to this idea as the *balance of rights* hypothesis and suggest that it can serve as a conceptual basis for making specific predictions about the effects of social organizational and sociolinguistic variables on academic achievement. . . .
>
> If the teacher exercises her authority by dictating the topic of discussion but allows the children to have some say about the roles they will assume as speakers and when they will speak, the cognitive and instructional focus of the lesson is more readily maintained.[40]

In a more experimental analysis of KEEP instruction, Au compared the reading lesson of two teachers, one who had had little experience with Polynesian children and the other who was an experienced teacher in the experimental KEEP program. On several proximal indices—amount of academically engaged time, number of reading-related and correct responses, and number of idea units and logical inferences—the same group of children performed better with the experienced teacher, who held the children to academic topics but gave them more freedom to choose when to speak, even if it meant overlapping another child's talk.[41]

The KEEP program works well for Polynesian children. But perhaps it would work as well for any children. How specific to Polynesian culture are these modifications? Which features of the KEEP reading lessons are simply features of good teaching for all children, and which are more culturally specific? In my opinion—and, I think, that of the KEEP researchers—some of the KEEP practices can be universally recommended, especially the teacher's role as mediator between the children and the texts, and the teacher's moment-to-moment responsiveness to her children's understanding rather than following a sequence of questions prescribed in a teacher's manual.[42]

"Relevance" is an important characteristic of good education, but sometimes we look for it in the wrong place. Relevance is often advocated as a necessary characteristic of curriculum materials. Instead, it should be considered a characteristic not of the materials but of the relationship between the materials—any materials—and the learners. It is a fundamental teaching responsibility to find ways to help students achieve that relationship. Our response to children who "hurt about school," as the Apache child put it so well, must be to find ways to make connections between their words, and their meanings, and ours.

But what about the cultural specificity of ways of speaking? In the KEEP program, the "balance of rights" or "shared control" involves the relaxation of turn-taking rules to allow children to speak out without being called on, and to chime in even when another child is speaking, as long as the content of their talk is relevant to the teacher-chosen topic. If the hypothesis of cultural compatibility is correct, other modifications of traditional lesson structure should be needed in order to achieve comparable shared control, student engagement, and academic growth for other groups of children.

To give this hypothesis of cultural compatibility a severe test, in 1983 the KEEP researchers took their program to a Native American community, where by now some schools are under tribal control. They went to the Rough Rock Demonstration School on the Navajo reservation in Arizona. A program successfully designed for one cultural group was deliberately transplanted to a very different cultural setting as a test of the cultural-specificity hypothesis.[43]

According to plan, Lynn Vogt, an experienced KEEP teacher, started out teaching the language-arts portion of each school day to a third-grade class of Navajo children. Gradually, the regular Rough Rock teacher, herself a Navajo, took over—still teaching in KEEP style. KEEP anthropologist Cathie Jordan observed the results, both directly in the classroom and on videotapes.

One feature of the KEEP reading-lesson structure seemed as appropriate at Rough Rock as in Honolulu: allowing the children to volunteer responses, rather than speaking only when called on by the teacher, seemed natural both to the children and to the Navajo teacher. But the length of child turns, and their relationship to the talk of their peers, was very different. There were no quick responses or overlapping speech. Instead, each Navajo child spoke for a longer time, volunteering questions as well as comments, while others waited patiently for their turn. "The ideas often seemed [to the KEEP outsiders] disjointed from one another, but in themselves, more complex and fully developed." As a result, the teacher asked fewer questions, and had to think very differently about relationships between the children's ideas and those in the text.

Admittedly, the contrast between Polynesian and Navajo cultures may be extreme. But this small piece of research confirms the importance of cultural differences in ways of speaking. It also suggests how sensitive teachers and observers can shorten the amount of ethnographic work necessary for adapting to such differences. In the Rough Rock situation, the most important resource for this adaptation was the indigenous teaching staff. Supplementary resources were other ethnographic descriptions of Native-American classrooms and of Navajo culture more generally, and observations of the children themselves out of school as well as in.

ADDITIONAL COMMENTS

Before we leave the topic of discourse variations, I want to add three comments.

First, another study of cultural differences is important for its alternative interpretation of why they cause problems. Ian Malcolm, an educational researcher in Western Australia, developed a comprehensive category scheme for analyzing classroom lessons and then studied classrooms of Aboriginal (black Australian) students. He found a set of speech acts that characterized the Aboriginal children's lesson behavior:

- Empty bidding—followed by silence.
- Declined replying—after a direct elicitation.
- Deferred replying—after a longer-than-normal pause.
- Shadowed replying—in the shadow of the next speaker.
- Unsolicited replying—without having been nominated.[44]

Malcolm analyzed the effect of these Aboriginal speech acts on the course of the lessons as distortions of the canonical form described in the last chapter, distortions caused "by incompletely shared acceptance or awareness of the norms of interaction by the participants."[45]

One explanation of this "incompletely shared acceptance or awareness" could be the reason suggested by Philips, Hymes, Heath, and the KEEP researchers—discontinuity between home and school—and there is some support for that interpretation from ethnographic descriptions of speech events in Aboriginal communities.[46]

But Malcolm offers "an additional perspective which does more justice to the active monitoring of the situation by Aboriginal pupils:"

> Aboriginal pupils are not simply incompetents in a white man's classroom; they are exercising their right as participants in a speech situation to help to "constitute" that situation. . . . The basics of communication to the Aboriginal pupil may well be summed up as: Who is this person who wants me to talk to him? Who is listening in? Do I want to say anything? Are my rights to noninvolvement being recognized? Have I the right to say something when I want to? If the teacher, and the school system, have treated these questions as of no account, then the Aboriginal child, by the management of his discourse role, will urge them toward acknowledging their significance.[47]

Malcolm's second interpretation may seem at first glance simply a rephrasing of the construct of interference, but his inference of more active student response offers a resolution of one puzzling aspect of cultural-discontinuity theory. We know that children can learn situationally appropriate ways of speaking and shift effectively among them at an early age. For example, a Native American toddler acquaintance of mine regularly took his pacifier out of his mouth and dropped it into his diaper bag as the car approached his day-care center and didn't retrieve it until safely back in the car hours later. That's style shifting where it hurts! Why, then, does such learning often fail to happen in the classroom? Or, in other words, what makes ethnic differences become ethnic borders?[48]

Second, a case study of science teaching reminds us that interventions can disrupt home-school continuity as well as create it. As part of a description of science education in the United States, British researcher Rob Walker describes a charismatic black teacher in a small town in the southern U.S. Bible Belt:

> Perhaps most striking is the way she stresses the students' oral expression. When they read, she listens, not just for the correct answer, but for the fluency and facility with which students use scientific terminology. This combination of teaching from the text and stressing oral expression . . . [is] particularly developed in religious communities. . . . The curriculum analyst may seek the replacement of existing styles of science teaching by a "discovery" approach . . . [but] the effect of success in this enterprise may be to cause a disjunction between school and community.[49]

The final comment comes from a journal entry by English/language-arts supervisor and Harvard graduate student, Paul Naso. After reading the research reports discussed in this chapter, in which mainstream teachers worked with minority students, he remembered his own first teaching experience "on the other side of the mismatch":

> When I began teaching in a sixth grade classroom of a suburban elementary school, I was unaccustomed to the ways of middle-class, college degree-oriented family life that most of my students knew so well. Because I went to college in the working class community I was raised in and had even lived in my parents' home while I attended college, I had rather fixed notions of how children, parents, and teachers interact. I considered differences between my childhood and my students' upbringing to be irrelevant. Most of the families of this particular suburban town came from other places all over the country; I thought that I could transplant myself as a teacher in their community as easily as they transplanted themselves as residents. That was not necessarily so. We were different and that seemed to matter. . . .

Who talked "school talk" better? I was astounded at how nonchalantly children handled what I considered exciting "new" material. At that time I was thrilled at what I was finding in my first search into children's literature. However, it seemed that whatever I came upon, children already owned it, read it, or had had it read to them. I was also struck at how matter-of-factly they referred to characters and situations that appeared in the stories they knew. One of my struggles as an undergraduate was with my inability to find common themes and to make connections between texts. It seemed not to be in my nature to cite. Yet, here were children saying that this character "reminds" them of that one or this situation in this book is "like the one" in that book, and those references were often to stories they had been introduced to at home, not in their earlier grades. Linking occurrences in literature is school work, and they were very good at it.

I suppose that now, thirteen years later I would be less impressed with that class of students. I would recognize that the description I just gave probably fits a much smaller percentage of children than my memory allows me to believe. But that was my first encounter with children whose families emphasized different things in their conversation than my family did. . . . I was struck by how conveniently school fit into the lives of these particular children; I was reminded of how incongruent school and home were for me as a child. . . .

Claims that children are unprepared for school excuse teaching (or schooling) that is unresponsive. . . . The teacher needs to find connections, in this case not in texts, but in contexts, to integrate what may easily stand as isolated school and home experiences. The unexpected or unfamiliar might alarm the teacher; or it might guide the teacher to see links where previously there appeared to be none. The teacher may, as Paolo Freire says, "enter into communion" or "remain nostalgic towards his own origins."[50]

THE SIGNIFICANCE OF VARIATION

Underlying all the variation we have considered in this chapter, one condition essential to education must remain the same: to communicate, to understand and be understood. Or, to put it another way, in order to keep this condition constant despite differences in purposes, size of group, medium of instruction, and participants, variation in discourse structure is necessary.

After reading reports of another set of studies—this time on mother-child communication—social psychologist Roger Brown found an answer to the often-asked question about what parents should do to facilitate their child's language development:

Believe that your child can understand more than he or she can say, and seek, above all, to communicate. To understand and be understood. To keep your minds fixed on the same target. In doing that, you will, without thinking about it, make 100 or maybe 1,000 alterations in your speech and action. Do not try to practice them as such. There is no set of rules of how to talk to a child that can even approach what you unconsciously know. If you concentrate on communicating, everything else will follow.[51]

Brown believes, as I do, that this fine-tuned articulation between what the child needs and what the environment provides happens un-self-consciously and nearly universally in the case of parents. Not so with teachers. We have to plan more deliberately for the many purposes for talk in our classrooms, and create the best environments—physical and interpersonal—for them.

As Naso puts it, the essential condition is still "entering into communion." Where cultural differences make that communion harder to achieve, at least at the beginning, we have to be ready to give up "nostalgia toward our own origins," including ways of speaking that have seemed so "normal" in our own past.

NOTES

[1] This set of features comes from Kuhn's 1984 analysis of discussions in college classrooms.

[2] The still-classic study of turn taking in conversation is Sacks, Schegloff, and Jefferson 1974. See also Irvine's 1979 discussion of dimensions of formality in communicative events.

[3] Paley 1981, 25–26. One reviewer of this manuscript wondered why Paley's transcriptions read so much more smoothly than others in the book. When asked how she made her transcriptions, Paley explained:

> In editing a child's speech, my aim is to preserve meaning, cadence, and inflection, and to avoid distractions for the reader. It is, I believe, the way we hear one another in the classroom.
>
> For example, Deepak, speaking of his toy snake, says, "His name is Snaky, um, and everybody calls him by his . . . um . . . not Snake, um, Tommy, um . . . and I had another . . . that other . . . um . . . it was a little bear . . . it was called Tommy . . . and the snake is . . . uh . . . Tommy the snake . . . I mean Tommy the snake is Tommy the bear's friend."
>
> Edited, the sentences might read: "His name is Snaky and everyone calls him Tommy. And I had another . . . a little bear . . . it was called Tommy. And Tommy the snake is Tommy the bear's friend." (personal communication, March, 1987).

I'm sure Paley is right that sensitive teachers (like normal conversationalists) hear children in this way. But making a transcript as an analyst is different from hearing speech as a participant and requires decisions contingent on purpose and focus (Ochs 1979b). Paley's editing is right for her books about her children. But for other purposes, the disfluencies themselves are informative, as I suggested in chapter 2, as both indications of cognitive load on the speaker and possible explanations of differential listener response. That's why I have not done editing similar to Paley's throughout the book.

[4] Dillon 1983, 18–19.

[5] Lemke 1982, 70–71.

[6] This class has been discussed by McLeod 1986, 42–43, from which this excerpt is taken; and by Hardcastle 1985.

[7] Philips 1983, 76. Goodwin 1981 is a comprehensive discussion.

[8] Rosenfeld, Lambert, and Black 1985, 106.

[9] In research on kindergarten children's learning of school scripts, Fivush 1984 finds that "the component activities of the school day seem to be marked at least partly by spatial cues."

[10] Dillon 1983, 1985.

[11] McLeod 1986, 42.

[12] Dillon 1983.

[13] Rowe 1986, 43. This article summarizes all her work. See also Tobin 1986 for a study of wait time in other curriculum areas.

[14] In shortened form from Rowe 1986, 45–46.

[15] Ibid., p. 43.

[16] Ibid, p. 46.

[17] Barnes 1976; Ochs 1979a.

[18] Kuhn 1984, 134.

[19] Barnes 1976, 113–114.

[20] Kuhn 1984. Erickson, personal communication, November 1983.

[21] Merritt and Humphrey 1979, 299; also Merritt 1982a, 1982b.

[22] Merritt 1982b, 143; second teacher utterance from Merritt, 1982a, 229.

[23] Meier 1985.

[24] Ibid., pp. 164–165.

[25] Ibid., pp. 170–171.

[26] Ibid., pp. 173–174.

[27] Ibid., pp. 175–176.

[28] Ibid., pp. 182, 172. The term *co-membership* is from Erickson 1975a. Michaels, whose research on sharing time was reported in chapter 2, has analyzed writing conferences in two sixth grades and compared them with sharing-time interactions (1985b). Staton, Shuy, Kreeft, and Reed 1983 describe dialogue journals, a hybrid of writing conferences and informal conversation in written form that originated in Leslie Reed's sixth-grade class in California and has since been adopted by teachers from primary grades to graduate school.

[29] Edwards and Furlong 1978, 121.

[30] Quinn, Mehan, Levin, and Black 1983, and Black , Levin, Mehan, and Quinn 1983.

[31] Erickson 1982a, 173.

[32] Her first, and still most influential report, was Philips 1972. Philips 1983 is a book-length version.

[33] Summarized from Philips 1972.

[34] Hymes 1981b, 59.

[35]Erickson 1984 reviews many of the classroom school ethnographies. Cazden 1983b explores why so much ethnographic research describes only the status quo. Foster 1987 is an analysis of a successful black teacher by an insider to that culture.

[36]Heath 1982b, and book-length version 1983.

[37]Heath 1982b, 124–125.

[38]For comprehensive accounts, see insiders Tharp, Jordan, Speidel, Au, Klein, Calkins, Sloat, and Gallimore 1984 and outsiders Calfee, Cazden, Duran, Griffin, Martus, and Willis 1981. On the reading program, see Au 1980 and Au and Mason 1981. For discussions of culture and the role of ethnographic research in improving education, see Jordan 1985 and Jordan, Tharp, and Vogt 1985 (ms.).

[39]The original research on talk-story was by Watson 1972, and is reported in Watson-Gegeo and Boggs 1977 and Boggs 1985.

[40]Au 1980, 149, 160.

[41]This research was Au's doctoral thesis, reported in Au and Mason 1981.

[42]Cochran-Smith 1983, 1986 gives the most detailed description of this "mediator" role in her analysis of reading and discussing stories with nursery-school children.

[43]Jordan, Tharp, and Vogt 1985.

[44]Malcolm 1979, 311, 313.

[45]Malcolm, 1982, 119.

[46]Harris 1980, abridged from Harris 1977.

[47]Malcolm 1982, 131.

[48]McDermott and Gospodinoff 1979. See Rosen's 1985 critique of Heath 1983 for her avoidance of explicit discussion of social class and racism.

[49]Walker 1978, 6.

[50]Paul Naso, journal entry, Harvard Graduate School of Education, March 4, 1985. His Freire reference is 1982, 47.

[51]R. Brown 1977, 26.

Chapter 5

Differential Treatment

In the discussion of cultural differences in chapter 4, I quoted Erickson's statement that mutual adaptation of learners and teachers seems to occur only between some students and the teacher. Studies of cultural differences and of differential treatment reflect complementary perspectives on this adaptive action. The cultural-difference perspective asserts that students would be better served if teachers took differences into account more than they now do. The differential-treatment perspective asserts that teachers now differentiate among their students in ways that may reinforce, even increase, inequalities of knowledge and skills that are present when students start school.

The two perspectives are related in other ways as well. In sharing time, cultural differences in children's narratives seem to elicit differential responses from many mainstream teachers. And sometimes well-intended presentations to teachers of information on cultural differences can unwittingly contribute to stereotypes and thereby to differential treatment.[1]

In this book so far, cultural differences have been discussed with respect to sharing-time narratives and variations in lesson structure. This chapter focuses on differential treatment in the one curriculum area where most research has been done—beginning reading—and one dimension of differentiation—higher versus lower levels of achievement. But the implications should be considered by all teachers. Just as the school curriculum becomes more differentiated in secondary and higher education, so, presumably, do teachers' responses to their students.[2]

Before the moment when children sit down with a teacher to get help in learning to read, they have been classified many times. All children receive assignments to a school, a grade, and a homeroom, then usually (at least in the United States) to a reading group. In addition, some children are further classified to receive additional reading-related services. Research on classroom discourse has focused primarily on the effect of within-classroom classification at the reading-group level. How is instruction differentiated between high-group and lower-group children? What are the likely outcomes of such differentiation? What causes such differentiation, and where are the best hopes for change?

HOW IS INSTRUCTION DIFFERENTIATED?

Before we turn to the results of recent observational research on differential instruction, it is important to state what does *not* happen. There is no consistent evidence that teachers favor high-group children in amount of instructional time or that teachers praise one group more than another. Blatant triage is not at work. The differences that turn up in systematic observations of instruction are both more subtle and more closely related to qualitative aspects of reading itself.

Recent observational studies include both survey research, in which teacher and student behavior is coded and counted in a number of classrooms, and more detailed qualitative case-study analyses of instruction in one or just a few classrooms, with audio or videotape recordings functioning as a zoom-lens camera. Ideally, information of both kinds would be available in a single study, but where that has not happened, findings from separate studies can be integrated. Fortunately for this research summary—though unfortunately, I believe, for the lower-group children—the findings across studies are so consistent that summarizing presents few problems.

Consider first Richard Allington's survey of teachers' responses to children's oral reading errors in 20 primary classrooms in three school districts in New York. Table 5-1 summarizes his findings.[3]

Note first that there is a difference in the overall rate of teacher correction of errors: more than two-thirds of the poor readers' errors were corrected, while fewer than one-third of the good readers' errors were corrected. Second, there were differences in timing of the corrections: teachers were more likely to interrupt poor readers immediately

TABLE 5–1

Group Differences in Twenty Primary Classrooms

	Lowest Reading Group	Highest Reading Group
Percentage of teacher correction of all student errors		
Immediately, at error	66	22
Later	8	9
Total	74	31
Percentage of teacher correction of semantically appropriate errors	55	11
Percentage of teacher correction of semantically inappropriate errors	79	48
Percentage of various types of cues supplied by teacher (totaling 100 percent within each group):		
Graphic/phonic	28	18
Semantic/syntactic	8	32
Teacher pronounce	50	38
Other	14	12

Note: From Allington 1980 (tables 2–4 and personal communication, 1982), with group norms translated into percentages. Copyright © 1980 by the American Psychological Association. Adapted by permission of the publisher and author.

at the point of error rather than waiting for the next phrase or clause boundary. Third, this difference in the timing of corrections applies both to semantically appropriate and semantically inappropriate errors; while more of the inappropriate errors were corrected in both groups (79 percent versus 55 percent and 48 percent versus 11 percent), the percentages are higher in both categories for the poor readers. The difference is especially notable for the semantically appropriate errors: whereas only one-tenth of such errors made by the good readers were corrected, the proportion corrected increases to more than one-half for the poor readers.

Because lower reading groups are apt to include a disproportionate number of ethnic-minority children, the influence on teacher behaviors of dialect differences and nonnative accents should also be considered. Cunningham investigated whether teachers' attitudes toward children's semantically appropriate errors differed for dialect-related errors (for example, reading "Here go a table" for "Here is a table") and nondialect errors (for example, reading "I will be home at 5:00" for "I shall be home at 5:00"). Two hundred and fourteen students in university graduate reading courses in four regions of the United States were asked on a questionnaire whether they would correct such errors when children were reading aloud. Seventy-eight percent of the dialect errors were corrected, but only 27 percent of the nondialect errors. Another section of the questionnaire probed the students' awareness of dialect differences. Because the students could not recognize the dialect errors as such, Cunningham infers that they acted out of ignorance—for example, not understanding that "here go" really does mean "here is" in many black children's language system.[4]

Luis Moll and his colleagues observed the reading instruction of second- and third-grade bilingual children in a California district bordering Mexico who were taught in Spanish by one teacher and in English by another. In general, the children were in the same relative groups in the two situations, but "the overriding concern of the lessons in English is decoding, pronunciation, and other forms related to the sounds of the second language."[5] Moll et al. believe that the English reading teacher mistook nonnative pronunciation for erroneous decoding and so subverted the children's progress in reading comprehension for the sake of a pronunciation lesson in English as a second language.

A fourth difference shown in Allington's study is in the kinds of clues teachers provide to help the children read the right word: for the poor readers, the clues are more likely to be graphemic or phonemic (that is, related to the spelling or sounds of the letters in a word), whereas for the good readers, the cues are more likely to be semantic or syntactic (related to the meaning of words or sentences).

Narrative descriptions from two first-grade case studies supplement these quantitative findings with a more qualitative picture of children's contrasting experiences in low- and high-group reading lessons. The first is from ethnographer Ray McDermott's intensive analysis of reading instruction in one first grade in New York City:

> [In the top group] occasionally, the children create problems by word calling instead of reading for meaning, and the teacher's main pedagogical task is to convince the children that there is living language . . . on the page. Thus, one child reads, "But Ricky said his mother . . ." in a dull monotone, and the teacher corrects her. "Let's read it this way, 'But Ricky, said his mother.' "
>
> With the bottom group, the teacher has rather different problems. Accordingly, the teacher and the children constitute rather different environments for each other in the different groups. The children in the bottom group do not read as well as the children in the top group, and the teacher attends less to the language on the book's pages and more to the phonics skills needed to interpret any given word in the text. Thus, there are many more stopping places in the children's reading, and the story line which is to hold the lesson together is seldom alluded to and never developed.[6]

The second description is from linguist John Gumperz's observations of two groups of children in a racially integrated first grade in California:

> We observed a reading session with a slow group of three children, and seven fast readers. . . . With the slow readers she [the teacher] concentrated on the alphabet, on the spelling of individual words. . . . She addressed the children in what white listeners would identify as pedagogical style. Her enunciation was deliberate and slow. Each word was clearly articulated with even stress and pitch. . . . Pronunciation errors were corrected whenever they occurred, even if the reading task had to be interrupted. The children seemed distracted and inattentive. . . .
>
> With the advanced group on the other hand reading became much more of a group activity and the atmosphere was more relaxed. Words were treated in context, as a part of a story. . . . There was no correction of pronunciation, although some deviant forms were also heard. The children actually enjoyed competing with each other in reading and the teacher responded by dropping her pedagogical monotone in favor of more animated natural speech.[7]

The third example comes from linguist James Collins's study of the collaborative nature of discourse during the comprehension segments of high- and low-reading-group lessons in two primary classrooms with working-class and lower-middle-class black children in Chicago. One of Collins's measures of collaboration was of "uptake"—the incorporation of a student's answer into a subsequent teacher question. Here are two examples with the critical teacher utterance marked with an arrow, followed by an indication (+ or −) of whether uptake occurred:

Uptake	No Uptake
T: All right, what are they looking for?	T: OK, when we think of a village, what do we think of? . . .
C: Signals.	
→ T: What signals? (+)	C: A little town.
	→ T: A small town, yes. And, uh, the son's name is what? (−)[8]

His "uptake" is similar to the measure of semantic contingency of caretaker's speech to younger children. The latter has been found to be one of the best predictors of children's subsequent language development.[9]

Collins's second measure of collaboration is of referential cohesion: the way in which topics are introduced by a noun phrase and then referred to subsequently by an anaphoric pronoun. Where this is not done, and topic shifts are made with potentially ambiguous pronouns, miscommunication can occur.

Collins found that the lower reading groups in both classrooms had fewer teacher uptakes and more sequences (one or two per lesson) where referential cohesion broke down and attention was diverted from discussion of the text to communication repair. After a subsequent out-of-classroom experiment in which he elicited narratives from both high- and low-group children and found no group differences in the way characters were introduced and referential clarity was maintained, Collins argued that the classroom differences must have been produced locally, in the reading groups themselves. He suggested that possible causes are less complete text knowledge on the part of the children, and more disrupted turns.

It might be argued that all such differences in instruction between low and high reading groups constitute pedagogically appropriate differentiation (a needs-based differentiation, in Maldonado-Guzman's words),[10] and that low-group children will receive the "high-group" kind of help at some later time. To confirm or disconfirm this possibility, we would need longitudinal studies following both the instruction and the progress of low-group children.

In one such study, Collins analyzed segments of lessons in which low-group children were reading stories comparable in difficulty to those the high-group children had read earlier in the year. In one of his comparisons, the two groups were taped while reading different parts of the very same story. A child in the high group read the following text:

> "John, I have your boat—" said Liza.
> "And I have a fly for your frog, too."
> "But you can't have your boat or the fly if I can't come in!"
> John looked at his frog, and he looked at Liza.
> Then he said, "Come in, Liza. Come in."

Later in the year, a child in the low group read the following passage from the same story:

> He ran out of the house with his things.
> And then he threw his boat into the garbage can.
> Liza was there. And she saw what John did.

Following are excerpts from Collins's transcription of the taped lessons (with intonation marks deleted).[11]

High Group

C: John I have your boat/said Liza and		1
T:	and	2

C: And I have a fly for your frog too / /   3

T: What's she mean by that   4

C: For the frog to eat / /   5

T: Okay / /   6

L: but . . . I . . . but   7

T: wait a minute till she gets through/ /   8

L: but   but   9

T: watch your books   watch your books   10

C: But you can't . . . have your boat/or the fly/If I can't come in/ /   11

   John looked at his frog/and he looked at Liza/ . . .   12

   Then he said come in Liza   13

T: What did he say/ /   14

C: Come in   15

T: How'd he say it / /   16

C: Come in Li—   17

T: Did he say come in Liza come in/ / Or did he say . . .   18

C: Come in   Liza/ come in/ /   19

T: Come in/ Liza   20

Low Group

M: Here   he/ . . . ran/ . . . out/ . . . of/ . . .   1

T: he   2

M: the house . . . wuh—   with his things/ /   3

T: with   4

M: And then . . . he . . .   threw his   5

T: sound it out/ threw   6

M: bu—(boat) boat/ . . . into the . . .   gahbag can/ /   7

                                    guh—   8

T: garbage/ / Say garbage/ /   9

M: gahbage   10

T: Don't say gahbage/ look at me/ /Say garbage/gar/ Say it / /   11

   Everybody say it/ /   12

CC: garbage   13

T: Celena/ say it/ /   14

Ce: garbage   15

T: Right/ /Marion / Liza   16

M: Liza . . .   was . . .   there and she was   17

T: where are we Sherrie   there   18

T: What   19

M:	she was	saw what . . .		19
T:	no/ /sss . . .	how does -j- sound/ /		21
M:	juh/ /			22
T:	What's the boy's name / / . . . John			23
M:	John . . . said			24
T:	did/ / She saw what John did/ / Marion/ what did he do / /			25
T:	She saw what he did/ / Now what did he do/ /			26
M:	He threw his things in the gahbage			27
T:	garbag/ / Right/ / Go on/ /			28

As Collins points out, the teacher helps the two readers in very different ways. With the high-group child, she interpolates one comprehension question (line 4), and she corrects the intonation necessary for indicating a clause boundary (line 2) and for separating spoken messages from addressee (lines 14, 16, 18). By contrast, with the low-group child she gives not only more help but qualitatively different kinds of help: directions to use phonic cues (lines 6 and 21), and a protracted attempt to correct the reader's pronunciation of one word (lines 9–15 and 28), after which even the teacher has lost her place.

Because of the consistency of the findings of these studies despite differences in researcher, classroom, and methodology, I believe that the classrooms studied can be considered representative of many—maybe even most—others that might be observed.

THE QUESTION OF OUTCOMES

Existing research suggests two ways in which the kinds of differentiation of instruction just described can restrict the progress of the low-group children. First, there is the effect of the more immediate timing of corrections. In a study similar in purpose to the wait-time research discussed in the chapter on lesson variations, New Zealand psychologists Stuart McNaughton and Ted Glynn conducted an experimental study of the effect of the timing of teacher correction—immediate (before the next word) or delayed (for five to ten seconds)—on children's self-correction behavior and reading-accuracy scores. Immediate correction depressed both children's self-correction and their accuracy scores, even on a second passage when no experimental correction occurred. McNaughton and Glynn suggest that teacher correction may interfere with children's progress by maintaining their "instructional dependence where they should be encouraging the children's self-corrections that are important both to early progress and eventual independent reading."[12]

Second, there is the effect on low-group readers of decreased attention to meaning. According to our best understanding of the reading process, it is neither just "bottom-up," driven by a reader's perceptions of letters, nor just "top-down," driven by the reader's hypotheses about what the text may contain. Instead, processing of different levels of text structure proceeds simultaneously and interactively. Many beginning readers may need to have their attention focused, temporarily but explicitly, on syllables and letters (as Resnick, for example, argues).[13] But even temporary focus at that level must be balanced by a complementary focus on the higher levels of text essential for meaning.

An important aspect of the much-used word *context* is the mental context—the context in the mind—provided by the reader's understanding of a larger unit of text than is being read at any one moment. Because of differences in preschool literacy experiences, children arrive at school with that context in the mind developed in different ways. All children in a literate society have experience with what has come to be called environmental print (labels, signs, and so forth), but that experience may not be the equivalent of being read to for building the context in the mind that is essential for reading larger units of connected text in books. It is unfortunate if attention to understanding larger meaningful units of text is most neglected during instruction for the very children who may need it the most.[14]

THE QUESTION OF CAUSES

If we assume, as I do, that teachers are dedicated to helping all children learn, how does this differential treatment come about? In other words, even if we agree that adults should, and do, tailor their instruction to the perceived needs of their students, we are still left with the question of why the instruction is differentiated in these particular ways, and what causes these unintended consequences.

Before we speculate on possible sources, a recent conceptualization of the problem may be helpful. In their book *Dilemmas of Schooling*, Ann and Harold Berlak describe teachers' resolutions of particular tensions and contradictions—"dilemmas"—inherent in all teaching. While any teaching act can be seen as a simultaneous resolution of multiple dilemmas, each dilemma is a separate heuristic lens for examining the teaching process.[15] Three of the Berlaks' dilemmas are especially relevant to differential instruction.

The first teaching dilemma is whether to respond to the ways in which children are alike or the ways in which they differ from one another. Differentiation of instruction by reading groups seems to indicate that teachers consider level of reading ability within a classroom as an indication of categorical differences in the ways children learn to read.

The second dilemma expresses the tension between conflicting theories about how people learn: by holistic practice or by attention to molecular parts. From the accumulated evidence, teachers seem to resolve this dilemma differently for different groups of children, believing that learning must be more molecular for those who have achieved less and can be more holistic only for those who have achieved more.

The third dilemma involves how teacher and students share responsibility for setting standards, monitoring progress, and correcting errors. If we assume that the goal of education is, in Marie Clay's felicitous words, to help all students construct "self-improving systems," then all students need the opportunity to make their own self-corrections.[16] But some teachers seem to believe that only some children can use the teacher's wait time toward that end. The errors of children in low reading groups are corrected more consistently and more immediately, as if the teachers were acting out of fear that the errors of these children (like the children themselves) might get out of control.

At first thought, this use of dilemma language as a conceptualization of differentiated instruction may recall the older "teacher expectation" literature, phrased in other terms. But whereas expectations differ simply in amount—a teacher expects more of some children, less of others—the dilemma language helps us see how the realizations of those expectations in actual teaching behaviors vary in complex qualitative ways.

Influences on teaching can be categorized as preactive and interactive (to use Philip Jackson's terms),[17] depending on their temporal relationship to the teaching act. Preactive influences are the dilemma resolutions, scripts, and pedagogical theories that teachers bring into the classroom. They are conscious ideas, accessible in an interview and often detectable in a teacher's written plans. Interactive influences, by contrast, are generated in the "in-flight" interactions with students. They are less conscious and may not result from decisions in the usual reflective sense.

Preactive Influences

If teachers do have differential theories of pedagogy based on perceived needs of students, where would such theories come from? Are they explicitly taught in preservice or in-service teacher education? Are teachers told that low-achieving children are more likely to develop "bad habits" and that therefore their errors should be corrected more frequently and more promptly? With respect to reading, are they told that low-achieving children need more attention to decoding skills and less to comprehension? What is the influence on instruction of the occupational culture of teachers—for example, informal staff-room chat?[18]

Messages about how the kind of instruction that different children need may also be transmitted through the way materials are designed. In her comparison of two beginning-reading programs, Distar and Open Court, Elsa Bartlett speculates about the possible effects of these programs on teachers' (and children's) conceptions of literacy—what it is and how it is achieved. First, does the altered alphabet and simplified orthography used in Distar I convey the impression to teachers that the children in Distar groups cannot cope with the "real thing"?

> In the search for an efficient instructional system, we may arrive at something that, at least superficially, seems to make life easier for beginners but that may hinder their subsequent development, either by teaching them inappropriate word-recognition routines or, more importantly, by limiting their concept of what it is that they can use their literacy to accomplish. Furthermore, . . . the limitations lie not just in the children's expectations but also in the expectations that any such curriculum will generate in a teacher about what it is that children can learn. With its emphasis on simplistic rules and rote memory, a program such as Distar may convey the impression (no doubt, unintended) that its children cannot absorb the "real thing"—the kind of orthography, diverse mapping rules, and flexible heuristics that are used in programs intended for other children.[19]

Second, does Distar's more limited set of comprehension tasks depress teachers' expectations about the kinds of questions the children are capable of answering?

> The disadvantaged child [learning with Distar] is given a simpler set of tasks: locating and remembering specific information from the immediately preceding text. In contrast, the goal for the middle-class child [learning with Open Court] is to integrate and reflect on material from the entire story. The point here is not that disadvantaged children do not need practice with this particular set of skills; probably all first graders do. The point is that in the first year, the program seems to go no further. And this can be limiting in two ways. First, it can limit children's expectations about what they can do with what they read—whether they will conceive of reflecting on it, having opinions about it, arguing with it, and so forth. Second, and perhaps more important, the limited tasks can limit the teachers' expectations about the kinds of questions that are used in other parts of the instructional program.[20]

Interactive Influences

Whatever the nature of teachers' conscious ideas, differentiation of instruction can also be created out of awareness in moment-to-moment "in-flight" interactions in the classroom. The best-laid lesson plans may go awry, because no lesson is under the teacher's unilateral control; instead, teacher behavior and student behavior reciprocally influence each other in complex ways.

The clearest examples of this reciprocal influence during reading groups come from analyses of how teachers allocate turns and generally try to keep the attention of the reading children focused on the reading task. One of the striking contrasts McDermott found in his contrastive study of high and low first-grade reading groups was in the turn-taking procedure: in the high group, children read in turn around the group, and no time was lost "off task" between readers; in the low group, children bid for a turn, and considerable time was lost after each child had finished. After reviewing turn-taking research, Lee Shulman argues against the century-old pedagogical rule that "pupils should be called upon promiscuously, and not in rotation." His arguments are based on exactly what McDermott found: "promiscuous" assignment produces unequal opportunities and substantial time spent attending to the turn-taking process rather than to reading.[21]

Sometimes, research can help us understand not only which teacher behaviors are "best" on some criterion but also why other behaviors continue to exist. McDermott suggests that the bidding process exists because it is itself functional for the teacher with her low group: it helps her avoid calling on children who basically cannot read. Then, because of the increased time off-task between readers, the low group is more interruptible, and is actually interrupted more frequently than the high group by other children who approach the teacher for help.

In a study of another first grade, Donna Eder also finds joint teacher-student production of attentiveness. In this room, children were assigned to reading groups by the first-grade teacher after a conference with the kindergarten teachers, who evaluated individual children in terms of their maturity ("attention span" and "listening skills") as well as reading readiness (more narrowly defined as knowledge of letters and so on). In this way, lower reading groups may have more inattentive behavior because children who have such problems are assigned there for that reason. Then the problems escalate. Inattentive behavior generates further inattentiveness when other children turn from their work to watch or get involved; and when the teacher shifts her attention from reading to the inattentive children, the lesson itself loses coherence and interest. If she avoids strictly managerial acts and tries to regain inattentive children's attention by calling on them when someone makes a mistake or just pauses to figure out a word, then the more frequent interruptions of low-group reading turns documented earlier is an understandable result.[22]

Teachers, like their students, are subject to the effects of reinforcement. McNaughton and Glynn suggest that hearing children read the right word correctly following immediate correction is a powerful reinforcer for the teacher's correcting behavior, especially with children who are making slow progress, even though there may be unfortunate longer-term effects on the progress of the corrected child.[23]

Two other analyses of reciprocal teacher-student influence are not of reading groups, but both contribute to our understanding. One is from a collaborative attempt in Tucson, Arizona, by language-arts coordinator Helen Slaughter and sociolinguist Adrian Bennett to create an interview in which bilingual children's oral language could be assessed. The aim of the interview was to elicit from a child extended multiclause discourse in both Spanish and English. As they listened to the audiotaped discourse, they realized that the adult's discourse style strongly influenced the complexity and coherence of language produced by the students. Particularly acute problems were encountered with the youngest and/or least proficient children:

> In analyzing the data, especially samples of elicited discourse of kindergarten children, it became clear that the task of establishing a topic of conversation, [and] eliciting clause or multiclause level responses from children, usually depended upon certain characteristics in the utterances of both adult examiner and students. Generally, the examiner in searching for a topic must suggest several topics that are within the child's experiential and conversational range, and must do so in a way that establishes a mutual conversational context. . . . Examiners must also help sustain a topic responded to by the child by continuing conversation on that topic rather than shifting to another. The mutual search for a topic of conversation also depends upon the child's utterances which must usually extend beyond some minimal one word or elliptical response to the elicitation. In other words, the child must provide some information that the examiner will be able to build upon in establishing the topic.
>
> Highly proficient students can often demonstrate conversational proficiency even in a less than optimal interview situation; also older students appear less affected by examiner characteristics. Conversely, some students appear to be low in language proficiency despite adequate examiner elicitation procedures. However, in general, the quality of student discourse appears highly dependent upon the quality of the interaction between examiner and students.[24]

In other words, if a child says only one or two words, the adult has less to build on in sustaining the topic and so is more apt to switch to another topic; as a result, a conversation in which the child is most apt to produce expanded responses never develops. The problem is magnified if the teacher is unfamiliar with the child's personal and cultural world. Remember, from the chapter on sharing time, Leona's teacher's honest reflections, and Tizard's more general comparisons of conversations at home and at school.

A similar reciprocal influence seems to have occurred in the changes in sharing time between two consecutive years in Ms. Wright's kindergarten–first grade observed by Dorr-Bremme. On his videotapes, the differences are clear: in Year II, talkativeness was less evenly distributed, and more children had little or nothing to say; and the most talkative children were more apt than in Year I to talk about topics that the teacher didn't value (like TV shows). The teacher was aware of differences in the two student groups, but she was not aware of the adaptive changes in her own behavior that Dorr-Bremme found on his videotapes. For example, during Year II sharing time, but not in Year I, she introduced topics, held students to them, and herself interpolated more comments and questions. Dorr-Bremme remarks:

> It is worth noting that in circumscribing the sharing topic [to the previous day's visit to a local hospital, for example], Ms. Wright may have inadvertently produced an interactional situation on which students had little to say. Children may not have remembered things they saw at the hospital. Alternatively, they may have understood that simply naming something that they remembered or liked best was all that was expected of them.[25]

Ms. Wright's adaptations (evidently made out of awareness) are understandable as a way of getting through sharing time without the domination of a few children. But they seem not to have helped the less proficient Year II children talk more like the children of the year before.

In summary, some of the recent videotape analyses of classroom discourse (sometimes called "microethnography") have enabled us to understand one important aspect of classroom speech events. In Dorr-Bremme's words:

> It seems that the ways of acting students bring to a classroom event can make a notable difference in how teachers teach in that event. It appears, in other words, that how students act can constrain the range of action choices that make sense for teachers to consider and choose. And as teachers teach (or "manage") the class in different ways, they constrain the range of actions that are appropriate and reasonable for students. But if students have a role in determining teachers' ways of doing teaching and/or "classroom management," then students play a collaborative part in structuring the classroom environment in which they are expected to learn and display what they have learned.[26]

But responsibility for doing everything possible to break into this circle of reciprocity remains with the teacher.

THE QUESTION OF CHANGE

My interpretation of these studies is that it will take special efforts to counteract widespread and powerful patterns if we are to ensure that the most effective teaching reaches all children.

The most obvious place to start is to present observations to the teachers themselves, in hopes that consciousness raising can begin. To my knowledge, none of the research on differential instruction has included discussions with the observed teachers. Such an effort is certainly worth making, including some kind of monitoring of deliberate attempts to change. The Kamehameha Early Education Program (KEEP) has developed one such monitoring system, designed to ensure that teachers focus children's attention on comprehension at least two-thirds of the teaching time.[27] Such a monitoring system will be helpful only if it is perceived by teachers not as an imposed policing by some evaluator (reading supervisor or building principal) but as a self-examination done periodically by one teacher-colleague for another.

But to the extent that patterns are functional in their present context, then change may be difficult to achieve, and even more difficult to sustain, unless the context of instruction itself can be changed. In other words, we shouldn't try to suggest to teachers, "Don't say X, say Y." I assume instead that some aspect of the larger activity structure will have to be changed.

That is what KEEP has done. In that program, homogeneous reading groups still exist, but the tasks to be accomplished have been changed. More time is spent discussing children's experiences relevant to the text to be read, and the reading itself is done silently, in order to let the children contribute text-based answers to the group discussion. A change from the traditional "round robin" oral reading to reading silently to find answers to questions should significantly decrease the excessive correction of oral reading errors with low-group children. As Allington points out, silent reading is judged by the adequacy of the reader's response to questions, while oral reading is more apt to be evaluated on the surface accuracy of the oral reproduction of the text.[28] I mention the KEEP program not to recommend its particular features as the solution for every classroom, but as an example of what change in the context of instruction, plus some kind of monitoring, can accomplish.

Changes within school itself are not the only possibilities. If, as I have suggested, teachers' familiarity with their children's personal and social world is critical to effective communication in school, then we also need to find ways to overcome the social and psychological distance between school and home.[29]

The problem of unintended bias is not specific to teaching. Lipsky discusses a similar challenge to social workers, another category of what he calls "street-level bureaucrats":

> The general argument . . . based on observations that street-level bureaucrats consistently introduce unsanctioned biases into client processing, suggests that it would be difficult to eliminate client differentiation without changing the structure of work for which these biases are functional.[30]

THE SIGNIFICANCE OF DIFFERENTIAL TREATMENT

The interpretation of particular teacher behavior as differential treatment can be supported by two kinds of evidence. First would be objective long-term evidence of detrimental effect. Since longitudinal studies are rare, such evidence is hard to find. In its absence, I have argued more circumstantially from what I believe to be good instruction.

Most of the research reported in this chapter is about early reading. My choice of words admittedly conveys a critical stance. For example, when a young oral reader utters a word that does not correspond to the word in the text, and the teacher speaks immediately to supply the correct word, what verb should we use to describe the teacher's action? I (and Allington before me) called it an "interruption" instead of "correction" or, even more positively, "help." "Interruption" can be defined only by the interpretation of an action, not by objective features of the action itself. My justification for using it is based on my understanding of the mental processes that reading requires. I believe that the low-group children are being denied opportunities to develop their own abilities for self-correction.

The second kind of evidence would be subjective reports by the student recipients. Do they perceive what I call differential treatment as differential experience? Older students could explain how they felt about their teachers' behavior. For example, Deena complained to researcher Sarah Michaels about her teacher's interruptions of her sharing-time narratives (given in chapter 2):

> She was always stoppin' me, sayin' "that's not important enough," and I hadn't hardly started talking![31]

Concern over unintended bias becomes for some educators an argument for highly scripted programs such as Distar or for computer-assisted instruction. If we want to retain, and expand, the arena for professional discretion rather than letting the problem be addressed in these more "teacher-proof" ways, we will have to find ways to reduce unintended bias in our actions. Of all classroom resources, our own behavior as teachers is the most precious.

NOTES

[1] See Fuchs 1966 for an example from the 1960s, and Kleinfeld 1975 and 1983 for more recent discussion.

[2] Trujillo 1986 reports a quantitative study of majority and minority students by sixteen white male college teachers from various disciplines: nonminority students were asked more complex questions, were pushed more to improve their answers, and received longer comments on their answers.

Another important dimension of possible differentiation is gender. In a meta-analysis of British and American quantitative studies of gender differences in teacher-pupil interactions, British sociologist Alison Kelly (in press) finds that girls get less teacher attention than boys, and that only some of the difference can be accounted for by the greater frequency of teachers' disciplinary contacts with boys. See also Wilkinson and Marrett 1985.

[3] Allington 1980.

[4] Cunningham 1976–77.

[5] Moll, Estrada, Diaz, and Lopez 1980, 57.

[6] McDermott 1978, 22–23.

[7] Gumperz 1970.

[8] Collins 1982, 1986. Examples from 1982, 151, 154.

[9] See Snow 1983 and Cazden, in press a.

[10] Maldonado-Guzman 1983, 1984 gives a conceptual framework and analysis of differential treatment in language arts and mathematics lessons in one of the bilingual classrooms (classroom S) described in chapter 9.

[11] Collins (unpublished ms.).

[12] McNaughton and Glynn 1981, building on Clay 1985.

[13] Resnick 1979. Anderson, Hiebert, Scott, and Wilkinson is an authoritative synthesis of research on reading.

[14] Cochran-Smith 1986, and book-length version 1984, give a detailed picture of how these mental contexts for literacy are built in one nursery school. Wong and McNaughton 1980 show experimentally that taking time to develop these mental contexts improves children's oral reading proficiency.

[15] Berlak and Berlak 1981.

[16] Clay 1985, 14.

[17] Jackson 1968. See Shavelson and Stern 1981 for a general research review.

[18] Hargreaves 1980 raises this question.

[19] Bartlett 1979, 234.

[20] Ibid., pp. 238–239.

[21] Shulman 1981. His century-old rule is from Stoddard 1860.

[22] Eder 1982a, 1982b.

[23] McNaughton and Glynn 1980.

[24] Slaughter and Bennett 1982, 61.

[25] Dorr-Bremme 1982, 397, n. 22.

[26] Ibid., p. 433.

[27] Calfee, Cazden, Duran, Griffin, Martus, and Willis 1981 includes a brief description.

[28] Allington, in press.

[29] Cazden 1976 reports my attempts to lessen the distance between myself and the black and Mexican-American children in San Diego.

[30] Lipsky 1980, 156.

[31] Michaels 1981, 439.

Chapter 6

Classroom Discourse and Student Learning

To talk about classroom discourse is to talk about interindividual communication. But the goal of education is intraindividual change and student learning. We have to consider how the words spoken in classrooms affect the outcomes of education: how observable classroom discourse affects the unobservable thought processes of each of the participants, and thereby the nature of what all students learn.

With such questions, we are in the difficult area of relationships between thought and language, or "thinking and speech," as the title of Vgyotsky's book, published as *Thought and Language*, should be translated. The change from "thought" to "thinking" and from "language" to "speech" is more than a quibble about the correct translation from the Russian. The shift in each case is to the more dynamic term: from thought as a product to thinking as a process, and from language as a symbolic system to speech as the use of language in social interaction.[1]

Given the difficulties of analyzing the thinking-speaking relationship, how should we consider that relationship in the classroom? Answers must differ depending on whether the talk is between learners and an expert (usually the teacher) or among peers. This chapter considers again teacher-led speech events. The next chapter asks the same question about interactions among peers.

In the past, the most common method for analyzing classroom discourse in cognitive terms has been categorizing teacher questions on some cognitive scale. First I shall review these attempts, and then I shall turn to more recent work.

CATEGORIZING TEACHER QUESTIONS

We all probably believe that questions at their best can stimulate thought. Duckworth interprets Piagetian "clinical interviews" in these terms:

> To the extent that one carries on a conversation with a child as a way of trying to understand a child's understanding, the child's understanding increases "in the very process." The questions the interlocutor asks in an attempt to clarify for him/herself what the child is thinking oblige the child to think a little further also. . . . What do you mean? How did you do that? Why do you say that? How does that fit with what was just said? I don't really get that; could you explain it another way? Could you give me an example? How did you figure that? In every case, those questions are primarily a way for the interlocutor to try to understand what the other is understanding. Yet in every case, also, they engage the other's thoughts and take them a step further.[2]

But categorizing teacher questions for their cognitive value is surprisingly hard to do. All categorizations depend on a distinction between questions that request factual recall or literal comprehension and questions that require more complex inferential cognitive work to go beyond the information easily available in memory or text. Bloom's Taxonomy of Educational Objectives for the cognitive domain has been the most influential scheme. It can even be considered the prototype taxonomy, representing commonalities among all the schemes developed in the last 50 years.[3]

Educational research has finally validated the educational benefits of teachers' asking more "higher-order" questions.[4] But the fact that it took a powerful meta-analysis to establish statistically what many teachers and researchers have long believed intuitively indicates that a lot of variation in cognitive impact is not caught by frequency counts of isolated question types.

For the teacher, that variation includes the importance of optimal placement of higher-order questions, and the difficulties in following up more complex questions addressed to a single student in a group lesson. For the researcher, there is the analytical problem of trying to decide the import (to the student) and the intent (of the teacher) of any question considered in isolation. The context in the mind of the student responder at the moment of answering will affect the amount of work any answer requires. And the real intent of the teacher's question is often clear only from her subsequent evaluation of student answers.[5]

Edwards and Furlong reflect on the difficulty of making even the seemingly simple two-value distinction between open and closed questions:

> Talk is not one distinct item after another. It involves what has been called "conditional relevance": the meaning of an utterance arises partly from something else which has been (or will be) said, perhaps some distance away in the interaction. . . . This point, of great importance for our own analysis of classroom talk, can be illustrated by considering a problem facing many systematic researchers, that of distinguishing between closed and open questions. . . . Many questions which appear to be open are closed because of the context in which they are asked (perhaps the teacher has recently provided "the" answer), or because the teacher has clear criteria of relevance or adequacy or correctness of expression to which he refers in evaluating the answers. The narrowness of the question only appears in what happens next.[6]

Barnes calls questions that are open in form but demonstrably closed in function "pseudo-open" questions. One of his examples is, "What can you tell me about a Bunsen burner, Alan?" This sounds completely open but, as the lesson ensues, it becomes clear that from all possible statements about a Bunsen burner, the teacher is seeking a particular statement about the conditions for luminous and nonluminous flames.[7]

I conclude from these difficulties that trying to apply some scale of cognitive difficulty to individual questions may be heuristically useful for teachers, but it is inherently imprecise for research. If, instead, we consider discourse in longer sequences, we can think about the potential cognitive value of classroom discourse as scaffold and as reconceptualization.

DISCOURSE AS SCAFFOLD

Near the end of a lengthy review of recent theories of cognition and instruction, educational psychologist Lauren Resnick writes about changes in how cognitive psychologists conceptualize teaching:

> Traditional views of the way in which social interaction affects learning focus on the adult as provider of new information, as a modeler of correct performance, and as a selective reinforcer of children's tries at producing the performance. . . . A different view of social processes in learning is attracting increased attention among cognitive psychologists interested in the development of general cognitive competence. The Soviet psychologist Vygotsky . . . has argued that cognition begins in social situations in which

a child shares responsibility for producing a complete performance with an adult. The child does what he or she can, the adult the rest. In this way, practice on components occurs in the context of the full performance. In naturally occurring interactions of this kind, the adult will gradually increase expectations of how much of the full performance the child can be responsible for.[8]

The metaphorical term *scaffold*, first introduced by Bruner and his colleagues, has come to be applied to social interactons of this kind. A familiar picture will make clear the concept and the pervasiveness of its exemplars. Imagine a picture of an adult holding the hand of a very young toddler with the caption, "Everyone needs a helping hand." Exactly as Resnick says, the child does what he or she can and the adult does the rest; the child's practice occurs in the context of the full performance; and the adult's help is gradually withdrawn (from holding two hands to just one, then to offering only a finger, and then withdrawing that a few inches, and so on) as the child's competence grows.

Before considering instructional activities that have been deliberately designed on this model, let's look at analyses of naturally occurring activities involving preschool children and their adult care givers that have been analyzed in these terms. I include here only scaffolds with dialogue. But, as developmental psychologists Fischer and Bullock point out in a review of post-Piagetian views of development, good computer software can also function as a scaffold, even if the learner works alone at the moment of use.[9]

Scaffolds for Preschool Children

Even before assistance to the toddler trying to walk, there is assistance to infants trying (at least as some mothers believe) to communicate. Psycholinguist Catherine Snow describes how hard mothers work to achieve a "conversation" despite the inadequacies of their three-to-eighteen-month-old conversational partners. At first they accept burps, yawns, and coughs as well as laughs and coos—but not arm waving or head movements—as the babies' turn. They fill in for the babies by asking and answering their own questions, and by phrasing questions so that a minimal response can be treated as a reply. Then, by seven months, the babies become considerably more active partners, and the mothers no longer accept all the babies' vocalizations, only vocalic and consonantal babbles. The mother raises the ante, and the child's development proceeds.[10]

Another example is Wertsch's analysis of a mother guiding her child through the task of making a copy puzzle just like a model. The task has three steps:

- Step 1: Consult the model to determine the identity and location of the piece needed next.
- Step 2: Select the piece identified in Step 1 from the pieces pile.
- Step 3: Add the piece selected in Step 2 to the copy object in accordance with its location in the model.

Here is a description of three episodes of interaction between a mother and her two-and-a-half-year-old child as they worked through the pieces of a single puzzle:

> The first two episodes began with the child asking where a piece was to go and the mother responding by directing the child's attention to the model puzzle. In both these episodes, the child's original question led to a response by the mother which, in turn, led to the child's response of consulting the model. All of these "moves" or "turns" were part of external, interpsychological functioning. The third episode began quite differently. First, the child did not produce a fully expanded question about where a piece should go. Second, and more importantly, her gaze to the model puzzle was not a response to an adult's directive. Rather than relying on an adult to provide a regulative communication, she carried this out independently using egocentric and inner speech. That is, in the case of some of the strategic steps required here, there was a transition from external social functioning to external and internal individual functioning.[11]

This description came from a research project, but essential features of the mother's guidance are common in naturally occurring puzzle activities at home.

Next are the early language games, such as peekaboo, that exemplify four features: a restricted format, clear and repetitive structure, positions for appropriate vocalizations, and reversible role relationships. And similar to peekaboo in its early versions, but open to greater complexity, is picture-book reading, also first analyzed by Ninio and Bruner in these terms. In all these early language games, as the child's development proceeds, he takes over more and more of the script.[12]

There can even be an analogue to cultural interference in this early learning. As Ninio and Bruner point out, picture-book reading has a different structure if the mother reads a nursery rhyme and leaves a slot for the child to fill at the end of each line. Sharon Haselkorn, while a graduate student at Harvard, reported interference between the patterns of mother and researcher that she encountered with book reading at this early age. Sharon was used to playing the "What's that?" game, but one of her young subjects had learned the "fill-in-the-blank" game, and they had a very hard time getting their book-reading acts together.[13]

In all these examples, the mother can and does enact the entire script herself in the beginning, but the child gradually assumes a more active role. Variations in the games over time are critical. The adult so structures the game that the child can be a successful participant from the beginning; then, as the child's competence grows, the game changes so that there is always something new to be learned and tried out, including taking over what had been the adult's role. Bruner's term *scaffold* has become a common caption for the adult's role in these games, and it is a good name if we remember that this is a very special kind of scaffold—one that self-destructs gradually as the need lessens and the child's competence grows.

Scaffolds in School

Figure 6–1 shows the basic structure of all the learning environments that fit the term *scaffold*. The authors, reading researchers Pearson and Gallagher, suggest that the model can be applied generally to education. Most instructional examples come from reading and other language arts, but there seems no reason why teaching skills in other areas couldn't be considered in the same terms.[14]

Because of problems inherent in fine tuning instruction to a group of children at the same time, instruction fitting this model probably occurs most often in teachers' interactions with individual students. One example comes from my San Diego classroom, when I instructed Leola

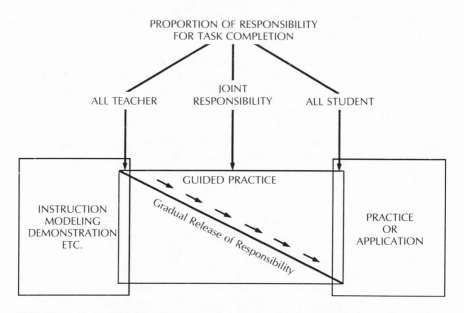

FIGURE 6–1   Basic Structure of Learning Environments That Fit the Term *Scaffold* (J. Campione, in Pearson and Gallagher 1983)

in a language-arts task that she would later teach to several of her peers. Here are the first two items on her worksheet in completed form, a sequential analysis of the task, and an edited version (minus repetitions, self-corrections, and so on) of my directions as I talked Leola through the first two items on the task (much as Wertsch's mothers talked their younger children through the copy puzzle):

1. new   1. Y∅lo∂u   2. tу́́éol∮d   3. m∅ńe
2. no
3. off   <u>You</u>   <u>told</u>   <u>me</u>

1. Read word on list at the left: new.
2. Think of its opposite: old.
3. Spell the opposite: O-L-D.
4. Find the set of letters with the corresponding number, and cross out letters that spell the opposite.
5. Copy letters that are left into spaces below: Y-O-U.
6. Read these letters as word: *you.*

(After all ten items are finished, the remaining words together make a funny sentence.)

Teacher's Instructions to Leola

Item 1		Item 2	
Teacher	**Leola**	**Teacher**	**Leola**
OK, now number one here says *new.*		OK, now number 2 here says—	No.
What's the opposite of *new?*	Old	*No.* What's the opposite of *no?*	Yes.
Old. How would you spell *old?*	O-L-D	OK, how do you spell *yes?*	Y-E-S
OK, in the letters that are on this paper, cross out the letter you just used for spelling *old.*	*(L does it)*	All right, now what are you going—	*(L crosses out the letters Y-E-S)* Told
Good. What word is left?	Y-O-U		
What does that spell?	You		
OK, and down here you'll write *you.*			

Evidence that such aid can indeed be gradually withdrawn, and that Leola did learn to do the task independently, can be seen in a comparison of the teacher's instructions for the first and second items. For the second item, I talked Leola through the first three parts; but then a vague and incomplete question, "Now what are you going—," was sufficient, and Leola took off on her own.

Another example of scaffolded instruction with individual students comes from Gillian McNamee's studies of help in children's story retelling. In her first observational study of one kindergarten teacher, McNamee analyzed the series of questions by which the teacher talked a child through a story retelling until the child could tell it alone. Then, in a more controlled experiment, McNamee read a story to 12 kindergarten children and asked each one to retell it three times. At each retelling, the adult helped with a series of questions designed to provide minimum help at first and then increasingly specific help as needed:

1. Repeat back the last sentence that the child said.
2. Ask: "What happened next?" or "So what happened?" or "What happened in the beginning/end?"
3. Ask a wh— question that probes for the next piece of information.
4. Supply the next piece of information needed in the narrative in the form of a tag question.[15]

In the second retelling, the children needed help with fewer story events. In the third retelling, the number of events on which the children needed help stayed the same, but the kind of help needed shifted from more specific to more general, from 4 to 3 or 2. When a second story was presented in order to see whether the children had internalized the story-retelling skills, the children reverted approximately to the second retelling stage: needing less help than with the first retelling, but more specific help than with the third.

As McNamee points out, we do not teach anyone to narrate a story by explanation or directions. We may provide models, but we also help by asking questions, thereby indicating the kind of information that should be included. Remember Mindy's teacher at sharing time.

Instruction designed on the scaffold model that is the best documented and evaluated is "reciprocal teaching." In 1981, Annemarie Palincsar, then a graduate student, and psychologist Ann Brown initiated a series of studies designed to improve reading comprehension through instruction in four cognitive strategies: predicting, generating questions, summarizing, and clarifying. The format they devised is a "dialogue between teacher and students in which participants take turns assuming the role of teacher." They worked first with remedial teachers and their junior high students, and have since extended the model, and evaluated it, with other grades and teachers. Basically:

> When classroom teachers are introduced to reciprocal teaching, it is within the framework of scaffolded instruction. That is to say, the teachers are told that the purpose of this instructional program is to guide students from the acquisition to independent application of the four strategies for the purpose of enhancing comprehension. They are instructed that this transfer of responsibility means that they will engage in different teaching strategies over the course of instruction. They initially provide explanation coupled with modeling, then fade out the modeling and function more in the role of coach providing corrective feedback and encouragement, promote self-evaluation, and reintroduce explanation and modeling as appropriate. The teachers are also told that the rate at which this transfer occurs will vary among their students, but no matter how slow the rate, each learner must always be challenged at his or her level of competence.[16]

After giving these examples, I want to emphasize the importance of three features of scaffolds: they make it possible for the novice to participate in the mature task from the very beginning; and they do this by providing support that is both adjustable and temporary. Palincsar credits KEEP researchers Ronald Gallimore and Roland Tharp for the term *metascript*: "verbal instruction that has a general format and general guidelines suggestive of a particular strategy but is not so highly prescriptive that there is no room for responsive teaching."

In current discussions, the term *scaffold* is frequently linked with Vygotsky's construct of "zone of proximal development." *Scaffold* refers to visible and audible support with the above characteristics. If, in fact, the novice takes over more and more responsibility for the task at hand, as demonstrably happens in all the examples we have seen, then we can infer, retrospectively, that our help was well timed and well tuned, and that the novice was functioning in his or her zone of proximal development, doing at first with help what he or she could very soon do alone.

Some General Comments on Scaffolds

In thinking about the generalizability of the model of discourse as scaffold, three issues need to be considered: the process of internalization, getting the answer versus getting the understanding, and the nature of knowledge being acquired.

The Process of Internalization. It is important not to have a mechanical conception of the process of internalization whereby overt social interaction (speaking and listening) becomes transformed into covert mental processes (thinking). About reciprocal teaching, Resnick points out that "the automatic nature of many reading comprehension processes, the speed at which reading proceeds, and its sequential nature make it implausible that in the normal course of skilled reading people actually pose questions or create summaries for themselves.[17]

In research on mathematics instruction, Resnick and her colleagues have distinguished between algorithms that are taught and more mature algorithms (that is, closer to the ones experts use) that the learners somehow figure out for themselves. For example, Resnick and her colleagues found that children who were instructed in one addition algorithm invented a more mature one for themselves. To add 3 + 4, they were instructed to count the two groups together: 1, 2, 3 and 4, 5, 6, 7. They then invented the strategy of starting with the larger number, whether it came first or second, and increasing by the smaller: 4 and 5, 6, 7.[18]

This is evidence against any simple version of internalization as covert imitation. In Soviet psychologist A. N. Leont'ev's words,

> The process of internalization is not *transferal* of all external activity to a pre-existing internal "plane of consciousness"; it is the process in which this internal plane is *formed*.[19]

In teaching, therefore, we should not assume a one-to-one relationship between the components of mature performance and the ingredients of the most effective instruction. As with children's language development, the models provided are samples to learn from, not examples to learn.

The heart of human cognition is the ability to discover new ideas, to "go beyond the information given," in Bruner's apt phrase. In the words of Finnish psychologist Yrjo Engeström, "The idea of scaffolding is restricted to the acquisition of the given." Engeström's final example, particularly striking from a non-American, is Huckleberry Finn's rejection of his society's norm of slavery, and his realization, in the final sentences of the book, that he must leave home to avoid resocialization to that norm by Aunt Sally. Whether or not one agrees with this interpretation of Huckleberry Finn, Engeström's general point is important: scaffolds as an instructional model cannot account for the mental leap to a new idea.[20]

Answering Versus Understanding. There is a critical difference between helping a child somehow get a particular answer and helping a child gain some conceptual understanding from which answers to similar questions can be constructed at a future time. Remember the "So . . ." sequence in chapter 3, in which the child gets the answer from cues available in the teacher's question.

One paradox of the teacher-question–student-answer structure is that pupil answers are essential for the progress of the lesson, and yet the answer expected by the teacher is often not obvious. As French and MacLure remind us, any question—even one as seemingly simple as "Who is that?"—has many potential answers, and providing the right one requires not only knowledge but "contextualized, interpretive work." In videotapes of infant-school classrooms collected as part of a longitudinal study of children's language development, French and MacLure find "two interactive strategies used by many teachers, which operate to give guidelines to the pupils in their attempt to get the answers teachers want."[21]

One strategy is called *preformulating*: "teachers preface the question they want the children to answer with one or more utterances which serve to orient the children to the relevant area of experience . . . essential to answer [the] question."

Preformulator	*T*: Can you see what the elephant's got at the end of his trunk?
Nuclear Utterance	What is it?

The second strategy is *reformulating*, when the initial answer is wrong. French and MacLure identify five types of reformulations, according to the degree to which they make the original question more specific:

Original Question	Reformulation
What are those people doing?	1. What are they planting?
What kind of an elephant?	2. Was he a very SAD elephant? (Here the reformulation includes a wrong answer, *sad*, but suggests the right semantic set.)
What else did you see?	3. Did you see a chest of drawers? (Here the reformulation includes the right answer.)
How did they go, Gary?	4. Did they go by bus or car?
What color have you used?	5. It's a brown, isn't it?[22]

Because these reformulators progressively decrease the cognitive task faced by the child, French and MacLure predict that teachers will prefer to use the less specific versions first, and that the above order will also be an order of sequence of use.[23]

Whether such simplifications do more in the end than help a child answer a particular question (and thereby also help the teacher "get through" the lesson) is an important empirical question, but one that's hard to answer. I argued that the questions I asked Leola to talk her through the worksheet did demonstrably have that generative effect. Reciprocal teaching has been shown to meet the even more stringent requirement of being more effective than alternative forms of instruction.

The Nature of Knowledge. Important value questions should be asked about conceptions of knowledge and education implicit in scaffoldlike structures. How one judges their pedagogical value depends on the content of particular sequences and on one's educational philosophy.

In chapter 2, I mentioned Searle's concern about "who's building whose building?" As an illustration of his concern, Searle refers to the sharing-time interactions between Mindy and her teacher:

> Cazden suggested and demonstrated intervention in young children's show-and-tell sessions to help the children learn to speak in focused, extended narrative. In Cazden's examples, however, the children's understanding, valuing, and excitement of the personal experiences were negated as the children were led to report the experience in an appropriate form. Applebee and Langer [also language-arts educators] (1983) advocate "instructional scaffolding" and provide examples in which teachers scaffold students' science experiment reports by providing a sheet of questions which outline the required steps. Undoubtedly, these outlines help the students report the experiment more completely, but do they really help them learn the purposes and nature of scientific writing? Why, for example, are the students performing and reporting the experiment? Whose intentions are being honored in the report?[24]

These are important questions, especially, it seems to me, where the construction—not just the comprehension—of oral and written texts is at issue. They prompted discussion in the chapter on sharing time about the problems inherent in any fixed standard for how the raw tape of experience should be edited. And the same question about "who is in control of the language" is raised in writing conferences, as we saw in chapter 4. Because instruction is effective as means doesn't make it worthy as end. Questions of value remain to be argued and answered, by teachers and researchers alike.[25]

DISCOURSE AS RECONCEPTUALIZATION

Important parts of the construction of most scaffolds are teacher questions—the first part of the IRE sequence—that guide the learner's mental attention to particular features of the task at hand. The term *reconceptualization*, by contrast, calls attention to the third part, usually considered simply "evaluation." But the name *evaluation* does not do justice to the full import of that third part—how it often serves not to deliver a verdict of right or wrong but to induct the learner into a new way of thinking about, categorizing, reconceptualizing, even recontextualizating whatever phenomena (referents) are under discussion.

When we think or speak or write about complex phenomena, we cannot avoid attending to, and using words to express, a partial picture. The limitation is one not of bias but of selectivity inherent in human perception. Think of the familiar "reversible figures": one can be seen as either a duck or a rabbit, another as an old woman or a young woman, but not both views at once.

Sometimes this mental context of speaker or listener, writer or reader, is called a "frame of reference," and any act of referring requires what linguist James Wertsch calls a "referential perspective." His examples come from the scaffolding conversations between mothers and their young children doing puzzles together that were described earlier in this chapter. Pieces of the puzzle may be called by different names. A round piece may be a circle or a wheel of a truck; a rectangular piece may be a rectangle or a window of a house.[26]

Wertsch calls labels like *circle* or *square* "common referring expressions." They apply across a wide range of situations but carry no special information about any one of them; they are labels that linguists would call "unmarked," and that may seem to express what the referent "really" is. Wertsch calls labels like wheel and window, by contrast, "context-informative referring expressions." They provide more information about the particular perspective from which the referent is being seen at the moment; they communicate effectively in a narrower range of contexts and are understandable only to those who see the situation in the same way; they thus require, and contribute to, a higher degree of intersubjectivity between speaker and listener, writer and reader.[27]

Initial Conceputalizations in the Preschool Years

We can consider as reconceptualization another and more familiar third part of a discourse sequence that happens also to begin with *e*: the "expansions" with which care givers respond to very young children. When psycholinguists Roger Brown and Ursula Bellugi began the study of the language development of three children—Adam, Eve, and Sarah —in the early 1960s, one of the first things they noticed was the frequency with which the parents responded to their young child's telegraphic utterances by repeating what they assumed the child meant and filling in the missing parts. Here are some examples from the first published report:

Child	Mother
Mommy eggnog	Mommy had her eggnog.
Eve lunch	Eve is having lunch.
Mommy sandwich	Mommy'll have a sandwich.[28]

In these three instances, the mother is putting into words the time of the action—past, present, or future—that is obligatory in English.

The existence of expansions has been widely documented in the speech of Western middle-class care givers, and has been widely discussed as well. Most of the discussion has focused on their possible contribution to the child's acquisition of grammar. But in that first article, Brown and Bellugi wrote, "It seems to us that a mother in expanding speech may be teaching more than grammar; she may be teaching something like a world-view." In these early conversations, children learn not only "how" to mean but "what" to mean as well.[29]

Reconceptualizations in School

A great deal of education is devoted to teaching students to see phenomena in a new way, to reconceptualize circles as wheels or wheels as circles. The teacher's response—semantically contingent on the student's response, as is the care giver's—continues to teach "something like a world-view." Instead of environmental assistance to the child's acquisition of grammar, consider teaching as environmental assistance to the student's acquisition of skills and knowledge. Instead of a semantically contingent utterance spoken in a dyadic relationship between mother and child, consider the semantically contingent utterances that teachers speak as the third part of the basic IRE sequence.

Griffin and Mehan give a simple example from a reading lesson:

> T: [Writes "tree" on paper attached to board] If you know what the word says, put up your hand . . .
> A: Tab.
> T: It does start with a "t."

> [The teacher's response] exemplifies a way of teaching called phonics. . . . By specifying, in fact by reifying, one of the possible interpretations of an utterance by a pupil, a teacher cooperates in the construction of that utterance as a learning of (or partial learning of, or steps toward learning) what is supposed to be learned.[30]

Only in literacy activities do we have to conceive of words as composed of letters.

Lemke has also identified this function of teacher utterances in his research on high school science lessons. He speaks of utterances in the E slot as "retroactively contextualizing" or "Retro" for short, and finds that they frequently reconceptualize the previous student response either structurally or thematically. Structurally, the teacher can reconstrue a student answer as only a bid. Thematically, "the strategy of retroactive recontextualization of SAs [student answers] is the most general such interactional strategy of thematic development in dialog." His transcripts of high school science lessons are difficult for the non–science specialist to appreciate, but here's one example of a Retro from a physics class, where the teacher "radically recontextualizes an SA (and the whole preceding dialogue) by saying: "Relativity! That's how Einstein made his fortune." (In this transcription, SF is female student and SM is male student; an empty parenthesis indicates unclear words.)

T: Electricity. Yes. And if you have electrons spinning, you get a magnetic field. So that that's why if they spin clockwise you get one kind of magnetic field; if they spin counterclockwise you get a different kind of magnetic field. And that's why you-you ( ) magnetic quantum numbers. [*T and Ss laugh*] Which, which way is this [*gesturing*], clockwise or counterclockwise?

SF: According to it—

SM: Depends on who you—

SF: to us—

SM: to us it's counterclockwise, but to you it's clockwise.

T: Relativity! That's how Einstein made his fortune.

Lemke comments: "In the new context thus created, the themes of 'relative motion' and 'relative to the observer' enrich the meaning of what precedes and signal the existence at least of a thematic system that links the present discourse to other scientific discourse. The thematic shift in this case is so radical as to be humorous and playful."[31]

Other observers have given other names to adult speech that has this function—whether initial conceptualizing in the home or reconceptualizing at school. Ryan speaks of the benefits of mothers' rich interpretation of children's ambiguous one-word utterances, and Vygotsky asserts that child and adult share reference before they share meaning. Edwards and Furlong speak of "this process of moving pupils toward the teacher's meanings . . . as the heart of most teaching."[32]

So far, the examples have shown how parent expansions and teacher evaluations can alter or enrich the propositional meaning of a previous student answer. The concept of reconceptualization can also be applied to the child's goal structure. Speaking from a Vygotskian perspective, James Wertsch says that one of the most important aspects of development is that children come to accept "a qualitatively different interpretation of the goal of joint activity."[33]

The work of Newman, Griffin, and Cole describes in detail how this can happen. They are trying to work out "a theory of the role of culturally organized experience in the development of mind." The short label for their focus, "cognition in context," is just a more general set of terms for "thinking and speech." They conduct research in educational contexts in part because "education is the form of culturally organized experience that is available as a tool of government policy."[34]

One task selected for analysis is a problem that has the same structure as the Piagetian chemical combination task. It involves stacks of cards (at first four stacks, and then five and six), each of a different TV or movie star. In interaction with a tutor (the researcher), the child is asked to find all the ways that pairs of stars can be friends. Briefly:

> When a child has done as many pairs as s/he could, the researcher instituted a short tutorial before doing another trial of pair making. She asked the child to check to see if s/he had made all the pairs. If the child did not invent a systematic procedure for checking, the tutor suggested one. She would ask, "Do you have all the pairs with Mork" (if Mork were the first star on the left). Then she would ask about the next star to the right. With these hints, we wanted to give the child the idea of systematically pairing each star with every other star. We could then see whether this systematic procedure [referred to by Piaget as "intersection"] carried over to the next trial at making combinations.[35]

Newman et al.'s analysis of the tutor-child interaction, and especially their interpretation of the adult "hints," is informed by the work of Soviet psychologists Vygotsky and Leont'ev.[36] I assume that Vygotsky's theories are more familiar to readers of this chapter than Leont'ev's. Briefly, according to Leont'ev, the structure of every human activity (which is energized by a motive) is composed of actions (which are directed by goals), and these actions in turn are composed of operations, selected and carried out automatically, depending on particular conditions. Any behavior can change in status from action to operation or vice versa. So, for example, shifting gears starts as a goal-directed action for a beginning driver; later it recedes in status to an operation, activated automatically in certain situations.

As Newman et al. say, "Implicit in [Leon'tev's] theory is the claim that instances of behavior have a property which makes them available for social negotiation and transformation. . . . We call this property of the units "non-unique analyzability." So, for example, making pairs of cards (or chemicals) can have the status of actions in different activities to tutor and child at the same moment (synchronically), and to the same participant (diachronically) as the child's understanding develops:

> The tutor's question "How do you know you have all the pairs" presupposes that the child was trying to get all the pairs. This may be a false presup-position but it is strategically useful. . . . The question treats the child's column of pairs as if it had been produced in an attempt to get all the pairs. The teacher than invokes the intersection procedure as a means to fix up the child's "failed attempt to produce all the pairs." In other words, she appropriates the child's pair-making, making it into an example of how to achieve the stated goal. We suspect that when their own "empirical" pro-duction of pairs is retrospectively interpreted in terms of the intersection scheme children begin to learn the (researcher's) meaning of "all the pairs."[37]

Newman et al. go on to suggest that, just as with the categorization of questions, there is an important difference between what's heuristic for teachers and for researchers:

> In education such assumptions [by the teacher about the child's actions] may be a useful way of importing the goal into the teacher-child interaction and from there into the child's independent activity. Our original coding scheme also treated many of the children's productions as poor strategies for getting all the pairs. In psychology, such overinterpretations can be dangerously misleading. Children are scored as doing poorly when in fact they are not doing the task in the first place.[38]

As Newman et al. apply Vygotsky and Leont'ev's theories, the pro-cess of "appropriation" (Leont'ev's term) is reciprocal and sequential. Appropriation by the teacher (as Newman et al. have described it) is followed—at least in some tutor-child dyads—by evidence in later tasks that the action of making pairs has been appropriated by the child and transformed into an action in a new and gradually understood activity —namely, the systematic procedure we call "intersection."[39]

I have deliberately included Lemke's term *recontextualization* for these phenomena in addition to the more familiar term *reconceptualization* in order to contrast this view of education with the more usual description of *decontextualization*.

Some phenomena can be considered relatively decontextualized. A picture of an airplane all alone on an empty page, as in some picture books, is more decontextualized than the real object up in the sky, or than a picture that portrays it in a more complete scene. Nonsense syllables are more decontextualized than meaningful words, and words on flash cards more decontextualized than words in connected text.

Psychological experiments also offer examples of more and less contextualized stimuli. For example, in two Soviet experiments, preschool children were able to stand still longer when asked to "be a guard" (contextualized instruction) than when asked simply to "stand still" (decontextualized instruction), and were better able to remember a list of objects when playing store (contextualized task) than when asked simply to remember a list (decontextualized task).[40]

When school language use is called decontextualized, it is because talk refers less often than at home to one particular kind of context: the physically present situation to which exophoric reference can be made. But the difficulties inherent in classroom discourse come not just from the relative absence of reference to shared physical context; they come as much from the more frequent reference to another kind of context: the words of other oral and written texts. Remember Naso's amazement when his middle-class students spontaneously made connections among texts. Whereas the physical context is always shared, the context of other words may or may not be shared. And reference to it is sometimes pointed out but often simply assumed.

Consider what happens at a professional conference. Much of the talk there has no relationship to the physical setting. It doesn't matter what room we're in, or what hotel, or even what city. An outsider to the profession would find interpretation difficult, but not primarily for this reason. It would be difficult because the talk is richly and complexly contextualized in worlds created and shared through words alone.

The same problem confronts readers of this book. I have tried to contextualize general ideas in two ways: first, by giving examples that should help all readers, and second, by giving references to other texts. If those texts are already familiar, then an author's name—for example, Bruner or Heath in a discussion of book reading—serves as an invitation to the reader to bring to mind those authors' ideas in interpreting what is written here. Reading researcher Richard Anderson speaks of text comprehension as recontextualization:

> It is generally believed that as people grow older they become more capable of abstract thinking and more capable, therefore, of coping with abstract, decontextualized language. . . . The problem is with the implication that since the language of text is abstract, the thinking that goes on with respect to this language is primarily abstract as well. Centrally involved in comprehending text . . . is the development of instantiated representations consistent with the message. Therefore, more of the picture has to be drawn unaided by the reader; the detail has to be generated based on what is stored in memory. If text is decontextualized, then we might think of the process of comprehending it as *recontextualization*.[41]

In Anderson's use, the term *recontextualization* emphasizes the critical importance of the active construction by each student of these "contexts in the mind," and the help that must be given by the teacher in the process. This help comes in the molar form of the entire curriculum, but it also comes in the more molecular form of what is said in the E slot.

Some General Questions About Reconceptualization

As with the metaphor of discourse as scaffold, so the metaphor of discourse as reconceptualization raises important issues: of teacher-student differences in age and culture; of the affective tone of the adult's response; and of values.

Differences of Age and Culture. Differences of age and culture can create significant barriers between teacher and student. In this respect, teachers face a different task than parents do. Through conversation at home, parents and others in the intimate community largely determine the child's foundation of what to mean (a world view) as well as how (a language system). Children take this world view, or their childish version of it, to school. Ideally, and frequently, the teacher works hard to understand and make connections, as Naso urged. Remember from chapter 2 Duckworth's words about "understanding the learner's understanding," and Bernstein's about the culture of the child becoming part of the culture of the teacher before the culture of the teacher can become part of the culture of the child. If this doesn't happen, as we saw in the chapter on sharing time, the result can be misunderstanding, conflict, and invalid inferences about a child's ability to learn.[42]

Affective Tone of the Adult Response. Consider again parental expansions and the difference between them and teacher corrections. The formal difference may be only in intonation and an optional initial yes or no. Yet that difference may have great significance for the child. Suppose that while looking at a book, a child says, "He fall down." Say to yourself the following alternative responses, stressing the underlined words:

Expansion: Yes, he fell down.
Correction: No, he fell down.

In her observations in infant classes, Willes looked for comparable responses. She found one example when the nursery rhyme about Humpty Dumpty was being turned into an action song. The children were expected to clench one fist to represent the egg, and place the other hand facing the body to represent the wall:

T: Where's your Humpty Dumpty sitting on a wall?
   Is he ready to fall off?
   Is he a bit wobbly?
S: I got *two* Humpty Dumpties.
T: Oh, you can't have two Humpty Dumpties! He has to sit on a wall![43]

In this situation, when the teacher is trying to get a whole class organized for a performance, there is understandably little time for negotiation of meaning. But it seems as if the person in higher status, who has the power to maintain her contextualization of the child's fingers, considers the child's view not as an alternative, but as a serious error.

The Issue of Values. We have to ask not just whose scaffold but whose world view. Here, in the domain of knowledge even more than in the domain of more value-neutral cognitive skills, imposition by authority should be questioned. Reconceptualization should add alternative meanings without denying the validity of meanings students bring to school.[44]

whose values?

NOTES

[1] Vygotsky 1962.
[2] Duckworth 1981, 51–52.
[3] Bloom 1956; Gall 1970.
[4] Redfield and Rousseau 1981.
[5] Gage 1977 and Berliner 1976 discuss problems of sequence. Levinson 1979 discusses the general problem of coding utterances for their function (as speech-act analyses require) with examples of question sequences from classrooms and elsewhere.
[6] Edwards and Furlong 1978, 41.
[7] Barnes et al. 1969, 24. The same ideas are discussed in different words in the third edition, Barnes, Britton, and Torbe 1986.
[8] Resnick 1985, 178–179. Her Vygotsky reference is 1978.
[9] Fischer and Bullock 1984.
[10] Snow 1977.
[11] Wertsch 1984, 10. Wertsch and Stone 1985, 175–176.
[12] Ninio and Bruner 1978. For discussions of peekaboo, see Ratner and Bruner 1978, Bruner 1983, and Cazden 1983a.
[13] S. Haselkorn, personal communication, 1978.
[14] Pearson and Gallagher 1983, 337. The chart is from an unpublished paper by J. Campione.
[15] McNamee 1980, 96. Her earlier study was McNamee 1979.
[16] Palincsar 1986, 78. She and Brown have published many articles on reciprocal teaching, most of which give transcripts from earlier and later sessions with a

single group of students. A particularly rich discussion is in Brown and Palincsar 1986.

17 Resnick 1985, 177.

18 Groen and Resnick 1977.

19 Leont'ev 1981, 57, emphasis in the original. See discussion by Wertsch and Stone 1985.

20 Engeström 1986, 32.

21 French and Maclure 1981. The larger study is reported in Wells 1986b.

22 French and Maclure 1981, 38–43.

23 In a footnote, French and Maclure, ibid., note similarities between their analysis of what teachers do and the "simplification techniques" advocated by Blank 1973, 90–97.

24 Searle 1984, 481; Applebee and Langer 1983.

25 Hammersley 1977 and Edwards 1980 also discuss these issues.

26 Wertsch 1985.

27 In different fields, the shared mental context that I call simply "perspective" has different names. In the field of scientific theories, Kuhn 1970 speaks of "paradigms"; in the field of literary theories, Fish 1980 speaks of "interpretive communities." I am extending their ideas to the everyday theories that everyone acts on and speaks from in everyday life.

28 Brown and Bellugi 1964.

29 Brown and Bellugi 1964, 143. For more recent discussion, see Cazden, in press a. Research by Watson-Gegeo and Gegeo 1985a in the Solomon Islands is important in documenting expansions in a non-Western culture.

30 Griffin and Mehan 1981, 196, 208.

31 Lemke 1982, 165, and accompanying transcription (with notation simplified).

32 Ryan 1974; Vygotsky 1962, 73; Edwards and Furlong 1978. Drawing on conversation analyst Emanuel Schegloff's 1972 related concept of "formulating," McHoul and Watson 1984 describe how an Australian geography teacher tried to transform students' "commonsense" knowledge into "formal" knowledge. See also Vygotsky's 1962 discussion of "spontaneous and scientific concepts."

33 Wertsch, in Rogoff and Wertsch 1984.

34 Newman, Griffin, and Cole, 1984 and unpublished version.

35 Ibid., in press.

36 Vygotsky 1962, 1978; Leont'ev 1981.

37 Newman, Griffin, and Cole, unpublished ms.

38 Ibid., 1984.

39 Researchers should note that the nonunique analyzability of units of behavior is an argument against the one-to-one correspondence between form and meaning that both speech-act theory and coding schemes assume.

40 Manuilinko 1975; Istomina 1975.

41 Anderson 1977.

42 Science educators face particularly difficult pedagogical issues in trying to help students understand, and not just verbalize, new ways of conceptualizing natural phenomena. See, for example, the work of New Zealand researchers Osborne and Freyberg 1986.

43 Willes 1983, 107.

44 For additional discussion, see the critical analysis of "teacher re-formulation

of pupil responses" by Australian educators Ken Watson and Robert Young 1980, 1986; Young 1980; and British sociologists Paul Atkinson and Sara Delamont's striking 1976 analysis of the "stage management" of discovery learning in a science classroom and clinical training in medicine.

Section II

Talk
with
Peers

Chapter 7

Peer Interactions: Cognitive Processes

When the British National Association for the Teaching of English (NATE) decided to put together a booklet celebrating 30 years of the association, they wanted to include the voices of students. Three young adults were located who had, in the 1960s and 1970s, been students in London comprehensive schools where heads of the English departments were active NATE members. They were interviewed about their memories of English lessons. Merle Chalon, who had immigrated to London from the West Indies, compared her Caribbean school, where "we sat in rows with the teacher in the front and even further at the front and elevated was the headmistress," with the London school, where "a group of children . . . could talk and help each other":

> We worked in groups a lot. The room was set out in tables. . . . We sat on an all girls table in one corner. There was myself and another West Indian girl and one Asian girl, and whatever the work was we had to read or write about, we could actually help each other, we could talk about it. . . . [This] was new and quite exciting to us.
>
> We did quite a lot of work where a group of us would go away with a tape recorder and talk about a particular topic or a particular book and then later on report it to the rest of the class. . . . One of the books which

we talked about was George Orwell's *Animal Farm* because our teacher found that the children were taking the book at different levels. For some of the children it was merely a book about animals, whereas for people like Fred, who was a boy in the class, he actually understood the political idea of it. . . . People who could understand at that level going away and talking about it, and then coming back and us listening to the tape, really helped in the class. And because the class was often working at different levels, . . . this [working in groups] would enable our teacher to have more time for those children who needed more specific help.[1]

Such interactions among students, focused on academic tasks and part of the discourse acceptable in official air time, are rare. In the introduction, I noted that although classrooms are as crowded human environments as restaurants or buses, the social organization of talk within them is strikingly different. In classrooms, it is planned and controlled by one person—the teacher—and she tries to permit only one person to talk at a time.

Large-scale observational studies in both the United Kingdom and the United States show the prevailing picture.[2] Even if seating in groups has replaced seating in rows, only the seating has been socialized, not the work. In both countries, two kinds of social organization seem to predominate, at least in elementary classrooms:

1. Traditional large-group instruction, with the teacher in control at the front of the room.
2. Individualized instruction, with children working alone on assigned tasks, and the teacher monitoring and checking their individual progress either at a student's desk or her own.

Because the kind of classroom organization Merle Chalon remembers seems now to be an endangered species of classroom discourse, threatened by pressures on both sides of the Atlantic, it is important to explore its special contributions.

Discussions of the role of social interaction in the development of cognition, learning, and knowledge often do not explicitly distinguish between interactions with experts (those who understand more about the particular matter at hand) and interactions with peers (other learners of generally equivalent understanding). Vygotsky, in his definition of the "zone of proximal development," speaks of both adults and "more capable peers":

[The zone of proximal development is] the distance between the actual developmental level as determined by independent problem solving and the level of potential development as determined through problem solving under adult guidance or in collaboration with more capable peers.[3]

Elsewhere, he says that "the higher functions of child thought at first appear in the collective life of children in the form of argumentation and only then develop into reflection for the individual child."[4] But his more detailed discussions of relationships between external and internal activity, between speech and thinking, seem to assume talk with an adult; the possible special values of talk in the child collective, in contrast to talk with an expert, are not analyzed.

Piaget's writings also display the same lack of explicit contrast, but an opposite emphasis on interactions with peers seems to be assumed. (Though, as we saw in the last chapter, Piagetian Eleanor Duckworth acknowledges the instructional value of adult questions.) To Piaget, social interaction is an essential antidote to egocentrism: in the confrontation with alternative points of view, one is stimulated to consider one's own limitations. His fullest discussion of this role of social interaction is in *The Psychology of Intelligence*.[5] But the introduction he wrote to *Group Games in Education*, by Piagetian early-childhood educators Constance Kamii and Rita DeVries, is a short retrospective summary of these ideas:

> Certain educators say sometimes that my theory is only "cognitive," and that I neglected the importance of social aspects of the child's development. It is true that most of my publications have dealt with various aspects of cognitive development, particularly the development of operativity, but in my first works I emphasized the importance of interindividual exchanges sufficiently not to feel the need afterwards to return to it. In fact, it is clear that the confrontation of points of view is already indispensable in childhood for the elaboration of logical thought, and such confrontations become increasingly more important in the elaboration of sciences by adults. Without the diversity of theories and the constant search for going beyond the contradictions among them, scientific progress would not have been possible.[6]

The importance to Vygotsky of interactions with experts (adult or child) and to Piaget of interactions with peers derives from their contrasting beliefs about how external talk affects internal thought. To Vygotsky, thought—or inner speech—clearly reflects its social origins in two senses of the word *social*: in its origin in interaction and its use of culturally organized symbolic systems, especially language.

> An important point to note about Vygotsky's ideas on the social origins of cognition is that it is at this point that he uses the notion of internalization. He is not simply claiming that social interaction leads to the development of the child's abilities in problem-solving, memory, etc.; rather, he is saying that the very means (especially speech) used in social interaction are taken over by the individual child and internalized. Thus, Vygotsky is making a very strong statement here about internalization and the social foundations of cognition.[7]

To Piaget, social interaction is important because of the cognitive conflict it stimulates; talk is a catalyst for internal change without direct influence on the forms and functions of thought. Genevan psychologist Perret-Clermont shares this view of development:

> Of course, cognitive conflict of this kind does not create the *forms* of operations, but it brings about the disequilibriums which make cognitive elaboration necessary, and in this way cognitive conflict confers a special role on the social factor as one among other factors leading to mental growth. Social-cognitive conflict may be figuratively likened to the catalyst in a chemical reaction: it is not present at all in the final product, but it is nevertheless indispensable if the reaction is to take place.[8]

In the rest of this chapter, I shall suggest four potential cognitive benefits of discourse among peers: discourse as catalyst, as the enactment of complementary roles, as relationship with an audience, and as exploratory talk instead of "final draft." I have categorized these contributions without regard to age. The only important age difference may be that older children and adults can learn from each other through words alone (as in a discussion of *Animal Farm*), while younger children benefit more from activities (like block building or science experiments) in which language refers to concrete objects and decisions about real actions have to be made.

DISCOURSE AS CATALYST

Two sensitive preschool teachers provide vivid examples of the catalytic function of discourse. First, from Sally Cartwright's notes on block building in her community nursery school in Tenants Harbor, Maine, where many of the children's fathers work on the sea:

1. Todd and Emily start building a lobster boat with large hollow blocks. The children make a good, pointed bow (for once!), a cabin, pretend winch to haul traps, helm, depth finder, lobster crates and traps, etc. Their building attracts a good many crew members, whose mingled voices come through: "Get aboard!" "We're going fishing!" "Did you bring lunch?" "It's in that basket." "Can't get this engine started, damn it." "Well, you've over-choked it and she's flooded." This from Travis, our mechanic, of course. "Rrmmm, rrmmmm! Going now. Cast off, you guys." "Untie those lines!" "What lines?" "The ropes to the dock! What are you, a farmer?" This from Noah, who goes out fishing with his dad.
   "Hey! Big seas ahead!" "Look at those waves! Gigantious!"
   "Wow! Put on your lifejackets!" "Got yours?" "Yup."

"My God, Mary! Phew, what a stink!"

"Why?"

"You're standing in my bait barrel!"

2. Five children are building in the large block area. Four of them have made a boat and gone out in a rough sea, while Michael is still on the dock, trying to untie the entirely imaginary rope by which they are—in his mind—still tied to the dock. (Michael's father is mate on the mail boat to Monhegan Island, and he's seen all kinds of action and may realize that untying a boat isn't done in a minute.) His back is turned to the boat, and he keeps trying to tell the others to wait. But they—in their minds—are already far out at sea, putting on life preservers in the rising storm. Finally, Michael finishes and calls out, "I've got you untied!" But far out at sea, they don't even hear.[9]

The second set of examples comes from Vivian Paley's kindergarten at the University of Chicago Laboratory School. Her book, *Wally's Stories*, is about her growing understanding of five-year-old minds. (Wally is a kindergarten boy who happens to be black and poor.) The conversations are Paley's transcriptions of tape recordings that she makes daily for herself. One discussion, about fairness, was included in chapter 4. Here's another from the same group of children, this time the beginning of a lengthy episode about how to measure rugs:

Wally: The big rug is the giant's castle. The small one is Jack's house.

Eddie: Both rugs are the same.

Wally: They can't be the same. Watch me. I'll walk around the rug. Now watch—walk, walk, walk, walk, walk, walk, walk, walk, walk—count all these walks. Okay. Now count the other rug. Walk, walk, walk, walk, walk. See? That one has more walks.

Eddie: No fair. You cheated. You walked faster.

Wally: I don't have to walk. I can just look.

Eddie: I can look too. But you have to measure it. You need a ruler. About six hundred inches or feet.

Wally: We have a ruler.

Eddie: Not that one. Not the short kind. You have to use the long kind that gets curled up in a box.

Wally: Use people. People's bodies. Lying down in a row.

Eddie: That's a great idea. I never even thought of that.[10]

In these examples, we certainly hear different points of view—on fairness, bait buckets and boats, and on measurement and conservation of length. Sometimes there is evidence of a child's conversion to a another child's view; but often there is no evidence of change, as with the uncoordinated perspectives in the block play, and the continued disbelief in the value of a constant unit of measurement.

Does this mean that there is no value to this talk among peers? Is immediate conversion the appropriate test of the value of experience? I think not. Confrontation with alternative ideas, whether from adults or peers, cannot be expected to produce immediate change. Language development is a case in point. There are times during all children's preschool years when their advancing knowledge of language as a rule-governed system produces words like "goed" and "holded," and, in answer to the question "What are you doing?", utterances like "I doing dancing." At those moments, the child seems impervious to contradiction, and no amount of correction has any obvious effect. Yet progress does occur, and we have to assume that exposure to alternatives plays a part, even though we can't track their influence in the silent processes of the child's mind.

Empirical support for the cognitive value of collaboration among school-age children comes from a series of training studies by a group of Genevan psychologists.[11] They examined the effects of peer collaboration on logical reasoning skills associated with the Piagetian stage of concrete operations. Perret-Clermont concludes from this body of work that peer interaction enhances the development of logical reasoning through a process of active cognitive reorganization induced by cognitive conflict. But none of these studies analyzed the interactions themselves.

In her doctoral thesis, Elice Forman did just that.[12] She gave pairs of fourth- and fifth-grade children eleven problem-solving sessions on a series of increasingly complex tasks in which the isolation of chemical reactants is required. The dyads were encouraged to work together throughout. She analyzed videotapes of the collaborative sessions, and also took individual pre- and posttest measures of logical reasoning.

Forman's study provides two kinds of information about collaboration: how collaborators differ from solitary problem solvers (from a prior study), and how collaborative partnerships differ from each other in interactional patterns and cognitive growth. All procedural interactions focusing on accomplishing the assigned task were coded for type of collaboration (parallel, associative, cooperative) and type of experimentation strategy (trial and error, isolation of variables, combinatorial). Forman found that the collaborators solved many more problems than the singletons in the same set of eleven sessions, and the pair who showed the most cooperative interactions and used the most combinatorial strategies—Bruce and George—also solved the most problems.

How does the nature of Bruce and George's collaboration relate to

their superior mastery of the series of problems? The Piagetian interpretation is cognitive conflict, and that did occur in some of the later
sessions when the results of their experiments were visible and the
children argued about what they had proved. Here is Forman's summary
of their interactions in the third session.[13]

> In this session, chemical C alone was the solution to the chemical problem.
> The two boys set-up and mixed the following set of experiments: B; C; BE;
> CD; CE; DE; BDE; CDF; DEF. In addition, they could examine the results
> of the two demonstration experiments: BCE; DEF. All experiments contain-
> ing chemical C turned purple, the rest remained clear.
>
> After all the experiments were mixed, the experimenter asked both
> children, "What makes a difference in whether it turns purple?" Bruce
> initially concluded that the answer was C and E. George expressed his
> surprise that a single element, e.g., C, produced the desired color change.
> In response to the standard prompt from the experimenter, "Can you be
> sure it's C and E?", Bruce reexamined some experiments, and found one
> which contained E (and not C) that did not change color. Bruce, however,
> did not conclude at this point that C was the only operative chemical. George
> then asked Bruce whether all the experiments containing C produced the
> desired color change. Bruce scanned each experiment containing C and
> announced that each did change color.
>
> Based on the experimental evidence and some information remembered
> from previous sessions, George concluded that C was the solution to the
> problem. Bruce, however, contradicted George by asserting it was F. At
> this point, they both reexamined the experiments. Afterwards, George still
> concluded it was C and Bruce concluded it was C and F.
>
> The experimenter asked whether they could be sure of their answers.
> George replied that he was sure of C but not of F. Once again, the evidence
> was examined. This time, Bruce identified the experiment CDF as indicating
> that F was an operational chemical. George countered this argument by
> comparing it with experiment DEF that did not produce the desired reaction.
> Bruce responded that D and E were more powerful liquids than F and
> therefore prevented F from working. George then tried another approach
> by asking Bruce how he could tell it was F and not C that made the mixture
> CDF turn purple. Bruce replied by asking George how he could tell it wasn't
> both C and F that made CDF turn purple. George's concluding remark was
> an assertion that he just knew it was C alone.

DISCOURSE AS THE ENACTMENT
OF COMPLEMENTARY ROLES

As Forman looked at her videotapes in order to figure out how Bruce
and George were so successful, she noticed productive interactions that
could not be considered instances of conflict. During the earlier setting-
up phase of each experiment, before empirical evidence was available

for discussion and argument, mutual guidance and support was evident. Here is Forman's summary of how Bruce and George enacted complementary roles:

> In their early collaborative problem-solving sessions, George and Bruce worked in parallel and each used empirical strategy similar to the one used on the pretest to generate combinations. After about a month of working together, they devised a social procedure for generating combinations empirically by assuming complementary problem-solving roles: one selected chemicals and the other checked their uniqueness.
>
> After two months, they had begun to organize their combinations into groups based on their number of elements. In addition, they had devised a deductive system for generating two-element combinations. This deductive procedure enabled the child who had previously done the checking to prompt, correct, and reinforce the selections of his partner. Higher order combinations were produced empirically using the familiar social procedure.
>
> At the last session, the boys continued to assume complementary roles but now used the blackboard as a recording device. They produced combinations in a highly organized fashion—singles, two-element combinations, three-element combinations, etc.—and were able to generate almost all of the 31 possible combinations. They used a deductive procedure for generating the two-element combinations but still relied on their empirical procedure for the higher order combinations.
>
> At the first posttest one week after the last collaborative session, the degree to which each boy had internalized a deductive combinatorial system was assessed by asking them to generate combinations independently. Bruce was able to generate all ten two-element combinations deductively on his own, but George was not. George used an empirical system to generate combinations. On the second posttest four months later, however, both boys had internalized a deductive procedure for producing two-element combinations.

Here Vygotsky's writings offer more insights. In Forman's words, "In tasks where experimental evidence was being generated and where managerial skills were required, by assuming complementary problem-solving roles, peers could perform tasks together before they could perform them alone. The peer observer seemed to provide some of the same kinds of 'scaffolding' assistance that others have attributed to the adult in teaching contexts."[14]

DISCOURSE AS RELATIONSHIP WITH AN AUDIENCE

In discussions of how speech (including classroom discourse) unites the cognitive and the social, we usually find the two meanings of *social* I mentioned earlier: the use of culturally transmitted products of human history—notably language itself and its expression in particular oral and written genres, and the transformation of social interaction into inner speech. In his analyses of collaboration in computer writing in a first grade, Heap suggests a third meaning: an orientation to the Other.[15]

Such orientation to the Other is achieved in speech through the availability of immediate feedback when something said is unclear. In solitary writing, achieving the same orientation to others—one's future audience—is harder.

One example comes from observations by Barbara Kamler, an Australian colleague of Donald Graves's research team while she was visiting a second grade. The teacher, Egan, held regular writing conferences with individual children. In addition, she encouraged the children to hold peer conferences about their writing with each other. Here is Kamler's account of conferences between two students, Jill and Debbie:

> On March 11, Jill was one of six children scheduled for a writing conference. . . . At Egan's direction, Jill and the other conferees went to the language table. Egan had requested that Jill first spend time with seven-year-old Debbie going over the book to be sure it was ready for a conference. . . .
>
> Jill began by reading each page aloud to Debbie. . . . As Jill listened to her own words, she made changes on pages 1, 2 and 3 without any prompting or comment from Debbie, and on pages 4, 5 and 8 in direct response to questions Debbie asked. . . .
>
> At the conclusion of this half-hour conference, Jill had made six content changes which affected the overall meaning of the piece. She had deleted information which made no sense or which she could not support; she added information to clarify or explain. Debbie's presence was crucial to the content revisions of the draft. Her physical presence forced Jill to reread the book for the first time since composing; Debbie seemed to make the concept of audience visible for Jill. Jill also needed an active reader to ask questions. . . .
>
> [Later] Debbie claimed her time: "OK, Jill, you help me now!" They reversed roles, returned to the language table to work on Debbie's book *Ice Follies*, until Mrs. Egan was ready to see Jill twenty minutes later.[16]

In this model of peer collaboration, the separation of roles between author and nonauthor-helper are more sharply defined than in the collaboration at the terminal described by Heap. As with Heap, the roles are reciprocal; unlike in Heap, the teacher has modeled the role for the helper to enact. Kamler and Graves assumed that, as in reciprocal teaching, the children learned what to do and say in the questioner role from the teacher's model in the conferences with her, a consistent model of how to ask questions about the content of writing, not form. The teacher believed that questions about content were more helpful to these young writers, and they were also the kinds of questions that children can ask of each other. The teacher's model thus made it possible for the children to take turns performing the teacher's role for each other—to the benefit of each child as author, through experiences with a responsive audience; and to the benefit of each child as critic, through internalizing such questions not only by answering them for the teacher but also asking them of peers.

For these benefits to occur, the teacher's model must be one the children can learn. Graves reports that the conference structure of another teacher in the same school was not as easily learned by the children, and so there was less of a multiplier effect via peer conferences in his classroom. This comparison suggests that the intellectual value of peer interactions in any classroom will be enhanced when the teacher models a kind of interaction that the children can learn to use with each other.[17]

Kamler suggests that the child writer benefits in two ways from the peer's presence. Most obviously, the peer asks questions, following the adult model but with content appropriate to the text at hand. (Some of Jill's changes were in direct response to Debbie's questions.) Less obviously, the peer silently but no less effectively represents the needs of an audience and makes "the concept of audience visible."

The covert effect of such a silent audience can be conceptualized in the empty cell created by the separation of function and form in Vygotsky's discussion of egocentric speech. We generally think of speech as social (intended for another) in function and external (voiced) in form, whereas inner speech is individual (intended for oneself) in function and internal (only thought, not voiced) in form. But talking aloud to oneself—"egocentric speech," in Vygotsky's terms, regardless of the age of the speaker—does not fit those distinctions. According to Vygotsky, egocentric speech is internal in psychological function and external in form. The changes Jill made in response to Debbie's silent presence were exactly the opposite: internal in form (though recorded in writing) and social in function, to make that writing communicate more effectively to another (Figure 7–1).[18]

Susan Sowers, formerly a research colleague of Donald Graves's, reports how Hilary, another second grader in Egan's classroom, engaged in such silent editing. She explained to Graves what she was doing when she read her draft to herself:

> "I have an individual conference—with myself," Hilary replied.
>
> Asked what she did in her solitary conference, she said she read her book again and again and thought of questions the other children would ask her about it. She gave an example of a question she anticipated about one page in her current book, *On the Farm*:

FORM

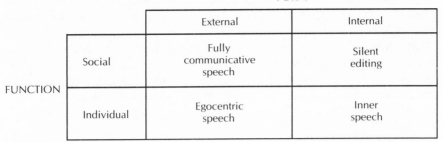

		External	Internal
FUNCTION	Social	Fully communicative speech	Silent editing
	Individual	Egocentric speech	Inner speech

FIGURE 7–1 Function and Form

"Your horse's name is Misty. Well, do you ride it or feed it or what?"
   [*Anticipated question*]
So I'm going to put, "I ride her every day unless it is raining."
   [*What she would write in response*][19]

DISCOURSE AS EXPLORATORY TALK

While watching one of Duckworth's clinical interviews with children working a problem in geometry, a teacher said, "I guess for the first time clearly I saw children learning—the process of learning without the answers fully intact." Speaking "without the answers fully intact" is what British educator Douglas Barnes calls "exploratory talk," in contrast to a "final draft."[20]

Barnes's use of these contrasting terms is interesting for its similarity to more recent discussions of writing in which a final draft is also the end of a process that begins with expressions of more exploratory ideas. In the light of that more recent work, Barnes can be read as arguing for classroom discourse as process rather than product. At one point, he explicitly relates oral language to writing:

> The distinction between exploratory and final draft is essentially a distinction between different ways in which speech can function in the rehearsing of knowledge. In exploratory talk and writing, the learner himself takes responsibility for the adequacy of his thinking; final-draft talk and writing looks towards external criteria and distant, unknown audiences. Both uses of language have their place in education.[21]

Barnes's concept of "exploratory talk" was mentioned, in chapter 4, as a feature of speech style during discussions, even if the teacher is a participant. But it is more likely to occur in discussions that are only among peers. Barnes recommends a teaching sequence that promotes the benefits of both kinds of talk and the relations between them, and describes an admittedly idealized example in an environmental-studies unit that begins with an introductory presentation by the teacher, then shifts to small-group discussions, and only later to a "report-back" discussion with the whole class. Critical to Barnes's argument is the hypothesis that the exploratory small-group talk "both strengthens class discussion and supports forms of learning which take place less readily in full class."[22]

THE SIGNIFICANCE OF TALK AMONG PEERS

Two final comments may provide further arguments for the value of talk among peers.

First, while such interactions take place at home and in the community as well as at school, they are especially important in school because of the limitations and rigidities characteristic of most teacher-student interactions in that institutionalized setting. In the last chapter, I called attention to a category of parent-child interactions, of which peekaboo and picture-book reading are familiar examples, that have special characteristics. There is a predictable structure, but the respective roles of parent and child change over time, with the child eventually speaking all the parts.

The contrast between such learning environments and the classroom is striking. In school lessons, teachers give directions and the children nonverbally carry them out; teachers ask questions and children answer them, frequently with only a word or a phrase. Most important, with the exception of reciprocal teaching, these roles are not reversible. Children never give directions to teachers, and rarely even ask them questions except to request permission. The only context in which children can reverse interactional roles with the same intellectual content, giving directions as well as following them, and asking questions as well as answering them, is with their peers.

But, someone may say, students talk all the time among themselves outside of school. Why use valuable school time for more of the same, when they could be talking with the (expert) teacher? My answer is that in out-of-school conversations, the talk is not about school subjects, and does not provide an opportunity for students to practice forms of academic discourse—the special ways of talking expected in school.

Second, while I have focused here on cognitive benefits of peer interactions, there are other justifications for including them deliberately in a teacher's plans. One justification is the potential value of such interactions for social development in a pluralistic society. It makes no sense (and seems almost dishonest) to "mainstream" children across some dimensions of diversity (for example, physical, mental, or emotional handicaps), and "integrate" children across other dimensions of diversity (officially recognized ethnic categories), unless the social organization of classrooms ensures the kind of equal-status interactions from which positive attitudes across those differences can grow. In the next chapter, we shall explore the conditions that make these benefits most likely to occur.

It also makes no sense to have learning so individualized in school when teams and committees are such a prominent part of adult life.[23]

NOTES

[1] National Association of Teachers of English, n.d., 14, 25, slightly edited.
[2] In the United States, Goodlad 1983, 1984, and his colleagues observed 1,016 classes. In the United Kingdom, Galton, Simon, and Croll 1980 observed 58 classrooms in 19 primary schools in three educational authorities.
[3] Vygotsky 1978, 86.
[4] Vygotsky 1981, 157.
[5] Piaget 1950, chap. 6. Piaget's revised thinking on egocentricity is available only as chapter 6 of British editions of *The Language and Thought of the Child*, based on the third (1959) edition.
[6] Piaget 1980.
[7] From Wertsch's editorial introduction to Vygotsky 1981.
[8] Perret-Clermont 1980, 178.
[9] Personal communication 1980.
[10] Paley 1981, 13–14.
[11] Perret-Clermont 1980.
[12] Forman 1981; also reported in Forman and Cazden 1985.
[13] These summaries are from Forman's unpublished notes.
[14] Forman and Cazden 1985, 343.
[15] Heap 1986.
[16] Kamler 1980, 683–685.
[17] Graves, personal communication 1980.
[18] The chart is adapted from the manuscript version of Wertsch and Stone 1985.
[19] Sowers 1984b, 9, reformated. See also Sowers 1984a.
[20] Duckworth 1981, 51; Barnes 1976.
[21] Barnes 1976, 113–114.
[22] Ibid., p. 200. In another study of peertalk, Barnes and Todd 1977 found, like Forman, that groups attained cognitive levels not attained by individuals working alone.
[23] As part of American interest in Japanese education, some observers have noted both the ability of Japanese adult groups to work together cooperatively and the prominent role of peer groups in Japanese schools. LeVine and White 1986 consider this an important part of Japan's adaptation of Western schooling to their social traditions.

Chapter 8

Peer Interactions: Contextual Influences

All speech is influenced by features of the context in which it takes place, and interactions among students are no exception. This chapter reports research that highlights some of those features.

DIFFERENTIAL EXPERIENCE

In chapter 5, I reported research on the differential treatment that some children receive from their teachers. But teachers are not the only source of variation in children's experience within a single classroom. Children have different experiences with their peers as well, whether the help is spontaneous or assigned by the teacher.

Spontaneous Helping

Collaboration and helpfulness among classmates that is spontaneous (unassigned) may be highly valued both as an expression of prosocial attitudes and as a multiplier of resources for the participants. But it also creates problems for students who are left out.

Developmental psychologist Catherine Cooper and her colleagues have conducted a series of studies on spontaneous helping in a second grade where it was not considered cheating and was even encouraged. Their sociometric comparison of the roles played by different children is striking:

> In this second grade classroom, the two children who received the most unsolicited information from their peers were also the ones most frequently sought as consultants. This pattern suggests that a small number of children may be at the crossroads of learning exchanges, and are both contributing to and benefiting from these interactions, whereas others miss both the challenge of questions and the benefit of instruction from their peers.[1]

Contrary to the researchers' expectations, academic ability was not the only important influence. Two children in this second-grade class were performing at the sixth-grade level, but only one of them was sought as a consultant.

In a study that complements Cooper's, Garnica compared the interactions of six kindergarten children who were at the bottom of the sociometric scale—called omega children—with six children picked randomly from the rest of the class.[2] Three 20-minute speech samples (collected by putting a small cassette recorder on the focal child) were analyzed for each of the 12 children. Their conversational behavior was compared on seven measures:

1. Number of conversational turns in all child-child conversations.
2. Number of different child conversational partners in all child-child conversations.
3. Number of attempts to initiate a conversation with the target child.
4. Number of attempts to initiate a conversation by the target child.
5. Number of times the target child's name is used by other children.
6. Number of insults or taunts received by the target child.
7. Amount of private speech produced by the target child.

The quantitative analysis showed a significant difference between the omega children and the others on all measures except the number of insults (6). The omega children were isolated and verbally neglected (1–5); they talked far more to themselves (7); and it appears from the qualitative analysis that they did not receive more insults and taunts simply because they rarely tried to step out of or challenge their neglected status.

If informal helping is important, then we need to understand not only the situations in which it works well but also how to change the status of isolated children. Neither the Cooper nor the Garnica studies suggests why some children both initiate and receive more interactions from their peers. As far as we can tell, in these particular classrooms the reasons come from individual characteristics. Two other studies of differential experience with peers show that characteristics such as sex, academic ability, and ethnicity are also influential; these are things that teachers should be able to do more about.

Sarah Michaels, whose research on sharing time was presented in chapter 2, has also been observing writing instruction in two sixth grades in which computers were introduced for word processing.[3] In order to use a computer, any writer needs to learn text-editing commands required by the software. In an end-of-the-year test, Michaels found strikingly different distribution of this knowledge in the two classrooms, and was able to explain the difference through extensive observations by research-team members throughout the year.

The test was a hands-on editing problem in which words of a popular song appeared on the screen with several mistakes. Each student individually was asked to fix them, and to explain what they were doing and why. Briefly, here's what Michaels found:

	Classroom A (N = 12)	Classroom B (N = 17)
Completed editing tasks	1	14
Used more sophisticated commands to do so	1	12
Understood mode organization of program	1	12
Used terms such as *cursor* and *Control C*	2	12

This distribution of knowledge cannot be explained by differences in the writing curriculum in the two classrooms; the students in Classroom B had no greater need for these editing skills than those in Classroom A. From the field notes, Michaels reports, "We know of 5 separate cases where a student in Classroom A retyped an entire composition into the computer (making only minor corrections) instead of using QUILL's editing capabilities." Critical influences seem to have been both the teacher's way of introducing knowledge about editing commands into the classroom, and then—important for our present discussion— her indirect influence on the patterns of peer relationships within which this knowledge could spread.

In Classroom B, where the knowledge was widespread among the students, the teacher herself became an expert, and so was able to give children individual help. She also displayed information about the commands on wall charts, which the children frequently consulted (including during the test). In Classroom A, by contrast, the teacher did not become an expert herself; she handed out Xeroxed copies of pages from a manual, which children were never seen consulting; and she depended on one boy, Richie, who had learned from the students and teacher in Classroom B, to help others. With respect to student-to-student diffusion of expertise,

> in Classroom B, the single most important factor is that students often worked in pairs at the computer (at least 30% of the time). Partners were assigned on the basis of the order in which first drafts were completed and edited by the teacher; hence, a certain unpredictability was introduced. Mixed sex and mixed computer ability pairings were common. Thus pair work (in addition to the wall chart) led to wide diffusion of computer vocabulary and editing information. There were no obvious sex differences related to which children had extensive information about the editing commands and the modes. . . .
>
> In Classroom A, there was no official partner policy at the computer (unlike Classroom B); students who had nothing to do were often allowed to hang out at the back of the room while a friend used the computer. As a rule, groupings at the computer divided along sex lines (as did groupings in the lunchroom and on the playground). For this reason, Richie spent more time at the computer with other boys, and only occasionally helped a girl. Not surprisingly then, on the computer quiz the only two other students to demonstrate some knowledge of the QUILL commands were boys who were close friends of Richie's. Not a single girl in Classroom A demonstrated that she knew how to insert or drop text.

This study offers a particularly clear picture of how information once introduced spreads through a small community, and the aspects of social organization that stimulate or restrain that spread. Much of the knowledge and skills taught in school is also available outside school, so schools cannot be held completely responsible for what is, or is not, learned. But these students were wholly dependent on school for text-editing skills. The few home computers were used only for games, and none of the students had had any computer experience at school before this year. Michaels points out important implications for teachers:

> The distinction . . . between introduction and diffusion of information should not be confused with the distinction between "formal" vs. "informal" learning, or teacher initiated vs. student initiated activities. Depending on the knowledge base of the students and the teaching approach of the teacher, the introduction of information in a classroom could fall at various points on continua of formality and student responsibility; that is, it can occur as a whole group lesson, a wall chart, peer tutoring, informal group discussion, etc. Similarly, how the information diffuses may depend on a wide variety of formal and informal processes, e.g. through peer experts with explicit tutorial duties, one-to-one conferences with the teacher, or casual peer chats.

All teachers depend on diffusion, on information spread, but teachers may not be fully aware of the extent of it, the multiple channels through which it occurs, or the barriers to it. If teachers can become aware of the complex relationship between the social organization of information transfer in their classrooms and learning outcomes, they might be better able to maximize the learning opportunitites that naturally occur and minimize previously unforeseen barriers to learning.

For example, in the case of computers, if a teacher wants to depend on student experts, then at ages where informal same-sex grouping is common, she should be sure that there are both boy and girl experts from the beginning, and/or establish a partner system that ensures mixed-sex pairing.

Interactions Within Assigned Groups

Sex is not the only likely line of cleavage within classrooms, nor does teacher assignment of students to peer groups eliminate all barriers to the spread of knowledge by means of peer help. In a series of studies, sociologist Elizabeth Cohen has been applying a theory developed in laboratory settings—Expectation States Theory (EST)—to classroom interaction. This theory attempts to explain how status characteristics of group members become the basis for others' expectations of competence and thereby affect the rate of interaction and influence in collective tasks.[4]

According to EST, several kinds of status characteristics can be salient in classrooms:

- Specific status characteristics directly related to the particular task, such as mathematical ability in a group assigned to work on a math problem.
- Specific status characteristics not directly related, such as reading ability in a group working on a task that requires no reading.
- Diffuse status characteristics, such as sex or ethnicity. (In previous studies of children playing a board game, whites were found to be dominant over blacks, Anglos over Chicanos and Canadian Indians, and European Jews over Middle Eastern Jews in Israel.)[5]

In one study of interaction in nine bilingual classrooms, grades two through four, groups were assigned challenging math and science tasks for an hour a day for fifteen weeks.[6] Each child was expected to complete individual work, but all the children were encouraged to ask each other for help, and were expected to give help when asked. The materials were in both English and Spanish, and the teachers used both languages, so students not yet proficient in English were at no disadvantage. The status of students as perceived by their peers was measured from a sociometric interview at the beginning of the year; rate of interaction was obtained from observations of the working groups; and learning was measured by tests of the curriculum content at the beginning and end of the curriculum unit.

In these classes, the rate of talking and working together was most closely related to the children's perceptions of which classmates were best at math and science, but it was also related to their perceptions of their peers' reading ability and to close friendships. Children who interacted the most were also the ones who learned most, especially about the more complex concepts. "Those children with high social status have more access to peer interaction that, in turn, assists their learning. In other words, the rich get richer." Cohen concludes:

> The use of heterogeneous peer groups in the classroom is like a two-edged sword. Talking and working together clearly has favorable effects on learning, especially conceptual learning. . . . However, heterogeneous groups also have distinctly negative effects. . . . Higher status students will have higher rates of participation and influence. These differences . . . are often accepted as inevitable consequences of individual differences in ability. . . . [But] they can also be seen as a product of the status structure of the classroom. . . . Thus it would seem incumbent upon those of us who advocate cooperative groupwork to consider the identification and treatment of these problems of status.

One such treatment, according to Cohen, is to convince children that many abilities, not just one, are important in the classroom and relevant to assigned tasks. Another, according to research by a student of Cohen's at Stanford, is to make sure that, in school, adults model the equal-status relationships that are encouraged among the students:

> Experimental results have shown that Expectation Training will *not* produce the desired effects in settings where the adults mirror the status order of the outside society, i.e. the Anglo teacher is the "boss" and the Hispanic aide clearly functions as subordinate. Unless the aide and the teacher model equal-status behavior for the children, the low-status child is likely to think that it is illegitimate in a desegregated setting to speak up and tell high-status children what to do.[7]

CULTURAL DIFFERENCES AMONG STUDENTS

In addition to the problems that status differences create for productive peer-group interactions, cultural differences may also affect the kind of group structure that works best.

One example comes from the transposition of the Hawaiian KEEP program into the Navajo school at Rough Rock, described in chapter 4. In the original KEEP program, mixed-sex groups of four or five children worked well in the learning centers. But not at Rough Rock:

> The children often seemed uncomfortable in the centers. They would become restless; they would get up and move to another table; they would pull their chairs away from each other to either isolate themselves or form into groups of two; [and] squabbling was frequent. The centers were not running comfortably, and they were not producing peer assistance.[8]

After considerable discussion between the KEEP researchers and the Navajo staff, the third-grade Navajo children themselves provided the clues to the necessary changes: " 'First we have to have smaller groups. . . . Then the girls could work together and the boys could work together.' And that in fact was the key: smaller groups of the same sex."

In this situation, the children could talk about the kinds of groups they would work best in. Where this is not so, teachers can learn much by observing the informal groupings and ways of interaction that their students tacitly choose in the classroom and on the playground.

There may also be cultural differences in the importance of "legal" peer interaction for students' attitudes toward school. Linguist William Labov has been studying relationships among dialect features, membership in peer-group gangs, and school reading achievement in black adolescents for twenty years, first in New York City and later in Philadelphia. He is convinced that one source of reading retardation is the conflict between the vernacular culture and the school, and that an important point of contrast is the value placed on group work versus independent achievement:

> School learning is, on the whole, a matter of individual study and competitive display before the group. The skills that are highly developed in vernacular culture depend on a different strategy. Sports, formal and informal, depend on close cooperation of groups. The same holds for music. . . . Vernacular skills are not developed in the quiet of the study chamber, but in close exchanges of group members. . . . There are powerful and positive forces available in the vernacular culture. . . . Once we have identified them, we can proceed to the constructive job of social engineering, to bring the forces of social cooperation and energy into the classroom.[9]

So far, in this book, I have reported research on cultural differences that come from differences in ethnicity (Native American, Hawaiian, black, and so on). Social class is another dimension of cultural difference, more prominent in recent educational research in England than in the United States. One recent study by reading educator Lowry Hemphill examines differences in discussion style between two small groups of unacquainted white high school girls—a working-class group in the inner city and a middle-class group in a suburb—in both informal and formal discussions.[10]

Hemphill herself led the informal discussions, on the topic "Should women have to register for the draft?" These discussions fit the characteristics I described in chapter 4: Hemphill refrained from nominating speakers, evaluating student comments, and so on. And it was in these informal discussions that the sharpest social-class differences occurred in the girls' conversational style.

One striking difference was in listeners' use of back-channeling utterances ("yeah" or "mmm," or content words that completed or repeated those of the speaker—the same features that increased in Meier's basic writing conferences described in chapter 4). Hemphill found the same frequency of back channels in the two informal discussions, but they functioned in different ways. In the middle-class group, nearly half of the back channels were uttered by girls who then became the next speaker; that is, they were uttered as a "floor-competing device," used to bid for the floor. Here's an example, followed by Hemphill's analysis[11]:

Leslie: Mmmhmm. So, I g— I don't know, I guess I just have a different perspective ⌈on it.
Rachel: ⌊Yeah.
Leslie: It's w—
Rachel: My grandfather was in the air force or the navy, one of the two, excuse me, during th— World War Two. And my mother always tells this funny story about he was home from a Navy base or Air Force or whatever he was doing . . .

(middle-class informal discussion)

Rachel inserts a "yeah" near the end of Leslie's turn, at a possible sentence ending. Since Rachel wasn't the speaker prior to Leslie, she doesn't have the automatic "prior speaker goes next" advantage. By inserting her "yeah," Rachel *becomes* the prior speaker and seizes the floor at a point where Leslie stumbles, presumably searching for the right word. Rachel then begins a long anecdote which she has clearly wanted to have the floor to relate at this point in the discussion. The maneuver Rachel has used here can be called a *bid*.

The working-class girls' back channels were different. They were longer and contained more content words, and only 10 percent of them predicted who would take the next turn. That is, they functioned more to contribute to the existing speaker's turn than to compete for the next one[12]:

Kelly: Guys get up in the mornin' and hop in the shower, maybe if they're lucky they hop— if we're lucky they hop in the shower. They throw on any clothes, they don't iron their clothes, they just throw on a pair of pants, a tee shirt, come to school doop dee doop. We got to get up in the mornin', take a shower, iron our clothes and ⌈get dressed up.
Eileen: ⌊Do our hair,
put on our makeup.   (working-class informal discussion)

Lowry: What would you do if they decided that next year that girls would have to register too, what would you do?
Eileen: Move out ⌈of state. Act mooney.
Kelly: ⌊Move out of state.
Eileen [continuing]: 'Cause then they won't draft you, if you're a little lunatic or somethin'. They won't draft you because they don't want any lunatics in the army.

(working-class informal discussion)

With this contrast in turn relationships, Hemphill found other related differences. Although speakers in both groups demonstrated their ability to construct syntactically complex sentences, the turns of the middle-class girls were, as a group, more complex. One conversational result was a longer interval between points in a speaker's turn when a sentence could be considered complete and the floor open to another speaker. For example, the following utterance

I mean you'd be forcing someone who possibly didn't believe the same way you do, to fight.

is not interruptible until the end. For middle-class speakers, just as back-channel bids help to gain the floor, complex syntax helps to keep it. Overall, the resulting contrast is between competition for individual-speaker topic development among the middle-class girls, and speaker-listener collaboration on topic development within the working-class group.

Some time after these informal discussions, each group participated in a more formal session on the topic "Should the drinking or driving age be raised?" For the adult participant, Hemphill trained a colleague to conduct a typical "lesson." She then focused her analysis on the effect of the shift to a lesson-participation structure on the speech of the two groups.

There was little change in the speech of the middle-class girls. They refrained from colloquialisms (like "scared shitless" in talk about the draft) and told fewer narratives of personal experience (though both topics were chosen in part to stimulate them). But the complexity of their utterances stayed high. For the working-class speech, the effects of the more formal session were greater. There were more silences (in response to teacher questions), less complex syntax, and more long narratives or minimal responses. In both groups, back channels were more often uttered while the adult was speaking than when peers were speaking. For the middle-class girls, whose back channels had been a turn-getting device, that function was now taken over by the teacher. For the working-class girls, whose back channels were a device for collaborative topic development, the effect of their absence on the content of individual utterances was greater.

Hemphill concludes:

A contrast which emphasizes the importance of individual speaker roles for middle-class students, and of speaker-listener collaboration for working-class students, can explain why each group responds differentially to "teacher talk." My research supports a claim that middle-class children and adolescents have grown up in families who value the ability to floor-hold in conversation and to construct monologues unsupported by listener responses. My work also suggests that working-class children and adolescents may have had not only less out-of-school experience with these styles, but may be accustomed in addition to another style, one that values collaborative topic development and elaboration in the role of listener. Classroom talk allows very few opportunities to display competence at this second set of abilities but almost exclusively creates opportunities where the first set of abilities can be displayed. Thus, working-class children may not only appear less competent to their teachers, they may also experience school as a place where oral language skills, as they understand them, are not valued.[13]

As Hemphill mentions in her concluding comments, this difference has implications for writing as well as speaking, and reinforces the special importance of student response groups for working-class student writers.

DIFFERENCES AMONG
CURRICULUM SUBJECTS

Peer interactions will have different functions in different areas of the curriculum. Stodolsky's study of peer work groups in fifth-grade math and social-studies classrooms in the Chicago area, mentioned in chapter 3, made that comparison. She found that groups were used more frequently in social studies, and were also qualitatively different in their assigned tasks. In social studies, children were more apt to be working on collaborative tasks: discussing, making maps, rehearsing a play, drawing or painting and doing crafts; in math, the most frequent interactions were during contests and games. In cognitive content, the math groups were working on basic skills, while the social-studies groups had a wider range—from higher mental processes to activities whose purpose was not considered primarily cognitive at all.

One traditional learning environment deserves mention here: the *chavrusas*—study teams of two young men who spend as much as ten hours a day together studying the Talmud in Orthodox Jewish yeshivas. (Some readers may have seen the movie *Yentl*, in which Barbra Streisand, dressed as a man, gains entry to a yeshiva, with many hilarious consequences.) There is a classroom teacher, the *rebbe*, but to at least one historian, his role is secondary to that of the *chavrusa*:

> The primary mode of study in the yeshiva is the chavrusa, or learning partner system. As the students examine the material they engage in an ongoing dialogue and debate. Each must defend his position while the other must challenge his partner's statements, even if they are only slightly inaccurate or incomplete. . . . Joint study is considered the best way to insure preciseness and clarity of thought.[14]

One must always be tentative about transferring learning environments from one culture to another. But asking students to study difficult texts in pairs or small groups, after some modeling of how to do it productively, is not unlike reciprocal teaching.[15]

AND WHAT ABOUT COMPUTERS?

Predictions about the long-term effect of computers on the social organization of education often emphasize their individualizing, even isolating, influence. For example, a 1957 science-fiction story by Isaac Asimov entitled "The Fun They Had" describes a scene in which siblings in a future century, getting ready to settle down to their computer terminals at home, reminisce about the olden days they've heard about from grandparents, when children actually went to school together at a central place in the community.

But in the shorter run, computers in the classroom seem to encourage more social interaction, not less. A front-page story in the Sunday *New York Times* (January 2, 1983), said, "The electronic revolution is beginning to alter social life" as well as work habits. So too in the classroom. A research team at the Bank Street College of Education has been observing these changes in many classrooms. They consistently find more peer interactions around computer work than on other classroom tasks. For example, in one classroom programing study (with LOGO), "We observed more collaboration among students, more solicitation of help from other students, and more 'dropping in' to make comments and suggestions, in programing than in noncomputer activities."[16]

There may be several reasons why placing computers in classrooms seems to result in increased collaboration among peers. One reason is a permanent feature of the technology: work in progress on the screen is public in a way that paper on a desk is not. Other reasons may be more temporary. Most classrooms today have one computer at most, and that makes it a scarce resource whose use can be doubled by asking children to work at the terminal in pairs. Expertise in the new technology is also a scarce resource, and student experts can supplement the limited availability of the teacher. Finally, perhaps there is something adventurous and experimental about the teachers who have been in the first wave of computer users, or something accepting of innovations about the principals and supervisors who become proud of the "computer revolution" happening in their schools.

Because of initial reports of increased student collaboration as well as visions of software as the new "teacher-proof" curricula, some critics of traditional classroom practices (such as IRE lesson sequences) hope that the computer can be an electronic Trojan horse that, once admitted into the classroom, will release its subversive power. Given the durability of traditional classroom structures, however, such a prediction seems unlikely to come true without deliberate action on the part of each teacher.

ROLES FOR THE TEACHER

I do not want to suggest that peer groups do, or should, work in complete independence of the teacher. We have already seen how important the teacher should be in setting up groups and monitoring carefully the groupings that form spontaneously. Teachers have important roles with respect to the content of the discussions as well.

One role is as model, as suggested in the report on reciprocal teaching in chapter 6 and the Kamler report on writing conferences in chapter 7. The role of teacher as model is an important link between interactions with an expert (teacher) and interactions among peers.

A second role is that of occasional participant in the discussion. We saw one example of this role in the excerpts from Vivian Paley's kindergarten in chapter 4. Another example comes from a film about Central Park East, an alternative public school in New York City.[17] The film, entitled *Kid Stuff*, shows vignettes of peer collaboration and discussion in one second-third grade. It was made while the class was deeply involved in a unit on ancient Egypt prompted by the King Tut exhibit at the Metropolitan Museum that they had visited.

One of the few occasions during the school day when the teacher,

Leslie Stein, demands that all the children do the same thing at the same time is a meeting on the rug when children tell a story, or read something they have written, to the entire group. In interviews, Stein explained:

> I think it's really important. This is one time when they absolutely can't do whatever they want, and they sit and listen. It's a situation where they're meant to ask questions of one another, and get information from one another, and help one another, and I like that.

The film includes a section of such a meeting just after Kevin has read aloud his story about "The Runaway Slave," set in ancient Egypt. It so happened that while the class was studying ancient Egypt, many of the children had seen a powerful television show, *Roots*, about slavery in the United States, and there was some understandable confusion about the common phenomenon of slavery in two settings so different in place and time. Here is a segment of the discussion, including participation by the teacher:

Jeff: That guy was strong. He used to move big big blocks from the pyramids by hisself. Only him.

Angie: You're talking about his roots, right?

Kevin: No, I was saying, If you were a slave it's like "Roots." Rhonda?

Rhonda: Why did he want to escape?

Kevin: Huh?

Rhonda: Why did he want to escape?

Kevin: Why did Kunta Kinte [a slave in *Roots*] want to escape? Marc?

Marc: Rhonda, he wanted to excape 'cause they made him work too hard and all that. So he wanted to get away from being a slave and working that hard.

Rhonda: That's about "Roots"? I thought he was talking about something else.

T: Wait. I'm sorry to interrupt you, but I think it's really important what Rhonda is saying. Kevin, do you want to explain what you said a little bit more because I think you went over it a little too quickly, and I think it's confused some people.

Kevin: If you was a slave for five or six years wouldn't you want to escape, moving big blocks of stuff? I'll show you the pictures.

T: Well, maybe you could explain it without the pictures. Could you try to explain it a little more without the pictures?

Kevin: Okay. See, he was making a pyramid and you know they had to use big blocks, big square blocks, big square-shaped boulders to make the pyramids, right? And he had to move them. And they weigh 700 pounds. Oni?

Oni: Kunta Kinta didn't work for six years. He worked more than that. And he still is, right? Wasn't he still a slave, no matter what? He didn't escape, did he? It was Harriet Tubman who escaped!

Kevin: Janala?

Janala: I got two things to say. Did they eat grits like Kunta Kinta did? . . .

The teacher understands more than any of the children about the comparison they are struggling to comprehend. Her role at the moment is to stop the flow of talk and ask Kevin to replay his ideas about slavery more slowly. But the complex combination of sociohistorical similarities and differences touched by Janala's wonderful question, "Did they [the slaves in ancient Egypt] eat grits like Kunta Kinte [a slave in the American South] did?" cannot be comprehended in one discussion. And so another role for the teacher is to listen to the children's ideas as input for her own planning of future situations in which important concepts can be revisited.

TALK IN THE UNOFFICIAL PEER CULTURE

Any classroom contains two interpenetrating worlds: the official world of the teacher's agenda, and the unofficial world of the peer culture. Most educational research is interested only in the first, and implicitly assumes the perspective of the teacher. Studies discussed so far in this chapter and the preceding one are limited in this way. They report peer interactions that are, or should be, included in the teacher's plans.[18]

Students, from their first year in school on, do not confine their actions and their talk to fulfilling the teacher's agenda, much as teachers might like that to be the case. And our observations should not be so confined either. To put the issue bluntly, to see children only in their relation to teachers and assigned tasks is to be like "colonial administrators who might be expected to write scientifically objective reports of the local populace . . . by ideologically formulating only those research problems that pertain to native behaviors coming under the regulation of colonial authority."[19] Being a teacher, unlike being a colonial administrator, is a valued social role that should be improved, not abolished. It is an important part of our task as teachers or researchers to uncover and understand the voice of students.

Other authors have addressed this issue. In narrative form, one of the themes of Saint-Exupéry's story *The Little Prince* is about the importance of trying to understand other people's understanding (remember the discussion at the end of chapter 2 on sharing time), and the conflicts between the perspective of a child—about what would be a good drawing of a boa constrictor, for example—and the perspective of adults who are always preoccupied with "matters of consequence."[20]

More than fifty years ago, Willard Waller devoted part of his classic study *The Sociology of Teaching* to the conflicts between students and teachers inherent in the institution of schooling. These conflicts do not exist, Waller pointed out, only when classroom participants come from different home cultures. More universally, there are age- and role-related conflicts between students and teachers over how situations are to be defined. "The fundamental problem of school discipline may be stated as the struggle of students and teachers to establish their own definitions of situations in the life of the school."[21] Much recent research can be seen as attempts to examine Waller's insights in more detail.

Of course, teachers do not need outsiders to tell them that students often speak and act in forbidden ways. But the observations of those who make the familiar strange by helping us see how life in classrooms is experienced by our students can make us more reflective about our behavior as well as theirs.

In a few particularly valuable cases, observers help us to see some segment of classroom life from both points of view (like helping us to see both the duck and the rabbit, or the young woman and the old woman in the familiar reversible figures). More often, researchers maintain one focus—either the view of the teacher because of the importance of her role (as in most of the research in this book thus far), or the view of the students because of their relatively powerless position.

One curriculum area that brings to the fore the inevitable tensions between the two perspectives is writing. One study that presents sympathetically the perspectives of both teacher and students is Michaels's analysis of writing conferences, referred to in chapter 4. Here students are complying willingly with the teacher's assignment to write a composition on a specific topic, but some are not doing it in ways that meet the teacher's expectations. How should we resolve the tension between encouraging the development of the student writer's "voice" and teaching directly or indirectly conventions not only of superficial details of spelling and punctuation but of more fundamental matters such as the selection and organization of ideas?

A second example, involving talk among peers, is Lemke's thoughtful commentary on the "asides" that students manage to make to one another at times when such side conversations are officially not allowed—asides that are usually out of recording range and so not even included on transcripts. In his study of high school science lessons, Lemke noticed one such aside during a teacher-student debate: one student, Erin, asked her question challenging the teacher and initiating the debate only after conferring with her neighbor in an aside that was illegal by the rules that give a teacher, in principle, total communication control. Lemke found, as did Mehan, that classroom discourse as it is actually talked doesn't always fit those rules, and suggests that both the rules and the violations may be useful. Where Mehan discussed the value of the violations in enabling the teacher to "get through" the lesson, Lemke explores their value to student's understanding of lesson content:

> In many cases one student will ask another about something the teacher said that he missed, or ask what the current task is, or even ask for an explanation of something heard but not understood. These asides often check for confirmation or support an idea or question which the student will later publicly contribute to the discussion, creating what most experienced teachers know are among the most important moments in any lesson. . . . [Classes] which have a lively and interesting dialogue usually have quite a bit of side conversation as well. Most teachers do not admonish students every time they talk to a neighbor, and it is a good thing they don't. . . .
>
> Consider the educational assumptions behind a strictly enforced rule against sidetalk. They presume that classroom learning is essentially an individual process between each separate, isolated student and the teacher. It is this assumption that justifies the rule, but observation of classes shows that what happens there is a highly social process; a complex, co-operative, self-adjusting pattern of interaction among all the participants. The rule belongs to a picture of classroom learning that distorts its social nature to make it seem as if each student is solely responsible, solely accountable for what they do or do not learn in class. . . . It is no accident that the only classroom situation in which the rule against talk between students *is* strictly enforced is that of *test-taking*—that moment in which the social process of the classroom *is* suspended, and replaced by an artificial set of separate isolated individuals.[22]

Here there is an interpenetration of the official and unofficial, legal and illegal parts of the total classroom-speech community. The dilemma for the teacher is not what her academic objectives should be, as it is in the case of student writing, but what rules about talking should be enforced to advance those objectives most effectively.[23]

Different questions are raised by observations of student behavior that cannot be seen as contributing to the teacher's goals. Such behavior starts young, even in seemingly ideal early-childhood environments. Hatch conducted both observations and interviews in a kindergarten with a very experienced teacher and a "whole-language" curriculum. He focused on those times of day when peer interactions were either forbidden (when a child was speaking during sharing time or the teacher was giving directions to the whole class) or discouraged (during large-group activities on the rug).

He found three patterns of illegal behavior: *forgetting expectations,* when abiding by the teacher's rules was overridden by the momentary stimulation of what someone said or simply by the proximity of another child; *secret communications,* or knowingly violating rules, as evidenced by "watch and whisper"; and *exploring the limits*—essentially watching, but without whispering. Hatch discusses these behaviors as examples of what sociologist Erving Goffman called, in his study of asylums, "secondary adjustments" to institutional expectations: behavior that does not conform to official norms.[24]

Striking evidence that such behavior seems inherent in the structure of schools, regardless of students' age or motivation, comes from educational anthropologist Jeffrey Shultz's reflections on his own graduate course in ethnographic research methods that included, as students, nine of his College of Education colleagues:

> I noticed my own students doing many of the same kinds of things that children do: passing notes to each other, surreptitiously reading the newspaper or working on material for other courses, laughing and giggling about something that has nothing to do with the class, etc. There seems to be something inherent in assuming the role of a student that elicits such oppositional behavior.

Shultz interprets this "oppositional behavior"

> as a way of dealing with a world in which what one does is often seen as not appropriate or correct and in which what one thinks is not considered relevant or interesting. Devising ways of manipulating and beating such a system becomes a challenge which is difficult to pass up, even to the extent that adults who assume the role of student become caught up in this oppositional process.[25]

In a footnote, he asks whether his students act this way because they feel they are being treated as incompetent and ignorant, or whether they are just repeating behaviors learned earlier in their lives. For his colleague volunteers, I also suspect that what is happening is a bit of what Goffman calls "role distancing"—occasional playful demonstrations that one is not "really" a student.[26]

THE SIGNIFICANCE OF THE CONTEXTS OF PEER INTERACTION

Whether as teachers or as researchers, we should not consider students only as filling the second slot in IRE sequences, thereby enacting a particular structure of classroom discourse and providing utterances that fill out the thematic content of a lesson. Events on the classroom stage are important even when the spotlight is not on the teacher, and even when we can only see students' mouths moving but cannot hear their spoken words.

NOTES

[1] Cooper, Marquis, and Ayers-Lopez 1982, 76.

[2] Garnica 1981.

[3] Principal investigators for this Microcomputers and Literacy Project were Bertram Bruce (one of the developers of the software QUILL at Bolt, Beranek, and Newman), Karen Watson-Gegeo, and Courtney Cazden. The information summarized in the table and all quotes are from Michaels 1985a.

[4] Cohen 1986.

[5] Schofield 1982 gives a detailed picture of black-white relationships in a newly integrated middle school, with extensive discussion of influences on "equal-status" relationships.

[6] The science curriculum is Finding Out/Descubrimiento by Linguametrics, n.d. Cohen emphasizes its importance: "The researcher [or teacher] who wishes to document learning gains as a result of peer interaction must be sure that the quality of the curriculum materials is good enough to produce learning; it does no good for peers to discuss unintelligible or poorly planned and chosen materials." The curriculum also includes detailed advice on teaching children the behaviors needed for effective group work.

[7] Cohen 1986, p. 108. See also Robbins 1977.

[8] Jordan, Tharp, and Vogt 1985.

[9] Labov 1982a 168–170.

[10] Hemphill 1986.

[11] Ibid., p. 41.

[12] Ibid., p. 39.

[13] Ibid., pp. 131–132.

[14] Helmreich 1982, 110–111.

[15] For ideas in other curriculum areas, see Moffett and Wagner 1976 for K-12 language arts (from a Vygotskian perspective), and Kamii and DeVries 1980 for a Piagetian perspective on games of all kinds, including mathematics, in early-childhood education.

[16] Sheingold, Hawkins, and Char 1984, 58. Also Hawkins, Sheingold, Gearhart and Berger 1982.

[17] The 16mm film *Kid Stuff*, and a longer videotape of the same classroom, *We All Know Why We're Here*, can be rented from The North Dakota Study Group, Center for Teaching and Learning, Box 8158 University Station, Grand Forks, North Dakota 58202. Copies of interviews with the teacher, Leslie Stein, held in October 1980 and January 1981, are available from the same address.

[18] Two exceptions were discovered in studies of the San Diego classroom described in chapter 3. Mehan 1980 describes a brief moment during the weekly distribution of classroom jobs when Carolyn successfully time-shares between attention to the teacher and to her own agenda with peers. Streeck 1983, 1984,

of the Free University of Berlin, reanalyzed the videotape of one of the four peer-teaching episodes discussed in Cazden, Cox, Dickinson, Steinberg, and Stone 1979—the one that was least successful, and most chaotic, from the teacher's point of view—to show how it could be seen as a concerted effort by the peer group to complete the assigned task, but in their own way.

[19]Speier 1976, 99.

[20]Saint-Exupéry 1943.

[21]Waller 1932, 297.

[22]Lemke in press, 32–35, edited.

[23]In case studies of children's learning in New Zealand, Alton-Lee 1984 found (contrary to her own expectations) similar evidence of the educational value of side conversations among peers during teacher-led lessons.

[24]Hatch 1986; Goffman 1961.

[25]Shultz n.d., 14–15 and 19–20, summarized.

[26]Outside the scope of this book are analyses of school culture from the perspective of Marxist "resistance theory," especially Willis's 1977 study of working-class boys in a British comprehensive school; Everhart's 1983 study of an American junior high school; and Connell, Ashenden, Kessler, and Dowsett's 1982 Australian study that includes girls as well as boys, parents as well as students, and a fee-paying upper-class school as well as a working-class comprehensive school.

Section III

---

*Ways
of
Talking*

Chapter 9

The
Teacher-Talk
Register

In the beginning of chapter 3, "The Structure of Lessons," I illustrated teacher talk with this example:

> What time is it, Sarah?
> Half-past two.
> Right.

That chapter discussed the features that place this talk in a classroom: the known-answer teacher question and the immediate evaluation of the student response. This chapter will explore other features of how people talk in the teaching role.

In the total repertoire of ways of speaking in any community, some of those ways will be identified with particular situations of use. The talk associated with occupational roles comes quickest to mind: the ways doctors talk, or lawyers, or sports announcers, when they are on the job. Varieties of language associated with such conditions of use are called registers. A *register* is a conventionalized way of speaking in a particular role, and is identified as a marker of that role.

Not all registers are occupational. One familiar and well-studied register is the baby talk (BT) that middle-class care givers typically use in speaking to infants and toddlers. In some ways, teacher talk (TT) with young children is similar to BT. Both are characterized by higher pitch, more exaggerated intonation and careful enunciation, shorter sentences and more frequent repetitions, and many more questions than the same adults would use in speaking (outside the parenting or teaching role) to other adults. As this list makes clear, a register is not a separate level of linguistic structure but a configuration of co-occurring features at many levels: pronunciation, syntax, speech acts, and so on.[1]

Other features differentiate teachers from parents and are more specific to teachers' role in the classroom, where teachers talk two-thirds of the time (in the I and E slots in the three-part IRE sequence), initiate almost all interactions, often with a set of boundary markers such as "now" and "well," and interrupt but are not interrupted.

One pervasive feature of the content of teacher talk is the expression of control—control of behavior and of talk itself. For example, in secondary-school classrooms in Scotland, linguist Michael Stubbs found eight kinds of metacommunicative talk—talk whose function is to monitor and control the classroom communication system. Here is his list, with examples from each category:

1. Attracting or showing attention.
   Now, don't start now, just listen.
   Yeah, well, come on now, you guys!
2. Controlling the amount of speech.
   Anything else you can say about it?
   I could do with a bit of silence.
3. Checking or confirming understanding.
   A very serious what? I didn't catch you.
   Do you understand, Stevie?
4. Summarizing.
   The rest all seem to disagree with you.
   Well, what I'm trying to say is . . .
5. Defining.
   Well, Brenda, does that mean anything to you?
   Can anybody put that in a different way?
6. Editing.
   That's getting nearer it.
   No, no, we don't want any silly remarks.
7. Correcting.
   [When a student has said that the meaning of *paramount* is "important"] Yes, more than that, all-important.
   [When the teacher is correcting a pupil's essay] The expression

"less well endowed" might be the expression you're wanting—
men don't usually pursue women because they're "well-built."
8. Specifying topic.
   Now, we were talking about structures and all that.
   Well, that's another big subject.[2]

As Stubbs explains, what is special about the classroom is not that somebody talks to get others' attention or check for understanding; such
language functions would be expected in any large group. What is special
is that talking in these ways is "radically asymmetrical . . . almost never
used by pupils and, when it is, it is a sign that an atypical teaching
situation has arisen."[3]

In his analysis of metacommunicative talk, Stubbs was interested in
a feature of the teacher-talk register common to all teachers by virtue of
their role, not stylistic differences in the enactment of that role from one
situation or one teacher to another. Both register and style are config-
urations of features at multiple levels of the language system, and both
depend on different frequencies of such features, not their presence or
absence. But there is an important difference between the two constructs:
we usually speak of a register in the singular but of styles in the plural.
It is useful to understand commonalities in the TT register, but it is also
useful to understand variability in styles: among more or less formal
situations within a single classroom, and among teachers who differ by
sex or cultural background.

Research on variability can also help validate hypotheses about underlying components of the register itself and why it is the way it is.
Again, research on BT provides an example. After reading a number of
research reports on BT, Roger Brown suggested that it is created by the
conjunction of two powerful intents on the part of the adult speakers:
to communicate clearly and to express affection. If he is right, then
situational variations in the importance of these intentions should influence BT forms in predictable ways. And there is some indication that
this is so. For example, psycholinguist Catherine Snow reports that
reading to young children elicited more complex speech from mothers
than free play, and suggests that "the extra situational support of pictures in the book reading situation limits the possible topics sufficiently
that the comments can be more elaborated [and still understood] than
in the less well-defined situations."[4]

In order to bring together research on variability in the TT register
and try to relate that variability to its underlying components, I shall
use a comprehensive model of politeness phenomena by two sociolinguists, Penelope Brown and Steven Levinson (henceforth referred to as
the B&L model).[5] Then, as an exercise in using the B&L model, we shall

look at the TT register features in one speech event in a bilingual first-grade class.

THE BROWN AND LEVINSON MODEL

To present the B&L model, the table below gives their assumptions in their words in the left-hand column, and my translation of those assumptions into classroom terms in the right-hand column. Briefly, the model includes the following three ideas:

1. Teachers inevitably engage in face-threatening acts (FTAs). They constrain students' freedom and criticize their behavior and their work, often in public.
2. Teachers can soften the effects of such acts by various politeness strategies. Two important strategies express intimacy ("positive" politeness) or deference and respect ("negative" politeness). Note that, in this model, "positive" and "negative" are terms of description, not evaluation.
3. The seriousness of any act, to teacher or student, depends on their perceptions of social distance (D), relative power (P), and a ranking (R) of the imposition of the teacher's act at a particular moment.

Now read the following, paragraph by paragraph, first the B&L model on the left and then my translation of that paragraph on the right.

Brown and Levinson (1978)	A Classroom Translation
Actors act rationally, though not necessarily consciously, and construct verbal strategies to achieve certain ends.	Teachers are rational actors.
These ends almost always include both conveying certain information, and doing so in a way that will minimize "face-threatening acts" (FTAs) to their addressee and to themselves.	Teaching is more than telling, more than even the most successful referential communication; it also requires the management of interpersonal relationships and the accomplishment of classroom control in face-saving ways.
"Face" has two aspects, either or both of which can be threatened by a particular act: negative face is a person's claim to freedom	Teachers, by the very nature of their professional role, are continuously threatening both aspects of their students' face—

Brown and Levinson (1978)	A Classroom Translation
from interference and constraint; positive face is a person's claim to be appreciated by others. Some acts, such as interruptions, threaten both negative and positive face.	constraining their freedom of action; evaluating, often negatively, a high proportion of student acts and utterances; and often interrupting student work and student talk.
Rational actors will usually not do FTAs "baldly, without redressive action," but will seek to minimize their threat by strategies of redressive action that can be divided into positive and negative politeness styles, or by going "off-record." Positive politeness phenomena are exaggerations of normal behavior among intimates and acquire their redressive force by association with intimate language use; negative politeness phenomena are forms used for social distancing, which minimize the impositions of particular FTAs by expressions of deference and respect. Off-record strategies use hints and metaphors to render the meaning deliberately ambiguous and therefore negotiable.	Teachers will soften their FTAs with some form of redressive action; and their strategic choices can be described as versions of positive or negative politeness styles, or, probably less frequently, as going off-record.
The seriousness of FTAs depends on participants' assessments of their social distance (D) and relative power (P), and their ranking (R) of the imposition of particular acts.	Teachers as a group are more distant than parents; the particular perception of psychological D between a group of students and their teacher will be influenced by, but not determined by, social facts of differences in ethnicity and social class. Perceptions of P will also vary, depending on a teacher's confidence in her authority, and on family and peer-group respect for that

Brown and Levinson (1978)	A Classroom Translation
	authority. R will vary, within classrooms, from one situation to another, depending on perceptions of the seriousness of the teacher's FTA to particular students at particular times.
The perceived seriousness of the FTA will determine the selection of redressive strategy. To do an FTA baldy, without redress, implies overwhelming urgency, minimal threat, or vastly superior power on the part of the speaker. The more serious the FTA, the more negative politeness forms will be selected, because the effectiveness of positive politeness depends on vulnerable assumptions about the hearer-speaker relationship.	While any one teacher will use a combination of negative and positive politeness forms, depending in part on R, interclassroom differences in D and P will produce different frequencies of these two kinds of redressive action and thereby two kinds of control style.

I'll try to make this abstract model come alive by giving some examples of TT that co-occur with variation in rank of imposition of the act (R), power relationships in the classroom (P), and social distance (D) between speaker and addressee(s). All three—R, P, and D—are aspects of the social context that affect ways of speaking. In considering them separately, we must keep in mind that any one utterance expresses some value in all three dimensions simultaneously. We shall consider them separately only for analytical convenience.

Variation in Rank of Imposition

Variation in the rank of imposition (R) emphasizes one particular aspect of the social context—the situation at the moment of speaking and the rights and obligations of the participants (teacher and students) in whatever activity is under way.

For example, Florio reports differences in the form of teacher directives in a single sixth-grade classroom between a crafts period and a more formal social-studies lesson. These differences can be understood as differences in R, the perceived seriousness of the teacher's acts of control. Directives in the crafts period tended to be phrased as either appeals to group solidarity or wh—imperatives. Here are her examples, with my B&L model categorizations in parentheses.[6]

> OK, the rest of you, let's get the chairs in a circle.
> Let's not embarrass him.
> > We would all do a different part of it.
> > (positive: include both speaker and hearer in the activity)
> Will you do me a favor, please, and shut off the light?
> > (negative: go on record as incurring a debt)
> Why don't you come down, and I'll give them to you to pass out?
> > (positive: give reasons)

If the crafts period is considered by both students and teacher as a time when students can carry out their own plans, then requests from the teacher that interfere with those plans require some kind of redressive or mitigating action.

In the social-studies lesson, the teacher's directives were more often direct imperatives.

> Get out your homework.
> Finish them up.
> Give me an exact location.
> > (baldly: without redressive action)

Within a lesson, when task focus has been achieved, students expect that the teacher will give directions for the work to be done, and there is no need for redressive action. The following two hypothetical directives are marked with an asterisk to indicate that they would be heard as odd and inappropriate:

> *Will you do me a favor and get out your homework?
> *Why don't you give me an exact location?

Unless such utterances are clearly marked intonationally for sarcasm, the use of such politeness forms, especially the negative form, "Will you do me a favor," for what should be a nonserious act (low R) is a telling example of Brown and Levinson's discussion of how such inappropriate selection communicates a seriousness of the act for non-R reasons. In this case, the teacher could easily be perceived by the students as admitting that she has, in fact, little power over them.

Another example shows how the rank of impositions can shift within a single episode. In my San Diego classroom, peer teaching was encouraged. One day, I wanted an often difficult third-grade boy, Greg, to take off a paper-bag mask and stop "jiving" around so that he could assume the role of tutor for two first-grade classmates. I approached him cautiously, with at least three co-occurring politeness features:

> Greg, um—I've got a job that I'd like to show you, so that you can, um, show, um, uh— (negative: "be conventionally indirect" and "give deference" with hesitations; positive: "give reasons")

At that point Greg broke in to express his willingness and took off his mask. It evidently wasn't nearly as big a deal to him as it had seemed to me! Presumably because I then realized that I had exaggerated the problem of rank, my subsequent directives became much less hesitant and were put in more direct imperative form:

> Come on over here and I'll show you.

Variation in Power

Variation in power (P) refers to a more pervasive aspect of the relationship among participants—not power in any absolute sense but relative power as perceived by the speaker, and as she (in this case the teacher) believes it is perceived by her addressees (the students).

One study by psychologist Robert Hess and his colleagues directly compared mothers and teachers in these terms.[7] Sixty-six mothers talking to an only child and 34 preschool teachers talking to a child from their school were compared in two situations: a referential communication game and a block-sorting task. While the mothers and teachers did not differ in their teaching effectiveness, they differed significantly in features of their talk. For example, "teachers have a higher percent of their questions, requests, and commands in indirect, moderated forms than the mothers." Here are some examples of the teachers' indirect, or more polite, style:

- I wonder how these blocks are alike.
- I wish you could tell me.
- Can you tell me why you put that one there?
- Please put this block where it belongs.

This difference between mothers and teachers was independent of educational level; that is, it was a difference between parent talk and teacher talk, not a difference in characteristics of the individual adults. When the mothers were divided into a low-education group (median 12 years) and a high-education group (median 15 years) and then compared with the teachers (median 16 years), the percentages of directives in indirect form were:

Mothers of lower educational level	45.5 percent
Mothers of higher educational level	48.5 percent
Teachers	60.6 percent

The difference between the two roles was thus a more significant influence on this aspect of their talk than the difference in educational level among the mothers.

Hess and his colleagues suggest several possible reasons why teachers use more indirect forms than mothers, including a more explicit authority relationship between mothers and children. Mothers may feel more secure in their "authority" and not feel the need to mitigate their control statements with indirectness as much as teachers do.

Some classroom observers have worried that such indirection may pose interpretive problems for young children, or for those of any age who are used to more direct expressions of authority.[8] But one pattern of indirection by means of metaphors seems to be used very successfully by some teachers of young children:

Be a sunflower. (Sit up tall.)
Are your pinchers ready? (Get hands ready to help make muffins.)
I see some chairs that need to go back in the house. (Put the chairs away.)
Can you hop your coat up to its hook? (Hang your coat up.)

and by a modern dancer, Hanya Holm, in speaking to a master class of young dance students:

Children, your bottoms are like sandbags. I want to come around and punch holes in them.[9]

The special characteristic of these examples is not only the change from direct imperatives to more indirect forms, but also the additional translation of nouns and verbs into metaphors from the child's play world. The teacher who spoke the first four, Jiiva Devi (in Portland, Oregon) explained to me that she talked this way because she found that young children were more apt to obey without a clash of wills. And psychologist Rochel Gelman notes how experimenters can often get two-to-three-year-old children to answer questions through a puppet when they won't speak for themselves. She calls these "status-mitigating devices," and suggests that when we understand why they work, we will understand more about young children as well as about research (and teaching, I would add).[10]

Teachers' perceived need to mitigate, or soften, their statements of control may be related, as the B&L model suggests, to their perception of uncertain authority. But the particular forms of mitigation, even the particular forms of indirectness, will be influenced by both their own personal background and what they find produces the fewest discipline conflicts with particular students.

Variation in Social Distance

Teachers are different from parents not only in their perceptions of authority (differences in power) but in their greater social distance (D) in contrast to the intimacy of parents. Many classroom observers have commented on the social distance that teachers either feel or wish to maintain between themselves and their students. I mentioned that the "Birthplaces" lesson was part of my attempt, through the curriculum, to lessen the distance I initially felt so keenly in San Diego.

Similarly, Hess and his colleagues, in seeking explanations of why teachers speak more indirectly than parents, mention the influence on teachers of such institutional characteristics as the need to deal with children in groups and the more transitory nature of teacher-student personal relationships. And Heath, speaking from her work with teachers in Appalachia, also explains the more indirect expressions of teachers' directive intent as strategies for coping with the role of care givers who are relative strangers.[11]

Indirect directives are not the only feature of TT that may be explained in terms of social distance. Registers can be characterized by what they don't include as well as what they do. Just as striking as the prevalence of expressions of control is the absence of expressions of humor and affect. One article by two British researchers, Walker and Goodson, is a rare discussion of humor in the classroom, and at least suggests its importance. For example, the folk advice to beginning teachers, " 'Never smile before Christmas,' implies that jokes are part of the process of letting yourself become a person in the eyes of the pupils."[12]

Like humor, expressions of affect are basic to social life. Yet they are mentioned by observers just as infrequently. Goodlad's observational study of more than one thousand U.S. classrooms found that "affect— either positive or negative—was virtually absent. What we observed could only be described as neutral, or perhaps 'flat.' "[13] Even if teachers start most school years feeling like strangers to their students, why do these features of distance persist? Is it possible, without expressions of humor and affect, to achieve a shared sense of community?

There is also evidence that differences in perceived social distance between the teacher and particular students within a single classroom are linguistically marked in ways that fit the B&L model. For example, in Ms. Wright's kindergarten and first-grade classroom, Shultz discovered that the teacher used a more joking style (positive politeness) with the first-grade students whom she had had for two years. "Comembership" is the label Erickson and Shultz give to the dimension of perceived social distance.[14] In these terms, Ms. Wright had higher comembership with the first-grade children than with the kindergarten children, who were relative newcomers to her classroom.

In a junior-college setting where they analyzed counseling interviews, Erickson and Shultz discovered ways, in addition to visually obvious characteristics of ethnicity, in which high comembership (low D) could be achieved:

> For each counselor studied, there were encounters in which a student who differed from the counselor in ethnicity and cultural communication style received as much friendliness and special help as did a student who was similar to the counselor. But these were exceptions, and in almost every one of them, situationally relevant, particularistic comembership was established between student and counselor—an Irish-American counselor and a Chicano student both revealing that they had attended the same parochial school, or an Italian-American counselor revealing that he had been a high school wrestling coach and a Polish student revealing that he was on the junior college wrestling team.

Degree of achieved comembership was related to features of the counselor talk. For example, one white counselor gave direct commands to white students but more indirect direction to black students:

> Why don't we give some thought to ah . . . to what you'd like to take there [next semester].

Comembership was also related to the success of the interview in terms of the amount of helpful information exchanged.

It is striking, in the light of the B&L model, that most of the particular politeness features mentioned in studies of teachers' language of control are in the negative or off-the-record categories. This suggests that other kinds of teacher talk are possible, that classrooms should exist in which the positive-politeness features characteristic of speech among intimates are used to redress the FTAs that teachers must perform, or in which a special combination of high perceived power and low perceived social distance, as in the high-comembership counseling pairs, makes politeness markers less necessary.

One such description is of Amish classrooms in Pennsylvania. According to anthropologist Ray McDermott:

The Amish teacher's way of handling talk flies in the face of much educational ideology in America. The teachers dominate their classrooms and an interaction analysis has shown a heavy use of imperatives and a high degree of direct instruction. The children are told what to do and when and how to do it. The teacher is in total control of the children's development. In terms of learning to read and in terms of enhancing an Amish identity, their system is most successful. The children and their teachers have been bathed in a closed community with highly specific routines for everyone to follow. In terms of these routines, everyone is accountable to everyone else. Common sense and mutual trust are strived for by community members according to a specific code. In this context, instructions are not blind imperatives, but rather sensible suggestions as to what to do next to further common cooperation. There is a warm relational fabric that underlies the instructions and transforms them from orders into sensible ways of routinizing everyday life. What to many appears an authoritarian and oppressive system for organizing a classroom may in fact make great sense to the children and, accordingly, allow them to feel good enough to learn whatever it is to which a teacher directs a class's attention. Outsiders simply miss the cues which ground teacher-student activities in trust and accountability.[15]

THE TEACHER-TALK REGISTER IN TWO BILINGUAL CLASSROOMS

Research in two bilingual first-grade classrooms in Chicago suggests where more examples of positive politeness strategies may be found. Over a two-year period, Frederick Erickson, Robert Carrasco, and I did extensive observations in two Spanish-English bilingual first grades in Chicago. In both classrooms, the teachers and all of the children were Mexican-American. Our purpose was to describe the social and cultural organization of interaction, especially as it differs from more mainstream Anglo classrooms.[16]

In some ways, the two classrooms differed noticeably. In one classroom, the teacher made more decisions about where the children should be in the room and what task they should work on, and all the children were working at a common task more of the time; in the second room, the children had more autonomy to decide where they should be and what they should work on, and more different learning tasks coexisted at any one time. An ethnography of how learning took place would yield two quite different pictures. In this respect, the classrooms can be considered more "structured" and more "open," respectively, and I'll refer to them here as Classroom S and Teacher S (for structured) and Classroom O and Teacher O (for open), respectively.

But in another respect, in their styles of classroom control, these two teachers were like each other and different from most of the descriptions in the published literature. In qualitative aspects of the teacher-student relationship, both teachers expressed a personalized style, a style Carrasco characterized as *cariño*—a close and caring relationship. To members of Hispanic communities, the concept of *cariño* is nothing new. One contribution of ethnographic description is to make explicit and more widely recognized what members of a community tacitly know and do.

Our most detailed analysis of *cariño* comes from Classroom S, which was conducted wholly in Spanish except for thirty minutes a day of English as a second language (ESL). To give a flavor of life in this room, here are my field notes, written immediately after my first visit in November 1978. They express the admiration of one first-grade teacher for another:

> I have never seen as well functioning a first-grade society. By this I mean the extent to which the children know where and when and what to do; there is a minimum of time spent giving directions (cues so reduced that often Robert Carrasco and I never were aware of them); little if any need for negative sanctions; maximum task focus on part of children. And yet all this without any sense of strong military-type discipline. The children can take "time out" to chat or dance and never get out of control. . . . Aside from making the room a pleasure to spend time in, such a smooth system should have tremendous educational advantages: minimum time spent on discipline and maximum available for learning.[17]

Our research task can be described as an attempt to explore how cultural congruence between the teacher and her children might contribute to this remarkable social organization.

Consider just the first event in each school day. We have five examples of this event on videotape, of which one typical instance from a day in December will be presented here. Briefly, before school begins, a few children arrive and put down the chairs. Without any noticeable signal from the teacher, they gradually move, quietly but not silently, into a circle on the floor in the open space in front of the blackboard, girls on one side of the teacher and boys on the other, bringing their homework papers with them. Several children wait and accompany the teacher as she walks over, morning coffee in hand, to join the children on the floor. During the next twelve minutes, two instrumental tasks are accomplished: collecting *tarea* (homework)—on this day, practicing the names of the days of the week—and calling the roll. What is obvious to even the first-time visitor or videotape viewer is the flawless execution; what we realized only in more careful videotape analysis is the particular style of TT register in which these functions are accomplished.[18]

In sequential structure, homework collection conforms to Mehan's description. The basic lesson sequence, addressed to each child in alphabetical order (which simplifies the nomination procedure), has the usual three parts:

1. T calls the name of the next child on her list.
2. The child hands the homework to T.
3. T acknowledges receipt by recording a mark in her grade book.

More extended conversations, Mehan's conditional sequences, are sometimes added onto this basic structure: when the teacher asks whether the child knows the work (to which some nod no with surprising honesty) or elicits a reason for the homework's absence or praises with words or applause. And there is clear evidence on the videotapes that this sequential structure is now—in December—well known to the children: they start forming a circle on the floor before the teacher gets there, and several individual children start to hand in their homework just before the teacher calls their name.

But during these twelve minutes of mainstream classroom discourse structure, there are frequent expressions of *cariño*: in-group forms of address, frequent use of diminutives, reminders to the children of norms of interpersonal respect, and expressions of the teacher's knowledge of her children's family life. Before looking at each of these features in more detail, it is important to see them in context. Figure 9–1 is a transcription of part of the homework collection: original Spanish in the left-hand column (with T's nominations of each child numbered in the margin), English translation in the middle, and comments on nonverbal action on the right. Note in passing that none of the directives is in indirect form, and some directives to speak are firm orders. In translation:

2. "Excuse me." Say that, hon.
13. I want you to tell me with your little mouth, honey. . . . You tell me. Tell me.

Forms of Address

Except when actually calling a child's name, during both homework collection and roll call the teacher addresses the children with terms of endearment: *papi* or *mami*, often shortened to *pa* and *ma*. (See nominations 1, 2, 3, 4, 7, and 13.) of the 20 children called on during homework collection on this particular day, T adds an affectionate term of address to ten.

Parenthetically, a very different social use of forms of address was pointed out by an English and language-arts supervisor, Carolyn Wyatt.

ORIGINAL SPANISH	ENGLISH TRANSLATION	COMMENTS ON NONVERBAL ACTION
1. *T:* Norma Guzmán.	Norma Guzmán.	Norma doesn't arise for period of three terminal pauses and Teacher meanwhile straightens papers. Teacher looks at Norma, stretches out her hand to take the homework.
T: OK, mami. Muy bien. ¿Tú lo hiciste solita?	OK, Mami, very good. You did it all by yourself?	
Norma: Sí.	Yes.	
T: Sí? Ok, me escribiste algo allí abajo.	Yes? OK. You wrote me something on the bottom.	Teacher looks from the child to the paper, to the child, and to the paper again.
2. *T:* Vicente Hernández?	Vicente Hernández?	Teacher looks up while boy tries to maneuver way through group of five boys sitting very close. Boy walks up and teacher takes paper from him, eyes still on the boy, who nervously adjusts his belt, then places hands in pocket.
T: Con permiso, di, pa. ¿Ya lo sabes, todo, sí? Yo te prehunto después. Pero encantada que lo entregaste.	"Excuse me." Say that, hon. Do you know it, all of it, yes? I'll ask you afterwards. But I'm delighted that you turned it in.	She looks down at list and boy turns around, hands in pocket, and walks four steps back to place behind other boys, face down, self-conscious walk.
3. *T:* Salúd Juárez? Tráemelo, ma. Gracias, ma. ¿Lo sabes todo, Salúd? No? ¿Pero los vas a practicar? Sí?	Salúd Juárez? Bring it to me, hon. Thanks, hon. You know all of it, Salúd? No? But you are going to practice it. Yes?	Salúd looks down at list. Teacher looks up to Salúd, who holds paper above her head. Teacher holds hand up. Child bends forward and reaches across circle to present paper to Teacher. Teacher looks down at list, places paper on homework stack. As Salúd says no, teacher looks up at Salúd, who is shaking her head.
4. *T:* Carlos López. Los estudiaste, papi? Sí? OK. ¿Ya los sabes todos? Sí?	Carlos López. Did you study them, honey? Yes? OK. And you know them all? Yes?	Teacher looks up at Carlos, who comes from off-camera to blackboard near teacher to hand her his paper. Teacher looks at him. She looks down to place paper on stack, then looks at him again.

(continued)

FIGURE 9–1 La Tarea (The Homework)

	ORIGINAL SPANISH	ENGLISH TRANSLATION	COMMENTS ON NONVERBAL ACTION
5.	*T:* Mario León. Ah, no. OK.	Mario Leon. Ah, no, OK.	Child directly across from teacher in circle reaches, on knees, and slides paper on the floor. Teacher reaches across for paper, doesn't look at boy, places paper on stack, looks at list again.
6.	*T:* Eugenia Molina.	Eugenia Molina.	Calls Eugenia's name. Child is sitting on opposite side of circle from teacher, reaches paper across to teacher, who takes paper and places it on stack, not looking at child.
7.	*T:* César Monjaras? ¿Aste, papi? Sí?	César Monjaras? Did you study, honey? Yes?	Teacher calls César; he reaches across circle and hands paper to the teacher. She looks at him, looks down again for next name.
8.	*T:* Jesús Monjaras? Ahora sí. Esto sí quiero ver, la tarea.	Jesús Monjaras? Now this is what I want to see, your homework!	Calls Jésus Monjaras. She then watches him as he rises and walks toward her with paper. He presents paper, turns, and returns to place, holding the top of his pants.
9.	*T:* Roberto Nigrete. Gracias. ¿Ya lo sabes? Para ponerte la estrellita?	Roberto Negrete, thank you. Now do you know it? So I can give you the little star?	Teacher calls child's name; he tosses paper across circle toward teacher. Teacher looks at him and accepts paper.

174

#		English	Action
10.	T: Edelia Padilla? ¿Lo sabes tú? Sí? Toditos?	Edelia Padilla. You know it? Yes? Every (little) thing?	Teacher calls Edelia's name, receives paper from her, and places paper on the stack.
11.	T: Ricardo Raygoza. Gracias.	Ricardo Raygoza. Thank you.	Teacher calls Ricardo; he delivers paper, turns, and sits again.
12.	T: Edith Roldán.	Edith Roldán.	Teacher quickly places paper on stack and calls next name, receiving paper from Edith, who is at her right side, without speaking or looking at her.
13.	T: Mario Escobedo? OK.	Mario Escobedo? Okay.	Teacher calls Mario's name, looks at him, gestures to her mouth as she calls for an explanation, in an irritated tone.
	Mario: No tengo nada.	I don't have anything.	
	T: Yo quiero que tú me degás con tu boquita, papi. "Yo no estuve ayer por eso no traigo la tarea." Tú dime. Dime. ¿Por qué no tienes la tarea?	I want you to tell me with your little mouth, honey. "I wasn't here yesterday and that's why I didn't bring my homework." You tell me. Tell me. Why don't you have your homework?	
	Mario: Porque tenía la tos.	Because I had a cough.	
	T: Porque tenías la tos.	Because you had a cough.	Child responds and teacher's tone softens.

FIGURE 9–1 (continued)

She noticed that a particularly effective black high school English teacher regularly called her students Mr. and Ms. in class:

> Mr. Patrick, can you explain that statement?
> Ms. Lewis, I haven't heard from you.

In some contexts, use of such forms could convey a sarcastic reprimand. Here, Wyatt's interpretation is that the teacher was conveying both respect for individual students and a seriousness of purpose about their course in minority literature.[19]

Diminutives

In the excerpt from "La Tarea," three diminutives appear: *estrellita* (9), *toditos* (10), and *boquita* (13). Later in the same event, the teacher uses two more:

Quiero que estén calladitos, eh?	I want everybody to be quiet, OK?
Gracias a Diosito por esas abuelitas.	Thank God for those grandmothers.

No translation carries the correct connotation of these diminutive endings. They do not change the meaning of the adjective or noun to which they are attached—quiet or God or grandmothers in the examples just above—but rather function, like the pronoun *tu* as opposed to *usted*, to express endearment toward the referent and closeness in the speaker-listener relationship. Evidence that the children and teacher share this stylistic feature apart from its literal meaning comes when a child refers earlier that day to Frederick Erickson, a more than six-foot-tall observer, as *un profesorcito!* The teacher had explained that Erickson had been her teacher, "like you have me as your teacher," when she had been at Harvard. Introduction of the visitor ended with this interchange:

T: El es mi maestro.	He is my teacher.
C: Maestro como un profesorcito.	Teacher like a (little) professor.
T: Como un profesorcito, de verdad que si.	Like a professor, that's right.

Importance of *Respeto*

The children were reminded of the importance of *respeto* (respect) when the teacher told Vincente, " 'Con permiso,' di, pa" ("Say, 'Excuse me,' honey") when he stepped in front of another child to hand in his homework (T nomination 2 on the transcript), even though the seating arrangement on the floor made that unavoidable.

Perhaps also a part of *respeto* is the expectation that children should explain their reasons for not having their homework, as in 13.

Teacher's Knowledge of Children's Family Life

Evidence of the teacher's knowledge of the children's families appears in sequences of noninstrumental talk at the end of both homework collection and roll call. When Edith—the child *comadre-informadora* (gossip know-it-all)—reports at the end of homework collection that Juan got upset in the lunchroom the day before, the teacher asks, "Were you mad, *papi*, at your mother?" knowing that his mother is a cafeteria volunteer. And at the end of roll call, the teacher accounts to the children for the absence of Anibal's mother, a classroom aide, with a long description of her illness, and then asks questions about Juanito's mother, whom she knew had also been sick. When Juan explains that he stayed with his grandmother while his mother was sick, the teacher expresses, in her thanks to God, her understanding of the extended family in Hispanic communities, and of the important role of grandparents in children's lives.

Gracias a Diosito por esas abuelitas que nos cuidan, por que si no, estamos muy tristes sin las mamis.	Thank God for those grandmothers who take care of us, because otherwise we are very sad without mommies.

This talk about families and health at the beginning of the school day is an aspect of Latino culture in timing as well as topic. In Hispanic communities, when people come together to transact any business, it is inappropriate—even rude—to begin the agenda immediately. Anthropologist Edward Hall describes the problems encountered by an Anglo businessman who expects to open an appointment with an immediate focus on business affairs. To be effective, he must learn to use that beginning slot in the conversation as this teacher has so effectively done.[20]

Another instance of this Hispanic pattern is included in a Radcliffe undergraduate honors thesis by M. J. Yanguas.[21] She interviewed 25 working-class Puerto Rican adults as part of a larger study of their acquisition of English as a second language. Yanguas herself is of Spanish background, and her mother worked as a seamstress in the Boston area. Some of her informants were co-workers of her mother's, or members of the same Catholic parish. Because her first interview was with a woman her mother knew well, her mother offered to come along. The mother's presence helped so much to create an informal speech setting, a culturally appropriate combination of social talk and interview, that her mother—or sometimes her father—accompanied Yanguas on almost all her interviews, even with strangers. Because such an interview setting seems so strange in mainstream Anglo culture, this example may dramatize cultural differences more vividly than examples from a classroom.

In addition to verbal stylistic features of address terms, diminutives, expressions of respect, and well-timed expressions of family knowledge, T exhibited nonverbal expressions of *cariño* in physical behavior toward the children that is associated with the behavior of parents: placing a child on her lap when working individually with the child, kissing the child as a reward for good work. Such nonverbal behavior is acknowledged in the B&L model, although only linguistic realizations are analyzed.

Some General Comments

This extended example is from Teacher S's classroom. But Teacher O also expressed *cariño* in her behavior toward her students, and both discussed their close relationships in interviews. Teacher S (who does not have children of her own) explained that she deliberately tries to get the children to do school tasks "through herself." Teacher O (who is a mother) commented that some children "bring out the parent" in her. And it is consistent with the influence of R on politeness strategies that features of *cariño* seemed more frequent and more exaggerated in Classroom S, where the teacher imposed more decisions on the children, and less frequent in Classroom O, where there was less differentiation of time and space and more fluid boundaries for what could happen where, when, and how.

Carrasco suggested the term *personalization* for the control style, or register, of these two teachers. Personalization as a quality of teacher style should be distinguished from *privatization*, a name for the strategy of not calling on children for public and competitive display, and correcting children individually and in private. The importance of privatization in Native American communities has been argued by both Philips and Erickson. In the B&L framework, *privatization* refers to one way of minimizing FTAs by changing the situation so as to decrease R; *personalization* refers to the style of redressive action when FTAs do occur.

Finally, in the light of the B&L model, we can reconsider one important aspect of language use in bilingual (or multilingual) settings: the social meaning of code switching, especially for procedural and disciplinary utterances. Brown and Levinson suggest that "Spanish is used for positive politeness, English for negative politeness"[22]—implying that code switching into English, the language of the dominant society, for control purposes would co-occur with other indicators of negative politeness, expressing more impersonalized reference to the English-dominated society of which school as an institution is a part, and grounding the teacher's authority in that society's norms of behavior. Code switching into Spanish for control, by contrast, should co-occur with positive politeness features, and serve to ground the teacher's authority not in the norms of the dominant society but rather in the *respeto* due teachers within the Hispanic culture.

The two Chicago teachers were very aware of this within-group support for their authority. We were told before school started that even if Mexican-American children knew enough English to cope with the monolingual English program, their parents often chose the bilingual program (in the same school) in order to get Latino teachers. They wanted their children to respect the teachers and were afraid that Anglo teachers could not get that respect.

On the basis of this hypothesis about the social meaning of code switching, one would predict that even if the use of English as the medium of instruction increased from fall to spring (as it did in Classroom O), the teachers would continue to code switch into Spanish for control. I would predict, for example, that utterances such as the following would recur:

> When Teacher O got mad at the children's behavior, she said (in reference to herself), "Miss X likes to hear stories and have games, but—" and then switched to Spanish to talk explicitly about *respeto*. (Note the use of *Miss*, a negative politeness feature of impersonalization, in the English clause.)

In these two classrooms, code switching to Spanish for the language of control could be explained more simply as switching into the language that the children know best. The hypothesis that it is instead a part of a positive politeness style rests not on frequency of code switching alone but on a fuller analysis of co-occurring features of the teacher-talk register.

THE SIGNIFICANCE OF STYLISTIC VARIATION IN THE TT REGISTER

Brown and Levinson believe that sociolinguistic analyses of the language of politeness and control offer "an ethnographic tool of great precision for investigating the quality of social relationships in any society.[23] More specific to our purposes, they suggest ways of thinking about part of the selectional structure of classroom discourse—the TT register and the ways in which it is used by particular teachers and how choices of particular politeness strategies both express, and dynamically reinforce, particular qualities of human relationships in the classroom.

The feelings and motives behind Teacher S's behavior are undoubtedly complex. From her behavior in the classroom and her words in interviews, we infer that she feels herself to be a hybrid of mother and teacher, and is playing that role in specifically Hispanic ways. But her behavior is not an importation of the style of teachers in Mexico or Latin America. It seems rather the expression of a protector and buffer in an enclave of young minority children in a non-Hispanic world.

Harder to infer is the contribution this style makes to Teacher S's success in creating with her children a very peaceful and orderly classroom world. I believe that it makes an important contribution, and that the challenge to every teacher is to find a personal style that is equivalent in contributing to a strong and positive sense of community with each year's group of learners.

NOTES

[1] Snow and Ferguson 1977 includes reports of many studies of BT. Anderson 1978 reviews research on both BT and TT as a preview to her dissertation research on children's knowledge of these and other speech styles.

[2] Stubbs 1976. Heyman 1986 analyzes the last kind of metacommunicative talk, specifying topic, as an example of what conversation analysts (a subgroup of microsociologists) call formulations.

[3] Stubbs 1976, 162.

[4] Brown 1977; Snow 1977.

[5] Brown and Levinson 1978.

[6] Florio 1978, 6–7.

[7] Hess, Dickson, Price, and Leong 1979.

[8] Willes 1983; Heath 1978, 1983.

[9] The first four examples come from my observations in a preschool in Portland, Oregon, in 1979. The last is from a Harvard term paper by Linda Nash, May 1984.

[10] Gelman 1978.

[11] Heath 1978.

[12] Walker and Goodson 1977, 206. See also Walker and Adelman 1976.

[13] Goodlad 1983, 467.

[14] Erickson and Shultz 1982, 176. See also Erickson 1975a.

[15] McDermott 1977, 157–58.

[16] Erickson, Cazden, Carrasco, and Maldonado-Guzman 1983.

[17] Cazden, field notes, Chicago, November 27, 1978.

[18] In a reanalysis of these same videotapes, Dickinson 1985 has compared this same speech event with the opening meeting in Ms. Wright's kindergarten–first grade, using Irvine's 1979 dimensions of formality.

[19] Transcription discussed in seminar on classroom discourse, Harvard Graduate School of Education, March 1984.

[20] Hall 1959. Purves and Purves 1986, 174, extend this comparison to letters: "In some cultures it is inappropriate to include personal matters in a business letter to a stranger; in other cultures it would be inappropriate not to include such matters."

[21] Yanguas 1980.

[22] Brown and Levinson 1978, 115.

[23] Ibid., p. 62.

Chapter 10

The
Student-Talk
Register

In John Hardcastle's class in a London comprehensive school from which a cross-discussion was presented in chapter 4, pairs of students often held peer writing conferences. In one such conference, between Kevin (whose family came from Montserrat in the West Indies) and Sunday (whose family came from Nigeria), we catch a glimpse of one student's idea about the kind of language expected in school. At one point in his composition, Sunday had written, "What I mean is . . ." Kevin suggests two alternative phrases:

> *What I'm trying to say is*—And you could add *What I'm trying to express in word terms . . .*

When Sunday says no, Kevin justifies his suggestions:

> Those big words could make you, right. You could look at O-level [a school-leaving exam] that way.

In the end, Sunday accepts Kevin's first suggestion and changes "What I mean" to "What I'm trying to say."[1]

We may disagree with Kevin's particular suggestions, but he is right that there are special forms of student language—oral as well as written—that teachers expect in school. These ways of speaking can be considered features of a student-talk register—not how students do talk, but how some teachers seem to want them to talk, at least for academic purposes in classroom lessons. To the extent that a special register is expected but not explicitly taught, it forms part of the hidden curriculum of the entire school day.

I was first alerted to a hidden curriculum in ways of speaking through my own university teaching. One fall I gave my child-language course to two different groups of students: two mornings a week to a class of graduate students at the Harvard Graduate School of Education, and one evening (as a double-length class) at the Harvard University Extension. The latter is a lower-tuition program whose older-than-college-age students are either working toward a college degree through part-time evening study or taking single courses for personal or professional interest. My extension class had a mixture of the two groups—degree candidates, like the tuna fisherman from California who was working as a bartender while progressing slowly toward law school, and teachers in local day-care centers and public schools. Each class knew of the other's existence, and students were encouraged to switch when convenient—as an evening make-up for the morning class, or the chance to experience "real Harvard" for the extension students.

One evening, I noticed two black students from the graduate class in the extension class. Instead of sitting in a far corner, they were near the front, and instead of remaining silent, they participated frequently in the evening's discussion. Finally, the man spoke publicly about his perceptions of the difference in the two classes. I paraphrase his unrecorded comments:

> In the morning class, people who raise their hand talk about some article that the rest of us have not read. That shuts us out. Here people talk from their personal experience. It's a more human environment.

Reflecting on this incident later, I remembered a similar contrast reported to me two years earlier by a Tlingit (Native American) woman graduate student from Alaska. She described discussions in another course during her first semester at Harvard. Here the contrast was not only between ways of speaking but how these ways were differentially acknowledged by the professor. Again I paraphrase:

> When someone, even an undergraduate, raises a question that is based on what some authority says, Professor X says, "That's a great question!" expands on it, and incorporates it into her following comments. But when people like me talk from our personal experience, our ideas are not ac-

knowledged. The professor may say, "Um-hm," and then proceed as if we hadn't even been heard.

She was saying that, in an important sense, contributions to class discussion based on narratives of personal experience do not "get the floor."[2] Evidently there is a subtle and implicit, or hidden, curriculum in some classrooms to denigrate such narratives and press for the substitution of other forms of explanation and justification.

The classroom status of narratives of personal experience spoken intraconversationally—not free standing and without ties to the surrounding discourse as in sharing time—exemplify the tensions between alternative goals, dilemmas, facing any teacher. On the one hand, as suggested by Richard Anderson in chapter 6, narratives can exemplify general ideas in a way that greatly aids their comprehension. Here is Hymes's example of narratives functioning cognitively in just this way:

> [A student] Joanne Bromberg-Ross had recorded consciousness-raising sessions of a women's group, and presented a portion to my seminar. One session in particular contained a marvelous demonstration of interdependence between two different modes of clarifying meaning. The topic was what was meant by "strength" in men and women. Discussion began with discussion of terms. An unresolved back and forth about terms was followed by a series of personal narratives. Suddenly definitional discussion returned, stated in a way that made it clear that there had been no break in metalinguistic focus. Narrative had solved the problem of differentiating two kinds of "strength" (one good, one bad), when direct definition had floundered. The second mode of language use continued the purpose of the first, coming successfully to its rescue.[3]

On the other hand, there is the problem of air time: narratives can take a long time to tell and teachers may feel they contribute little to the rest of the class. As I argued in chapter 7, peer groups are one solution to this dilemma, giving time for simultaneous exploratory conversations in small groups that can then contribute in shorter, less narrative, and more generalized form to a whole-class summary.

The rest of this chapter gives examples of ways of speaking expected in particular classrooms. They have been recorded at different grade levels by different researchers. I hope they will stimulate readers to reflect on their own justifications for preferring particular speech styles.

TIMING

In order to be heard as appropriate, a student not only has to speak the right words but also has to say them at the right time. Many observers of classroom discourse have commented on this feature of the communicative competence that teachers expect. We saw examples in the "Birthplaces" lesson in chapter 3.

Another example comes from Lemke's study of high school science lessons. Janice correctly answers the teacher's question about a diagram on the blackboard before being called on, but her answer is not acknowledged until it is produced in its proper slot (marked with an arrow), after T's nomination[4]:

> T: Hydrogen would have *one* electron—somewhere in there—and helium would have . . .?
>
> S: *Two* electrons.
>
> T: Two. This is 1S, and the white would be? Mark?
>
> Mark: 2S.
>
> T: Two S. And the green would be?
>
> [*Janice says "2P" twice, and then is called on.*]
>
> T: Janice?

→   Janice: 2 ⎡P.

    T: ⎣2P. Yeah, the green one would be 2Px and 2Py.

Lemke comments:

> [The teacher] is trying now to enforce the rule that students should wait to be called on before answering, even though he does not enforce this rule all the time. When Janice repeats her answer again [marked by arrow], it is less loud and clear than before, and the teacher in fact doesn't bother to wait till she has finished but overlaps her speech with his own confirming repeat of "2P." Both these features suggest that Janice and the teacher know that her last repeat was purely pro forma (i.e. a mere formality), since her earlier answer had been clearly heard by everyone. The teacher has sacrificed the efficient development of the science themes here to an enforcement of order in the interaction pattern, a particular order that gives him the power to control who will speak when.[5]

In addition to being an example of the importance of timing, the teacher's nomination of Janice after he must have heard her volunteered answer can also be considered an example of structural recontextualization, mentioned in chapter 7. The teacher's nomination publicly reinterprets Janice's volunteered answer as a bid, thus making it acceptable in his preferred terms.

STANDARD SYNTAX

One criterion of appropriateness that many teachers feel responsible for enforcing is the use of standard syntax. The first example comes from a high school mathematics class in the Philippines in which English is the students' second language. What the teacher wants the student to say is, "The sentences in group A [on the blackboard] are number sentences, while the sentences in Group B are set sentences," but it takes many turns to get that answer produced:

T: Ro?

Ro: The group—the group A—

T: The sentences—

Ro: The sentences—sentences—

T: in group—

Ro: of group—

T: in—

Ro: in group A is a number sentence—

T: are—

Ro: are—number sentence—

T: -ses—

Ro: sentences—while the—set B—is
     set—set—

T: [*chuckles*]: Who can say it again?

[*Four more children are called on to produce the answer, only one of whom does it without error.*][6]

To this teacher, learning mathematics seems to mean learning not only to use mathematical terms in particular ways, but also to use them in syntactically correct English sentences.

Corrections of nonstandard syntax are found not only in second-language classrooms, but also in classrooms where students are native speakers of a nonstandard dialect of English. Formally or informally, many teachers take on the job of language standardization.

In either situation, the standard version can be provided in the form of a correction that effectively stops the thematic action and focuses attention on form, as we have just seen; or it can be provided less intrusively, and with intonation that affirms rather than criticizes, as in the following example from a British classroom. The topic is the function of sea creatures' shells:

T: What does protection mean? Any idea, Carl?

S: Sir, to stop other things hurting it.

T: Right, stops other things hurting it. Now if it came out of its shell, and waggled along the seabed, what would happen to it? Yes?

S: It might get ate.

T: It might get eaten by something else, yeah.[7]

The contrast in the teacher's utterances in these two examples parallels exactly the contrast between adults' corrections and expansions of toddlers' utterances in chapter 6. But there is an added (and rarely considered) influence in the classroom examples: the dual audience for the students—teacher and peers.

In an extensive review of two decades of sociolinguistic research, New Zealand linguist Alan Bell puts forth "a unified theory of intraspeaker linguistic variation" based on "audience design."[8] Of particular importance to the classroom is his analysis of the seemingly simple concept of "audience." Many speech situations, including classrooms, include more than the speaker and a single addressee. Also present are "auditors" (not addressed directly but officially present as listeners) and sometimes also "overhearers" (neither addressed nor officially ratified as listeners). In the classroom, the students not being directly addressed are ever-present auditors, and they exert an influence on the teacher and student speakers.

We have already seen examples of the effect of multiple addressees on the teacher. Remember the examples of multifunctionality of directives in the lesson discourse in chapter 3: asking one student (addressee) to say something again while simultaneously reprimanding another (auditor) for speaking out of turn.

For the student speaker, the audience includes the teacher (usually the official addressee) and peers (as auditors in group lessons, or overhearers when they are supposedly doing their own individual work). Except when engaged in a truly private conversation, student speakers in the classroom always have this dual audience of teacher and peers, and have to cope somehow with the dilemma posed by their different expectations.

Michaels and Foster describe sharing time in a first grade where the teacher set the rules but then withdrew from active participation.[9] She became, in Bell's terms, an overhearer, not officially a participant, but listened enough while attending to other chores to be ready to step in if the rules weren't being followed. Under this condition of a homogeneous peer audience, the stories of some of the children—especially the black girls—became "performed narratives," with the gestures and sound effects of a dramatic monologue. This report is interesting in itself, and it also helps us understand the complex demands student speakers face in the more common dual-audience situation.

One acknowledgement of this dual audience is a brief autobiographical comment by linguist Roger Shuy:

There is a natural conflict between acceptability by teacher and acceptability by peers even *within* the classroom. Personally I can remember very clearly my school conflicts between peer pressure and teacher expectations. One strategy to avoid this conflict is to give the right answer to the teacher but to do so in either non-standard or informal English.

Shuy calls these dual demands of teacher and peers "vertical" and "horizontal" acceptability, respectively. In oral lessons, an example would be, "La Paz ain't the capital of Peru." And, when reading aloud, the good reader who wants to avoid being considered the teacher's pet may find ways to read the correct words but in an informal, peer-group style.[10]

Another example of this conflict in expectations is reported by sociolinguist Leslie Milroy while she was recording the speech of adolescents in northern Ireland. In an initial group interview, one boy shifted his speaking style to fit the formality of the interview situation, but he was laughed at by his peers. "On the next occasion, he shifted his speech style markedly in the direction of the [peer] vernacular. Obligations to the group were powerful enough to override the influence of the recording equipment and outside interviewer."[11]

What should be the teacher's response to such student speech? To correct, even gently? Or to recognize that the student has found what the Berlaks (discussed in chapter 5) call a "transformational solution" to an important dilemma, a solution that, if accepted, may help to prevent a forced choice between peer group and school?[12]

DECONTEXTUALIZATION
AND EXPLICITNESS

In chapter 6, I reported that school language use is often characterized as "decontextualized." Examples of teacher evaluations of student speech that fit such a characterization—and the related characterization of explicitness—can be found.

One example of decontextualization was observed by a Harvard graduate student, Gail Perry, in a preschool. In a discussion of "different places we see water in," Sharanda offered a specific lake—Lake Fairfax—instead of the more generic "lakes." And like the narratives of personal experience, her contribution never got the floor and remained unacknowledged in the teacher's summary (marked with an arrow):

T: What are some different places we see water in?

S: The ocean.

T: The ocean, and what else?

S: Swimming pools.

T: Swimming pools.

S: Sea.

S: Lakes

T: Sea, lakes.

Sharanda: Lake Fairfax.

Nathan: Rivers.

Sharanda: Lake Fairfax

S: [*Inaudible on tape*]

→ *T:* Right. . . . Rivers, oceans, swimming pools. Where else do you find water . . . ?[13]

There is no developmental evidence that children have more trouble with common names (lake) than with proper names (Lake Fairfax). But Sharanda may not realize that the former, less contextualized alternative sometimes has a privileged status in school.

A second example comes from a metalinguistic discussion of word meanings in a kindergarten. When teachers request a definition, they may reject a contextualized answer (given by the first child, C1) and press for the classic Aristotelian form conventional in dictionaries (superordinate category plus differentiation, given in part by C2):

T: What is a lullaby?

C1: It helps you to go to sleep at night?

T: But what is it?

C2: It's a song.

T: That's right.[14]

Sometimes, student speech is evaluated not for the choice of individual words but for the explicitness of an entire proposition. The following examples come from a second-grade reading-group lesson in a class where Sarah Michaels and I were recording sharing time. The text was a basal-reader story about an early space flight that sent up monkeys, and, whether by coincidence or careful plan, the lesson took place on a day when a manned space flight was actually being launched. Twice during the discussion of the story, the teacher requested more explicit formulation of a student answer. These requests are marked by an arrow.

Example 1

T: OK, Janine, what about this rocket ride? Is this the one that the astronauts are going to be taking today? Is it the same kind? [*Janine shakes head no*] How is it different?

J: Monkeys are in it.

T: Monkeys are in it. What will be in the rocket that's going up today? The space shuttle.

J: Astronauts.

T: There'll be astronauts instead of monkeys. Good. OK. [*45-second interlude during which three children working at their seats are reprimanded for talking and another child is helped in finding a book*] OK, are we all looking at page 129?

Ss: Yes.

T: And Janine has just told us that the difference between today's space shuttle and this rocket ride was what, Janine? [*four-second pause*] Who's going up today, and who went up in this story?

J: Astronauts.

T: Tell me about that.

J: The astronauts went up today.

→   T: And in this story—[*said as if speaking for Janine, telling her how to continue*]

J: In this story the monkeys went up.

T: OK, very good. Monkeys went up instead.

Example 2

T: OK, can you tell us about their coming back to earth? Tell us about that part. How do they do it? How do they get back? [*three-second pause*] They're way out there in space, traveling at a very high speed. Paul, how do they get back?

P: They used their parachute. They went down into the water.

→   T: Tell me more about that. You mean they put a parachute on the monkeys?

P: They used the parachute on the, on the rocket and went, went down into the water.

T: Very good.[15]

Although the students demonstrate correct understanding of the story and its relationship to the events of the day through their elliptical answers, the teacher presses for more syntactically elaborated statements.

THE LANGUAGE OF SCIENCE

Some ways of speaking are specific to particular school subjects. Two examples come from science teaching. In one, students have not adopted the school way of speaking; in the other, they have learned it, but perhaps too well.

The inappropriate speech comes from a C (lower-stream) biology class in a British comprehensive secondary school. In a footnote to an article on classroom knowledge, Keddie reports:

> There is probably . . . a problem for teachers in how C pupils actually phrase their comments or questions. When I reported to the humanities department on the research, I gave as [one example] of pupils asking questions from their own commonsense views of the world . . . from the key lesson in which pupils were shown slides of the foetus in the womb, when a C boy asked about the foetus: "How does it go to the toilet then?" This latter question, which seems to be an intelligent one, probably could not be asked more precisely without a concept of the body's "functions." When I gave [this example] . . . one teacher said the boy "must have been joking." At the least he implied that [this] question [was] not appropriate to the business of learning.[16]

More generally, Keddie suggests that one of the important differences between A- and C-stream students is their prior familiarity with, or willingness to adopt, the teacher's definition of the lesson situation and what counts as knowledge—and, I would add, ways of talking about it.

The example of appropriate scientific talk, at least according to one view of school science, comes from Lemke's study of high school science lessons. Here students as well as teachers have come to expect that science will be talked about in certain ways:

- A diagram is a "representation" of an atom, not a "picture," and nothing is said about who first conceived this kind of picture or why.
- Evolution "occurs," but nothing is said about who first made sense of some bits of evidence in this way.
- In general, the all-important human agency has disappeared from view. Instead of scientists doing and deciding, there is only "it is."

When the teacher reintroduced the human agency by means of stories, Lemke found that the students were particularly attentive. But he also found that both teachers and students indicated by their laughter or joking tone of voice that such stories were not part of the real business of the lesson.[17]

RELEVANCE AND CONCISENESS

Two criteria on which considerable variation is possible are relevance to the lesson topic as the teacher defines it and conciseness in expression. As part of research on children's functional language competence at the

Center for Applied Linguistics, sociolinguists Peg Griffin and Roger Shuy asked primary-school teachers to rank their pupils on the effectiveness of their language use without defining what "effectiveness" meant. Then in oral interviews, they gave the teachers statements such as "acts as leader," "acts on instructions," "gets point across," and asked them to name children who did those things all of the time, sometimes, or hardly ever. Of all the statements offered to the teachers, ability to get points across was the most predictive of ranking as a highly effective language user, and several teachers specifically mentioned conciseness, in contrast to going on too long, as important in all classroom talk.[18]

In many adult-child conversations outside school—around the dinner table, driving in a car, while working in the kitchen—there is no such pressure to get to the point as quickly as possible. When being concise is valued in the classroom, it is probably as much because of situational pressures on the teacher, as she worries about the attention of the rest of the group or thinks about all the other children who need a chance as well, as because she is trying to teach children a particular way of speaking.

While there may be situational reasons for pressing children to speak relevantly and to the point, there are developmental and cultural reasons why it may be difficult for children to meet such expectations. Most adults have had the experience of waiting for a chance to speak in a discussion only to find, when the chance finally arrives, that the topic has shifted and what we wanted to say may not be heard as relevant at all. But, unlike children, we have verbal remedies, ways of marking our contribution as "out of place" but worth hearing anyway. To introduce a comment that is not related to immediately preceding talk, we can say, "By the way . . ." or "Speaking of . . ." or, even more specifically, "I want to go back to what X was saying a few minutes ago." Children don't use such metalinguistic connectors—whether because of lack of awareness of the problem or unavailability of potential solutions—and so are more apt to be ruled out of order.

An example of this in the San Diego classroom was picked up for comment in a review of Mehan's book by sociolinguist Deborah Tannen. In discussing Mehan's concept of "reflexive trying," she asks whether his assignment of utterances to the IRE categories may sometimes distort the speaker's intentions and hide the very tying he asserts as important:

For example, consider the following segment. In connection with a lesson on Martin Luther King [Jr.], the class has been discussing people's ages at

the time of King's death. The teacher then signals a shift of focus by an-
nouncing she will read a story . . . :

Initiation	Reply	Evaluation
T: I'm just going to start this story on Martin Luther King / /		
Greg: Well, my mama was 19 when he died.		*T:* [*Touches Greg's knee*]

Mehan's analysis is clearly correct: Greg's comment is not a reply to the
teacher's initiation of story reading but rather a new initiation [and ruled
out-of-order by the teacher's non-verbal action]. However, in a broader
view, Greg is responding, belatedly, to an earlier initiation, adhering to the
prior topic of talk [how old children and teacher were when King died].[19]

Philips's research on discussions in one Native American community
suggests that there may also be cultural reasons for different assumptions about relevance. In council meetings on the Warm Springs Reservation, she noticed that responses on a single topic were often widely
separated, by as much as half an hour, without explicit tying. She comments, "It may be worth noting that with this approach to sequencing,
conflict between persons can be muted and obscured."[20]

Teachers will differ on the tightness of their control of the lesson
topic. In an analysis of high school lessons in England and Australia,
McHoul found that teachers did not permit students the conversational
practice of changing topics.[21] They dealt with attempts to do so by what
Mehan calls "bounding off": treating such a student attempt as a side
sequence to the main events of the talk.

We have to be sympathetic to pressures on teachers to get through
their lesson plans and cover the curriculum. But it is also important to
remember the arbitrariness of any definition of what the topic is, and
what is relevant to it. Relevance is not as subjective as the criterion of
importance that some teachers invoke in responding to sharing-time
stories, but there can still be legitimate differences of beliefs and expectations.

GENERAL COMMENTS

This chapter's examples of an expected student-talk register do not form a homogeneous set. The feature of timing is part of the sequential structure of discourse—when an utterance is supposed to be spoken. The others are part of the selectional (paradigmatic) structure—forms of "English for academic purposes."

The early work of Barnes and his colleagues in England focused on the language of secondary-school teaching. Barnes categorizes the vocabulary of this language of instruction in several ways: if it is subject specific or more general; if it is explicitly explained or not; and whether it has a conceptual function in making important referential distinctions or simply a sociocultural function in identifying the speaker in a certain role.

As Barnes points out, it is difficult to distinguish between the conceptual and sociocultural functions, because the distinction may not be made in the same way by speaker and hearers:

> From the point of view of the teacher, everything he says has for him a more or less important socio-cultural function in supporting his roles as teacher and as teacher-of-mathematics; yet everything he says could also (in theory) be placed on a scale for its conceptual function, according to how far it is also being used to organize the subject matter of the lesson. But this is only for the teacher; for the pupil it must be different. Each new item must first appear to have a socio-cultural function—that is, to be "the sort of thing my physics teacher says"—and then, insofar as the pupil is able to use the item in talking, thinking, or writing, it will take upon itself a conceptual function.[22]

In a comparison of working-class and middle-class speech styles, linguist William Labov makes a related distinction between "pretension" and "precision." And in an unusual guide to academic writing, sociologist Howard Becker argues that "classy locutions" (like the ones Kevin was suggesting to Sunday at the beginning of this chapter) function only "ceremonially, not semantically."[23]

None of these researchers claims that there is no intellectual value in specialized ways of speaking. They only ask, as do I, that we distinguish between forms that have such value and forms that don't. Once we have made that distinction, we can then explain our expectations to students, and explore strategies for helping them learn to use the intellectually valuable forms. I assume that such strategies will require a combination of interesting contextualized activities plus occasional metalinguistic attention to language itself.

NOTES

[1]Transcriptions from Alex McLeod, personal communication, November 1986.

[2]For discussion of "getting the floor in the classroom," see Philips 1983.

[3]This and the examples from my university teaching are from Cazden and Hymes 1980, which includes further discussion by Hymes of the importance of personal-experience narratives, and yet their differential acceptability across situations and speakers.

[4]From Lemke 1986, 3–4. See also Mehan 1979; Erickson and Mohatt 1982; Erickson and Shultz 1977.

[5]Lemke 1986, 19.

[6]Campbell 1986.

[7]Edwards 1980.

[8]Bell 1984.

[9]Michaels and Foster 1985.

[10]Shuy 1981, supplemented by personal communication, 1985.

[11]Reported in Romaine 1984, 183.

[12]Berlak and Berlak 1981. For more on the important topic of dialect differences among students, see Romaine 1984 for a cross-national review of the sociolinguistic literature; Cazden 1972 for a still-relevant discussion of educational issues; Lucas and Borders 1987 for a study of dialect use in kindergarten, fourth, and sixth grades; and Hewitt 1986 for an ethnographic study of cross-dialect influences on peer speech in England.

[13]Perry, unpublished term paper, Harvard Graduate School of Education 1985.

[14]Edwards 1980, 182. See also R. Watson 1985.

[15]Michaels and Cazden 1986, 133–134.

[16]Keddie 1971. Readers familiar with the work of the British sociologist Basil Bernstein may see some of my examples as illustrations of his ideas. The C-stream student's speech can be seen as a violation of the boundary between the sacred (science) and the profane (bathroom). The teacher's press for more decontextualized language use can be formulated in Bernstein's terms as a press for "universalistic orders of meaning." And the hidden curriculum of ways of speaking is what he calls "invisible pedagogy." See Atkinson 1986 for further discussion.

[17]Lemke 1986; also reported in *The Age*, Melbourne, Australia, September 13, 1983.

[18]Griffin and Shuy 1978.

[19]Tannen 1981, 277.

[20]Philips 1983, 54.

[21]McHoul 1978.

[22]In Barnes et al. 1969, 58.

[23]Becker 1986, 31; Labov 1972.

Chapter 11

Afterword

I started this book with the story of my return to teaching primary-school children in San Diego to try to put into practice some of the ideas about language and education that I had been teaching and writing about, and to rethink ideas for future research. The ideas about language and education that were in my head at that time were about language structure: its development, dialect variation, and situational influences. As I wrote then:

> This focus on structure separate from use, on linguistic means separate from social and cognitive purposes, is not only where I had been, but where the language development field as a whole has been.

Not all discussions of language in the classroom were so limited, even in the mid-1970s. In England, for example, Connie and Harold Rosen wrote "The Language of Primary School Children," not by working down from theory and research but by working up from instances of the best classroom practice. The Rosens began their book with a chapter on "the context of the school situation," and ended it with notes that speak optimistically about a sociolinguistic theory of context that "could perhaps lead teachers to decide more precisely what features of the situation they wish to alter and in what way so that children may speak more powerfully and act more effectively."[1]

This book is my progress report on what we have learned about the classroom as a context for the language of teaching and learning. Now, at the end, I want to underline three cautions in thinking about relationships between context and speech.

First, there are two kinds of relationships. One is more obvious. Context is the situation as the speaker finds it, antecedent to the moment of speaking; and it is the rules for speaking in that context to which the speaker's utterances must be appropriate. Much research on classroom discourse attempts to explicate the implicit rules governing appropriate language use that teachers know and children must learn.

But speakers not only conform to rules and fit their speech appropriately to a preexisting context; they also actively speak so as to change contexts and create new ones, "redefining the situation itself in the process of performing it."[2] We have seen examples of both relationships between speech and context, and examples of both teachers and students as context-creating speakers.

Second, we need to be aware of the limits of the "classroom as culture" metaphor. To assume that classrooms are cultures highlights the implicit norms, the teacher as "native" member, and the induction of "immigrant" children. But classrooms are, or should be, very special cultures—a community of people who are changing, and whose change the environment should be specifically designed to support.

Third, contexts are nested, from the most immediate to the act of speaking to the more distant: classroom, school, school system, community, and so on; and the classroom context is never wholly of the participants' making. Heath has written a poignant epilogue about the external influences on the Appalachian teachers she worked with in the 1970s as an explanation of why "the methods used by these teachers have all but disappeared".[3] Bracketing out such influences and considering classroom discourse as if it were autonomous may be necessary, or at least expedient, for teachers. But those who help to shape the contexts that surround the classroom have to realize their responsibility as well.

Finally, a word from one teacher to others. Thinking about the research reported in this book will inevitably lead to greater self-consciousness, at least temporarily. It did for me, and I wish this didn't have to happen. I wish we as teachers could be as successful as parents on intuition alone. But as anthropologist Edward Sapir explains, "It is sometimes necessary to become conscious of the forms of social behavior in order to bring about a more serviceable adaptation to changed conditions." Or, in his blunter words, analysis and conscious control are "the medicine of society, not its food."[4] Because of conditions both within the classroom and outside it, we need the "medicine" of more careful analysis and conscious control so that our implicit theories of the language of teaching and learning can be open to continual re-vision. Nothing less does justice to our profession and our children.

NOTES

[1] C. and H. Rosen 1973, 260.
[2] Erickson 1975b, 484.
[3] Heath 1983. See also H. Rosen's 1985 review.
[4] Sapir 1951.

References

Allington, R. L. 1980. Teacher interruption behaviors during primary grade oral reading. *Journal of Educational Psychology* 72:1–377.

———. In press. The reading instruction provided readers of differing reading abilities. *Elementary School Journal.*

Alton-Lee, A. G. 1984. Understanding learning and teaching: An investigation of pupil experience of content in relation to long-term learning. Doctoral dissertation, University of Canterbury (New Zealand). Submitted to University Microfilms.

Anderson, E. S. 1978. Learning to speak with style: A study of the sociolinguistic skills of children. Doctoral dissertation, Stanford University. University Microfilms no. 78-8755.

Anderson, R. C. 1977. The notion of schemata and the educational enterprise: General discussion of the conference. In *Schooling and the acquisition of knowledge*, edited by R. C. Anderson, R. J. Spiro, and W. E. Montague. Hillsdale, N.J.: Erlbaum.

Anderson, R. C., E. H. Hiebert, J. A. Scott, and I. A. G. Wilkinson. 1985. *Becoming a nation of readers: The report of the commission on reading.* Washington, D.C.: National Institute of Education.

Applebee, A. N., and J. A. Langer. 1983. Instructional scaffolding: Reading and writing as natural language activities. *Language Arts* 60:168–175.

Atkinson, P. 1986. *Language, structure and reproduction: An introduction to the sociology of Basil Bernstein.* New York: Methuen.

—— and S. Delamont. 1976. Mock-ups and cock-ups: The stage-management of guided discovery instruction. In *The process of schooling: A sociological reader,* edited by M. Hammersley and P. Woods. London: Routledge and Kegan Paul.

Au, K. H. 1980. Participation structures in a reading lesson with Hawaiian children: Analysis of a culturally appropriate instructional event. *Anthropology and Education Quarterly* 11:91–115.

—— and J. M. Mason. 1981. Social organizational factors in learning to read: The balance of rights hypothesis. *Reading Research Quarterly* 17:115–152.

Barnes, D. 1976. *From communication to curriculum.* London: Penguin. (Also available from Boynton/Cook, Montclair, N.J.).

——, J. Britton, and H. Rosen. 1979. *Language, the learner and the school.* Baltimore: Penguin Books. (Revised edition 1971).

——, J. Britton, and M. Torbe. 1986. *Language, the learner and the school* (3rd ed.) Harmondsworth, Middlesex, England: Penguin. (Also Upper Montclair, N.J.: Boynton/Cook Publishers.)

—— and F. Todd. 1977. *Communication and learning in small groups.* London: Routledge and Kegan Paul.

Bartlett, E. J. 1979. Curriculum, concepts of literacy, and social class. In L. B. Resnick & P. A. Weaver (Eds.), *Theory and practice of early reading* 1:229–242.

—— and S. Scribner. 1981. Text and context: An investigation of referential organization in children's written narratives. In *Writing: The nature, development and teaching of written communication,* edited by C. H. Frederiksen and J. F. Dominic. Hillsdale, N.J.: Erlbaum.

Becker, H. S. 1986. *Writing for social scientists: How to start and finish your thesis, book, or article.* Chicago: University of Chicago Press.

Bell, A. 1984. Language style as audience design. *Language in Society* 13:145–204.

Berlak, A. and H. Berlak. 1981. *Dilemmas of schooling: Teaching and social change.* London: Methuen.

Berliner, D. 1976. Impediments to the study of teacher effectiveness. *Journal of Teacher Education* 27:5–13.

Bernstein, B. 1972. A critique of the concept "compensatory education." In *Functions of language in the classroom,* edited by C. B. Cazden, V. John, and D. Hymes. New York: Teachers College Press. (Reprinted by Waveland Press, 1985.)

Black, S. D., J. A. Levin, H. Mehan, and C. N. Quinn. 1983. Real and non-real time interaction: Unraveling multiple threads of discourse. *Discourse Processes* 6:59–75.

Blank, M. 1973. *Teaching learning in the preschool: A dialogue approach.* Columbus, Ohio: Charles E. Merrill.

Bloom, B. S., ed. 1956. *Taxonomy of educational objectives: Handbook I: Cognitive domain.* New York: Longmans, Green & Co.

Boggs, S. T. 1985. *Speaking, relating and learning: A study of Hawaiian children at home and at school.* Norwood, N.J.: Ablex.

Brown, A. L., and A. S. Palincsar. 1986. Guided, cooperative learning and individual knowledge acquisition. Champaign, Ill.: Center for the Study of

Reading, Technical Report 372. Also in *Cognition and instruction: Issues and agendas*, edited by L. Resnick. Hillsdale, N.J.: Erlbaum.

Brown, P., and S. Levinson. 1978. Universals in language usage: Politeness phenomena. In *Questions and politeness: Strategies in social interaction*, edited by E. N. Goody. Cambridge: Cambridge University Press.

Brown, R. 1977. Introduction. In *Talking to children: Language input and acquisition*, edited by C. E. Snow and C. A. Ferguson. New York: Cambridge University Press.

———— and U. Bellugi. 1964. Three processes in the child's acquisition of syntax. *Harvard Educational Review* 34:133–151.

Bruner, J. 1983. *Child's talk: Learning to use language*. New York: W. W. Norton.

Calfee, R., C. B. Cazden, R. B. Duran, M. P. Griffin, M. Martus, and H. D. Willis. 1981. *Designing reading instruction for cultural minorities: The case of the Kamehameha Early Education Program*. Report to the Ford Foundation, December. ED 215 039.

Campbell, D. R. 1986. Developing mathematical literacy in a bilingual classroom. In *The social construction of literacy*, edited by J. Cook-Gumperz. Cambridge: Cambridge University Press.

Cazden, C. B. 1972. *Child language and education*. New York: Holt, Rinehart and Winston.

————. 1976. How knowledge about language helps the classroom teacher—or does it: A personal account. *Urban Review* 9:74–90.

————. 1983a. Peekaboo as an instructional model: Discourse development at school and at home. In *The sociogenesis of language and human conduct: A multidisciplinary book of readings*, edited by B. Bain. New York: Plenum.

————. 1983b. Can ethnographic research go beyond the status quo? *Anthropology and Education Quarterly*, 14: 33–41.

————. 1986. Classroom discourse. In *Handbook of research on teaching* (3rd ed.), edited by M. E. Wittrock. New York: Macmillan.

————. In press a. Environmental assistance revisited: Variation and functional equivalence. In *The development of language and language researchers*, edited by F. Kessel. Hillsdale, N.J.: Erlbaum.

————. In press b. Language in the classroom. In *Annual review of applied linguistics*. Vol. 7, 1986–87, edited by R. Kaplan. Rowley, Mass.: Newbury House.

————, M. Cox, D. Dickinson, Z. Steinberg, and C. Stone. 1979. "You all gonna hafta listen": Peerteaching in a primary classroom. In *Children's language and communication. Twelfth Annual Minnesota Symposium on Child Development*, edited by W. A. Collins. Hillsdale, N.J.: Erlbaum.

———— and D. Hymes. 1980. Narrative thinking and storytelling rights: A folklorist's clue to a critique of education. In D. Hymes, *Language in education: Ethnolinguistic essays*. Washington, D.C.: Center for Applied Linguistics.

————, V. P. John, and D. Hymes, eds. 1972. *Functions of language in the classroom*. New York: Teachers College Press. (Reprinted by Waveland Press, 1985.)

————, S. Michaels, and P. Tabors. 1985. Self-repair in Sharing Time narratives: The intersection of metalinguistic awareness, speech event and narrative style. In *The acquisition of writing: Revision and response*, edited by S. W. Freedman. Norwood, N.J.: Ablex.

Chaudron, C. 1980. Those dear old golden rule days. *Journal of Pragmatics* 4: 157–172.

Chomsky, C. 1972. Stages in language development and reading exposure. *Harvard Educational Review* 42:1–33.

Chomsky, N. 1957. *Syntactic structures.* The Hague: Mouton.

Cicourel, A. V., K. H. Jennings, S. H. H. Jennings, K. C. W. Leiter, R. Mackay, H. Mehan, and D. R. Roth. 1974. *Language use and school performance.* New York: Academic Press.

Clay, M. M. 1985. *The early detection of reading difficulties* (3rd ed.). Auckland (New Zealand) and Portsmouth, N.H.: Heinemann.

Cochran-Smith, M. 1983. *The making of a reader.* Norwood, N.J.: Ablex.

———. 1986. Reading to children: A model for understanding texts. In *The acquisition of literacy: Ethnographic perspectives*, edited by B. B. Schieffelin and P. Gilmore. Norwood, N.J.: Ablex.

Cohen, E. G. 1986. *Designing group work-strategies for the heterogeneous classroom.* New York: Teachers College Press.

Collins, J. P. 1982. Discourse style, classroom interaction and differential treatment. *Journal of Reading Behavior* 14:429–437.

———. 1986. Differential instruction in reading. In *The social construction of literacy*, edited by J. Cook-Gumperz. Cambridge: Cambridge University Press.

Connell, R. W., D. J. Ashenden, S. Kessler, and G. W. Dowsett. 1982. *Making the difference: Schools, families and social division.* Sydney: Allen and Unwin.

Cooper, C. R., A. Marquis, and S. Ayers-Lopez. 1982. Peer learning in the classroom: Tracing developmental patterns and consequences of children's spontaneous interactions. In *Communicating in the classroom*, edited by L. C. Wilkinson. New York: Academic Press.

Cuban, L. 1984. *How teachers taught: Constancy and change in American classrooms 1890–1980.* New York: Longmans.

Cunningham, P. M. 1976–77. Teachers' correction responses to black-dialect miscues which are non-meaning-changing. *Reading Research Quarterly* 12: 637–653.

Delamont, S. 1983. *Interaction in the classroom.* London: Methuen.

Dickinson, D. K. 1985. Creating and using formal occasions in the classroom. *Anthropology and Education Quarterly* 16:47–62.

Dillon, J. T. 1983. *Teaching and the art of questioning.* Bloomington, Indiana: Phi Delta Kappa Educational Foundation.

———. 1985. Using questions to foil discussion. *Teaching and Teacher Education* 1:109–121.

Dinsmore, D. F. 1986. "Has anyone got any news?": The nature of "News Times" in an infants' class. Ms., University of Lancaster.

Dorr-Bremme, D. W. 1982. Behaving and making sense: Creating social organization in the classroom. Doctoral dissertation, Harvard University. UMI #82-23, 203.

Duckworth, E. 1981. Understanding children's understandings. Paper presented at the Ontario Institute for Studies in Education, Toronto.

Dunkin, M. J., and B. J. Biddle. 1974. *The study of teaching.* New York: Holt, Rinehart and Winston.

Eder, D. 1982a. The impact of management and turn-allocation activities on student performance. *Discourse Processes* 5:147–159.

———. 1982b. Difference in communicative styles across ability groups. In *Communicating in the classroom*, edited by L. C. Wilkinson. New York: Academic Press.

Edwards, A. D. 1980. Patterns of power and authority in classroom talk. In *Teacher strategies: Explorations in the sociology of the school*, edited by P. Woods. London: Croom Helm.

——— and J. J. Furlong. 1978. *The language of teaching: Meaning in classroom interaction.* London: Heinemann.

Engeström, Y. 1986. The zone of proximal development as the basic category in educational psychology. *Quarterly Newsletter of the Laboratory of Comparative Human Cognition* 8:23–42.

Erickson, F. 1975a. Gate-keeping and the melting pot: Interaction in counseling interviews. *Harvard Educational Review* 45:44–70.

———. 1975b. Afterthoughts. In *The organization of behavior in face-to-face interaction*, edited by A. Kendon, R. M. Hams, and M. R. Key. The Hague: Mouton.

———. 1982a. Taught cognitive learning in its immediate environment: A neglected topic in the anthropology of education. *Anthropology and Education Quarterly* 13:149–180.

———. 1982b. Classroom discourse as improvisation: Relationships between academic task structure and social participation structures in lessons. In *Communicating in the classroom*, edited by L. C. Wilkinson. New York: Academic Press.

———. 1984. School literacy, reasoning and civility: An anthropologist's perspective. *Review of Educational Research* 54:525–546.

———, C. B. Cazden, R. Carrasco, and A. Maldonado-Guzman. 1983. Social and cultural organization of interaction in classrooms of bilingual children. Final report to the National Institute of Education.

——— and G. Mohatt. 1982. Cultural organization of participant structures in two classrooms of Indian students. In *Doing the ethnography of schooling: Educational anthropology in action*, edited by G. D. Spindler. New York: Holt, Rinehart and Winston.

——— and J. Shultz. 1977. When is a context? Some issues and methods in the analysis of social competence. *Quarterly Newsletter of the Institute for Comparative Human Development* 1:5–10. Also in *Ethnography and language in educational settings*, edited by J. Green and C. Wallat. Norwood, N.J.: Ablex.

——— and J. Shultz. 1982. *The counselor as gatekeeper: Social interaction in interviews.* New York: Academic Press.

Everhart, R. B. 1983. *Reading, writing and resistance: Adolescence and labor in a junior high school.* Boston: Routledge and Kegan Paul.

Fischer, K. W., and D. Bullock. 1984. Cognitive development in school-age children: Conclusions and new directions. In *Development during middle childhood: The years from six to twelve*, edited by W. A. Collins. Washington, D.C.: National Academy Press.

Fish, S. 1980. *Is there a text in this class? The authority of interpretive communities.* Cambridge, Mass.: Harvard University Press.

Fivush, R. 1984. Learning about school: The development of kindergartners' school scripts. *Child Development* 55:1697–1709.

Florio, S. 1978. Learning how to go to school: An ethnography of interaction in a kindergarten/first grade classroom. Doctoral dissertation, Harvard University.

Forman, E. A. 1981. The role of collaboration in problem solving in children. Doctoral disseration, Harvard University.

——— and C. B. Cazden. 1985. Exploring Vygotskyian perspectives in education: The cognitive value of peer interaction. In *Culture, communication and cognition: Vygotskian perspectives*, edited by J. V. Wertsch. New York: Cambridge University Press.

Foster, M. 1987. "It's cookin' now": An ethnographic study of the teaching skills of a successful black teacher in an urban community college. Doctoral dissertation, Harvard University.

Freire, P. 1982. *Pedagogy of the oppressed*. New York: Continuum.

French, P., and M. Maclure. 1981. Teachers' questions, pupils' answers: An investigation of questions and answers in the infant classroom. *First Language* 2: 31–45. Reprinted in *Readings on language, schools and classrooms*, edited by M. Stubbs and H. Hillier. London: Methuen, 1983.

Fuchs, E. 1966. *Pickets at the gates*. New York: Free Press.

Gage, N. L. 1977. *The scientific basis of the art of teaching*. New York: Teachers College Press.

Gall, M. D. 1970. The use of questioning in teaching. *Review of Educational Research* 40:707–720.

Galton, M., B. Simon, and P. Croll. 1980. *Inside the primary classroom*. Boston: Routledge and Kegan Paul.

Garnica, O. K. 1981. Social dominance and classroom interaction—The omega child in the classroom. In *Ethnography and language in educational settings*, edited by J. Green and C. Wallat. Norwood, N.J.: Ablex.

Gee, J. P. 1985. The narrativization of experience in the oral style. *Journal of Education* 167:9–35.

———. 1986. Units in the production of discourse. *Discourse Processes* 9:391–422.

———. In press. Two styles of narrative construction and their linguistic and educational implications. *Discourse Processes*.

Gelman, R. 1978. Cognitive development. *Annual Review of Psychology* 29:297–332.

Goffman, E. 1961. *Encounters: Two studies in the sociology of interaction*. Indianapolis: Bobbs-Merrill.

Goodlad, J. I. 1983. A study of schooling: Some findings and hypotheses. *Phi Delta Kappan* 64:465–470.

———. 1984. *A place called school: Prospects for the future*. New York: McGraw-Hill.

Goodwin, C. 1981. *Conversational organization: Interaction between speakers and hearers*. New York: Academic Press.

Graybeal, S. S., and S. S. Stodolsky. 1985. Peer work groups in elementary schools. *American Journal of Education* 93:409–428.

Griffin, P., M. Cole, and D. Newman. 1982. Locating tasks in psychology and education. *Discourse Processes* 5:111–125.

———— and H. Mehan. 1981. Sense and ritual in classroom discourse. In *Conversational routine: Explorations in standardized communication situations and pre-patterned speech*, edited by F. Coulmas. The Hague: Mouton.

———— and R. Shuy. 1978. *Final report to Carnegie Corporation of New York: Children's functional language and education in the early years.* Washington, D.C.: Center for Applied Linguistics.

Groen, G. J., and L. B. Resnick. 1977. Can preschool children invent addition algorithms? *Journal of Educational Psychology* 69:645–652.

Gumperz, J. J. 1970. Verbal strategies in multilingual communication. In *Roundtable on languages and linguistics 1970*, edited by J. E. Alatis. Washington, D.C.: Georgetown University Press.

Hahn, E. 1948. An analysis of the content and form of the speech of first grade children. *Quarterly Journal of Speech* 34:361–366.

Hall, E. T. 1959. *The silent language.* Greenwich, Conn.: Premier Books.

Halliday, M. A. K. 1978. *Language as social semiotic: The social interpretation of language and meaning.* Baltimore: University Park Press.

Hammersley, M. 1977. School learning: The cultural resources required by pupils to answer a teacher's question. In *School experience: Explorations in the sociology of education*, edited by P. Woods and M. Hammersley. London: Croom Helm.

Hardcastle, J. 1985. Classrooms as sites for cultural making. *English in Education* (Autumn) 8–22.

Hargreaves, D. H. 1980. The occupational culture of teachers. In *Teacher strategies: Explorations in the sociology of school*, edited by P. Woods. London: Croom Helm.

Harris, S. 1977. Milimgimbi Aboriginal learning contexts. Doctoral dissertation, University of New Mexico.

————. 1980. *Culture and learning: Tradition and education in Northeast Arnheim Land.* Darwin (Australia): Northern Territory Department of Education, Professional Services Branch.

Hatch, J. A. 1986. Alone in a crowd. Ms., Ohio State University at Marion.

Hawkins, J., K. Scheingold, M. Gearhart, and C. Berger. 1982. Microcomputers in schools: Impact on the social life of elementary classrooms. *Journal of Applied Developmental Psychology* 3:361–373.

Heap, J. L. 1986. Sociality and cognition in collaborative computer writing. Paper presented at the University of Michigan School of Education Conference on Literacy and Culture in Educational Settings.

Heath, S. B. 1978. *Teacher talk: Language in the classroom.* Washington D.C.: Center for Applied Linguistics.

————. 1982a. What no bedtime story means: Narrative skills at home and school. *Language in Society* 11:49–76.

————. 1982b. Questioning at home and at school: A comparative study. In *Doing the ethnography of schooling: Educational anthropology in action*, edited by G. Spindler. New York: Holt, Rinehart and Winston.

————. 1983. *Ways with words: Language, life, and work in communities and classrooms.* Cambridge: Cambridge University Press.

Helmreich, W. B. 1982. *The world of the yeshiva: An intimate portrait of Orthodox Jewry*. New York: Free Press.

Hemphill, L. 1986. Context and conversational style: A reappraisal of social class differences in speech. Doctoral dissertation, Harvard University. UMI #86-20, 703.

Hess, R. D., W. P. Dickson, G. G. Price, and D. J. Leong. 1979. Some contrasts between mothers and preschool teachers in interaction with 4-year-old children. *American Educational Research Journal* 16:307–316.

Hewitt, R. 1986. *White talk black talk: Interracial friendship and communication among adolescents*. Cambridge: Cambridge University Press.

Heyman, R. D. 1986. Formulating topic in the classroom. *Discourse Processes* 9: 37–55.

Hoetker, J., and W. P. Ahlbrand, Jr. 1969. The persistence of the recitation. *American Educational Research Journal* 6:145–167.

Hymes, D. 1971. Competence and performance in linguistic theory. In *Language acquisition: Models and methods*, edited by R. Huxley and E. Ingram. New York: Academic Press.

———. 1972a. Introduction. In *Functions of language in the classroom*, edited by C. B. Cazden et al. New York: Teachers College Press. Reprinted by Waveland Press, 1985.

———. 1972b. Models of the interaction of language and social life. In *Directions in sociolinguistics: The ethnography of communication*, edited by J. J. Gumperz and D. Hymes. New York: Holt, Rinehart, and Winston.

———. 1981a. Ethnographic monitoring of children's acquisition of reading/language arts skills in and out of the classroom. Final report to the National Institute of Education. ED 208 096.

———. 1981b. Ethnographic monitoring. In *Culture and the bilingual classroom: Studies in classroom ethnography*, edited by H. T. Trueba et al. Rowley, Mass.: Newbury House.

———. 1982. Ethnolinguistic study of classroom discourse. Final report to the National Institute of Education. ED 217-710.

Irvine, J. T. 1979. Formality and informality in communicative events. *American Anthropologist* 81:773–790.

———. 1986. Review of *Conversational routine: Explorations in standardized communication situations and prepatterned speech*, edited by Florian Coulmas. *Language in Society* 15:241–245.

Istomina, Z. M. 1975. The development of voluntary memory in pre-school age children. *Soviety Psychology* 13: 5–64.

Jackson, P. W. 1968. *Life in classrooms*. New York: Holt, Rinehart, and Winston.

Jordan, C. 1985. Translating culture: From ethnographic information to educational program. *Anthropology and Education Quarterly* 16:105–123.

———, R. Tharp, and L. Vogt. 1985. Compatibility of classroom and culture: General principles, with Navajo and Hawaiian instances. Pre-publication draft, Kamehameha Schools/Bishop Estate: Center for Development of Early Education.

Kamii, C., and R. deVries. 1980. *Group games in early education*. Washington, D.C.: National Association for the Education of Young Children.

Kamler, B. 1980. One child, one teacher, one classroom: The story of one piece of writing. *Language Arts* 57:680–693.

Keddie, N. 1971. Classroom knowledge. In *Knowledge and control: New directions in the sociology of education*, edited by M. F. D. Young. London: Collier Macmillan.

Kelly, A. In press. Gender differences in teacher-pupil interactions: A meta-analytic review. *Research in Education*.

Kleinfeld, J. 1975. Positive stereotyping: The cultural relativist in the classroom. *Human Organization* 34:269–274.

———. 1983. First do no harm: A reply to Courtney Cazden. *Anthropology and Education Quarterly* 14:282–287.

Kuhn, M. 1984. A discourse analysis of discussions in the college classroom. Doctoral dissertation, Harvard University. UMI #84-21, 215.

Kuhn, T. S. 1970. *The structure of scientific revolutions*, 2d ed. Chicago: University of Chicago Press.

Labov, W. 1972. The logic of nonstandard English. In W. Labov, *Language in the inner city: Studies in the black English vernacular*. Philadelphia: University of Pennsylvania Press.

———. 1982. Competing value systems in the inner-city schools. In *Children in and out of school: Ethnography and education*, edited by P. Gilmore and A. Glatthorn. Washington D.C.: Center for Applied Linguistics.

Lambert, W. E., R. C. Hodgson, R. C. Gardner, and S. Fillenbaum. 1960. Evaluational reactions to spoken languages. *Journal of Abnormal and Social Psychology* 60:44–51.

Lashley, K. S. 1961. The problem of serial order in behavior. In *Psycholinguistics: A book of readings*, ed. by S. Saporta. New York: Holt, Rinehart and Winston.

Lazarus, P., and S. L. Homer. 1981. Sharing time in kindergarten: Conversation or question-answer session? *Journal of the Linguistic Association of the Southwest* 4:76–1000. ED 194 930.

Leinhardt, G., C. Weidman, and K. M. Hammond. In press. Introduction and integration of classroom routines by expert teachers. *Curriculum Inquiry*.

Lemish, D., and M. L. Rice. 1986. Television as a talking picture book: A prop for language acquisition. *Journal of Child Language* 13:251–274.

Lemke, J. L. 1982. Classroom and communication of science. Final report to NSF/RISE, April. ED 222 346.

———. 1986. *Using language in classrooms*. Victoria, Australia: Deakin University Press.

———. In press. The language of classroom science. In *Locating learning across the curriculum*, ed. by C. Emihovich. Norwood, N.J.: Ablex.

Leont'ev, A. N. 1981. The problem of activity in psychology. In *The concept of activity in Soviet psychology*, edited by J. V. Wertsch. Armonk, N.Y.: M. E. Sharpe.

LeVine, R. A., and M. I. White. 1986. *Human conditions: The cultural basis of educational development*. New York: Routledge and Kegan Paul.

Levinson, S. 1979. Activity types and language. *Linguistics* 17:365–399.

Linguametrics Groups. N.d. Finding out/descubrimiento: Science and mathematics for primary age students. San Rafael, Calif.: Author.

Lipsky, M. 1980. *Street-level bureaucracy: Dilemmas of the individual in public services.* New York: Russell Sage Foundation.

Lucas, C., and D. Borders. 1987. Language diversity and classroom discourse. *American Educational Research Journal* 24: 119–141.

Lundgren, U. P. 1977. *Model analysis of pedagogical processes.* Stockholm: Stockholm Institute of Education, Department of Educational Research.

Malcolm, I. 1979. The West Australian Aboriginal child and classroom interaction: A sociolinguistic approach. *Journal of Pragmatics* 3:305–320.

———. 1982. Speech events of the Aboriginal classroom. *International Journal of Sociology of Language* 36:115–134.

Maldonado-Guzman, A. 1983. An ethnographic framework for analyzing differential treatment in the classroom. In *Social and cultural organization of interaction in classrooms of bilingual children,* edited by F. Erickson et al. Final report to the National Institute of Education.

———. 1984. A multidimensional ethnographic study of teachers' differential treatment of children in two Mexican American classrooms: The dynamics of teachers' consciousness and social stratification. Doctoral dissertation, Harvard University. UMI #84-21, 194.

Manuilenko, Z. V. 1975. The development of voluntary behavior in preschool-age children. *Soviet Psychology* 13(4):65–116.

Martin, G. 1987. A letter to Bread Loaf. *In Reclaiming the classroom: Teacher research as an agency for change,* edited by D. Goswami and P. S. Stillman. Upper Montclair, N.J.: Boynton/Cook Publishers.

McDermott, R. P. 1977. The ethnography of speaking and reading. In *Linguistic Theory: What can it say about reading,* edited by R. Shuy. Newark, Del.: International Reading Association.

———. 1978. Pirandello in the classroom: On the possibility of equal educational opportunity in American culture. In *Futures of exceptional children: Emerging structures,* edited by M. C. Reynolds. Reston, Va.: Council for Exceptional Children.

——— and K. Gospodinoff. 1979. Social contexts for ethnic borders and school failure. In *Nonverbal behavior: Application and cultural implications,* edited by A. Wolfgang. New York: Academic Press. Also in *Culture and the bilingual classroom: Studies in classroom ethnography,* edited by H. T. Trueba et al. Rowley, Mass.: Newbury House, 1981.

McHoul, A. 1978. The organization of turns at formal talk in the classroom. *Language in society* 7:182–213.

McHoul, A. W., and D. K. Watson. 1984. Two axes for the analysis of "commonsense" and "formal" geographical knowledge in classroom talk. *British Journal of Sociology of Education* 5:281–302.

McLeod, A. 1986. Critical literacy: Taking control of our own lives. *Language Arts* 63:37–50.

McNamee, G. D. 1979. The social interactive origins of narrative skills. *Quarterly Newsletter of the Laboratory of Comparative Human Cognition* (University of California at San Diego) 1 (4): 63–68.

———. 1980. *The social origin of narrative skills.* Doctoral dissertation, Northwestern University.

McNaughton, S., and T. Glynn. 1980. *Behavioral analysis of educational settings:*

Current research trends in New Zealand. New Zealand Association for Research in Education, Delta Research Monographs no. 3.

———. 1981. Delayed versus immediate attention to oral reading errors: effects on accuracy and self-correction. *Educational psychology* 1 (1): 57–65.

Mehan, H. 1978. Structuring school structure. *Harvard Educational Review* 48: 32–64.

———. 1979. *Learning lessons.* Cambridge, Mass.: Harvard University Press.

———. 1980. The competent student. *Anthropology and Education Quarterly* 11: 131–152.

Meier, T. 1985. The social dynamics of writing development: An ethnographic study of writing development and classroom dialogue in a basic writing class. Doctoral dissertation, Harvard University. UMI #86-01, 984.

Merritt, M. 1982a. Distributing and directing attention in primary classrooms. In *Communicating in the classroom,* edited by L. C. Wilkinson. New York: Academic Press.

———. 1982b. Repeats and reformulations in primary classrooms as windows on the nature of talk engagement. *Discourse Processes* 5:127–145.

——— and F. Humphrey. 1979. Teacher, talk and task: Communicative demands during individualized instruction time. *Theory into Practice* 18:298–303.

Michaels, S. 1981. "Sharing time": Children's narrative styles and differential access to literacy. *Language in Society* 10:423–442.

———. 1983. Influences on children's narratives. *Quarterly Newsletter of the Laboratory of Comparative Human Cognition* 5:30–34.

———. 1985a. Classroom processes and the learning of text editing commands. *Quarterly Newsletter of the Laboratory of Comparative Human Cognition* 7:70–79.

———. 1985b. Hearing the connections in children's oral and written discourse. *Journal of Education* 167:36–56.

———. 1986. Narrative presentations: An oral preparation for literacy with first graders. In *The social construction of literacy,* edited by J. Cook-Gumperz. Cambridge: Cambridge University Press.

——— and C. B. Cazden. 1986. Teacher/child collaboration as oral preparation for literacy. In *The acquisition of literacy: Ethnographic perspectives,* edited by B. B. Schieffelin. Norwood, N.J.: Ablex.

——— and M. Foster. 1985. Peer-peer learning: Evidence from a kid-run sharing time. In *Kid watching: Observing the language learner,* edited by A. Jagger and M. Smith-Burke. Urbana, Ill.: National Council of Teachers of English.

Miller, P., A. Nemoianu, and J. DeJong. 1986. Early reading at home: Its practice and meanings in a working-class community. In *The acquisition of literacy: Ethnographic perspectives,* edited by B. B. Schieffelin and P. Gilmore. Norwood, N.J.: Ablex.

Moffett, J., and B. J. Wagner. 1976. *Student-centered language arts and reading: A handbook for teachers.* Boston: Houghton Mifflin.

Moll, L. C., E. Estrada, E. Diaz, and L. M. Lopes. 1980. The organization of bilingual lessons: Implication for schooling. *Quarterly Newsletter of the Laboratory of Comparative Human Cognition* 2:53–58.

National Association of Teachers of English (NATE). N.d. *The first twenty-one years: 1963–1984.* Sheffield, England: NATE.

National Institute of Education. 1974. Conference on studies in teaching. Report of Panel 5: Teaching as a linguistic process in a cultural setting. ED 111 805.

Newman, D., P. Griffin, and M. Cole. 1984. Laboratory and classroom tasks: Social constraints and the evaluation of children's performance. In *Everyday cognition: Its development in social contexts*, edited by B. Rogoff and J. Lave. Cambridge, Mass.: Harvard University Press.

Ninio, A., and J. Bruner. 1978. The achievement and antecedents of labeling. *Journal of Child Language* 5:1–15.

Ochs, E. 1979a. Planned and unplanned discourse. In *Syntax and semantics*. Vol. 12. *Discourse and syntax*, edited by T. Given. New York: Academic Press.

———. 1979b. Transcription as theory. In *Developmental pragmatics*, edited by E. Ochs and B. B. Schieffelin. New York: Academic Press.

Osborne, R., and P. Freyberg. 1986. *Learning in science: The implications of children's science*. Portsmouth, N.H.: Heinemann.

Paley, V. 1981. *Wally's stories*. Cambridge, Mass.: Harvard University Press.

Palincsar, A. S. 1986. The role of dialogue in providing scaffolded instruction. *Educational Psychologist* 21:73–98.

Pearson, D. P., and M. C. Gallagher. 1983. The instruction of reading comprehension. *Contemporary Educational Psychology* 8:317–344.

Perret-Clermont, A. N. 1980. *Social interaction and cognitive development in children*. New York: Academic Press.

Philips, S. 1972. Participant structures and communicative competence: Warm Springs children in community and classroom. In *Functions of language in the classroom*, edited by C. B. Cazden et al. New York: Teachers College Press. Reprinted by Waveland Press, 1985.

———. 1983. *The invisible culture: Communication in the classroom and community on the Warm Springs Indian Reservation*. White Plains, N.Y.: Longman.

Piaget, J. 1950. *The psychology of intelligence*. London: Routledge and Kegan Paul.

———. 1959. *The language and thought of the child*. 3d ed. London: Routledge and Kegan Paul.

———. 1980. Foreword. In C. Kamii and R. DeVries, *Group games in early education*. Washington, D.C.: National Association for the Education of Young Children.

Pratt, M. L. 1977. *Toward a speech act theory of literary discourse*. Bloomington: Indiana University Press.

Purves, A. C., and W. C. Purves. 1986. Viewpoints: Cultures, text models, and the activity of writing. *Research in the Teaching of English* 20:174–197.

Quinn, C. N., H. Mehan, J. A. Levin, and S. D. Black. 1983. Real education in non-real time: The use of electronic message systems for instruction. *Instructional Science* 11: 313–327.

Ratner, N., and J. Bruner. 1978. Games, social exchange and the acquisition of language. *Journal of Child Language* 5:391–401.

Redfield, D. L., and E. W. Rousseau. 1981. A meta-analysis of experimental research on teacher questioning behavior. *Review of Educational Research* 51: 237–245.

Resnick, L. B. 1979. Theories and prescriptions for early reading instruction. In *Theory and practice of early reading*. Vol. 2, edited by L. B. Resnick and P. A. Weaver. Hillsdale, N.J.: Erlbaum.

———. 1985. Cognition and instruction: Recent theories of human competence and how it is acquired. In *Psychology and learning: The Masser lecture series*. Vol. 4, edited by B. L. Hammond. Washington, D.C.: American Psychological Association.

Robbins, A. 1977. Fostering equal-status interaction through the establishment of consistent staff behaviors and appropriate situational norms. Unpublished doctoral dissertation, Stanford University.

Romaine, Suzanne. 1984. *The language of children and adolescents*. New York: Basil Blackwell.

Rosen, C., and H. Rosen. 1973. *The language of primary school children*. Baltimore: Penguin.

Rosen, H. 1984. *Stories and meanings*. Sheffield, England: National Association for the Teaching of English. (Also Upper Montclair, N.J.: Boynton/Cook Publishers.)

———. 1985. Review of S. B. Heath, *Ways with words*. *Harvard Educational Review* 55: 448–456.

Rosenfeld, P., N. M. Lambert, and A. Black. 1985. Desk arrangement effects on pupil classroom behavior. *Journal of Educational Psychology* 77: 101–108.

Rowe, M. B. 1986. Wait time: Slowing down may be a way of speeding up! *Journal of Teacher Education* 37:43–50.

Ryan, J. 1974. Early language development: Towards a communicational analysis. In M. P. M. Richards, *The integration of a child into a social world*. London: Cambridge University Press.

Sacks, H., E. A. Schegloff, and G. Jefferson. 1974. A simplest systematics for the organization of turn-taking in conversation. *Language* 50:696–735.

Saint-Exupéry, A. 1943. *The little prince*. New York: Harcourt, Brace, Jovanovich.

Sapir, E. 1951. The unconscious patterning of behavior in society. In *Selected writings of Edward Sapir*, edited by D. G. Mandelbaum. Berkeley: University of California Press.

Schegloff, E. 1972. Notes on a conversational practice: Formulating place. In *Studies in social interaction*, edited by D. Sudnow. New York: Free Press. Also in *Language and social context*, edited by P. P. Giglioli. Harmondsworth, England: Penguin.

Schofield, J. W. 1982. *Black and white in school: Trust, tension, or tolerance?* New York: Praeger.

Schön, D. 1983. *The reflective practitioner: How professionals think in action*. New York: Basic Books.

Searle, D. 1984. Scaffolding: Who's building whose building? *Language Arts* 61: 480–483.

Shavelson, R. J., and P. Stern. 1981. Research on teachers' pedagogical thoughts, judgments, decisions, and behavior. *Review of Educational Research* 51:455–498.

Sheingold, K., J. Hawkins, and C. Char. 1984. "I'm the thinkist, you're the typist": Social life of classrooms. *Journal of Social Issues* 40:49–61.

Shulman, L. S. 1981. Educational psychology returns to school. Invited address, American Psychological Association, Los Angeles.

Shultz, J. 1979. It's not whether you win or lose, it's how you play the game: A microethnographic analysis of game-playing in a kindergarten/first grade classroom. In *Language, children and society*, edited by O. K. Garnica and M. L. King. New York: Pergamon.

―――. N.d. The child as student, the student as child. Ms., University of Cincinnati.

――― and S. Florio. 1979. Stop and freeze: the negotiation of social and physical space in a kindergarten/first grade classroom. *Anthropology and Education Quarterly* 10:166–181. ED 181 008.

Shuy, R. 1981. Learning to talk like teachers. *Language Arts* 58: 168–174.

Sinclair, J. McH., and R. M. Coulthard. 1975. *Towards an analysis of discourse: The English used by teachers and pupils.* London: Oxford University Press.

Slaughter, H. B., and A. T. Bennett. 1982. Methods of analyzing samples of elicited discourse in English and Spanish for determining student language proficiency. Final Report to the Inter-America Research Associates and the National Institute of Education.

Smitherman, G. 1977. *Talkin' and testifyin': The language of black America.* Boston: Houghton Mifflin. Reprint, Detroit: Wayne University Press, 1986.

Snow, C. E. 1977. Mothers' speech research: From input to interaction. In *Talking to children: Input and acquisition*, edited by C. E. Snow and C. A. Ferguson. New York: Cambridge University Press.

―――. 1983. Literacy and language: Relationships during the preschool years. *Harvard Educational Review* 53:165–189.

――― and C. A. Ferguson, eds. 1977. *Talking to children: Input and acquisition.* New York: Cambridge University Press.

――― and B. A. Goldfield. 1982. Building stories: The emergence of information structures from conversation. In *Analyzing discourse: Text and talk. Georgetown University Round Table on Language and Linguistics, 1981*, edited by D. Tannen. Washington, D.C.: Georgetown University Press.

Sowers, S. 1984a. Learning to write in a workshop: A study in grades one through four. In *Advances in writing research.* Vol. 1. *Children's early writing development*, edited by M. Farr. Norwood, N.J.: Ablex.

―――. 1984b. Theoretical perspectives on the writing conference. Qualifying Paper, Harvard Graduate School of Education.

Speier, M. 1976. The child as conversationalist: Some culture contact features of conversational interactions between adults and children. In *The process of schooling: A sociological reader*, edited by M. Hammersley and P. Woods. London: Routledge and Kegan Paul in association with The Open University.

Staton, J., R. Shuy, J. Kreeft, and L. Reed. 1983. *Analysis of dialogue journal writing as a communicative event.* Washington D.C.: Center for Applied Linguistics.

Stoddard, J. F. 1860. *Stoddard's American intellectual arithmetic.* New York: Sheldon.

Stodolsky, S. S., T. L. Ferguson, and K. Wimpelberg. 1981. The recitation persists, but what does it look like? *Journal of Curriculum Studies* 13:121–130.

Streeck, J. 1983. *Social order in child communication: A study in microethnography.* Amsterdam and Philadelphia: John Benjamins.

―――. 1984. Embodied contexts, transcontextuals, and the timing of speech acts. *Journal of Pragmatics* 8:113–137.

Stubbs, M. 1976. Keeping in touch: Some functions of teacher-talk. In *Explorations in classroom observation*, edited by M. Stubbs and S. Delamont. London: John Wiley. Revised version, chap. 3 in Stubbs 1983.

———. 1983a. *Discourse analysis: The sociolinguistic analysis of natural language*. Chicago: University of Chicago Press.

———. 1983b. *Language, schools and classrooms*. London: Methuen.

——— and S. Delamont, eds. 1976. *Explorations in classroom observation*. London: John Wiley.

——— and H. Hillier, eds. 1983. *Language, schools and classrooms: A reader*. London: Methuen.

Tannen, D. 1981. Review of H. Mehan, *Learning lessons. Language in society* 10:274–278.

Tharp, R. G., C. Jordan, G. E. Speidel, K. H.-P. Au, T. W. Klein, R. P. Calkins, K. C. M. Sloat, and R. Gallimore. 1984. Product and process in applied developmental research: Education and the children of a minority. *Advances in Developmental Psychology* 3:91–144.

Tizard, B. 1986. The care of young children: Implications of recent research. London: Institute of Education, Thomas Coram Research Unit Working and Occasional Papers.

——— and M. Hughes. 1984. *Young children learning*. Cambridge, Mass.: Harvard University Press.

Tobin, K. 1986. Effects of teacher wait time on discourse characteristics in mathematic and language arts classes. *American Educational Research Journal* 23: 191–200.

Tracy, K. 1984. Staying on topic: An explication of conversational relevance. *Discourse Processes* 7:447–464.

Trujillo, C. M. 1986. A comparative examination of classroom interactions between professors and minority and non-minority college students. *American Educational Research Journal* 23:629–642.

Vygotsky, L. S. 1962. *Thought and language*. Cambridge, Mass.: MIT Press.

———. 1978. *Mind in society: The development of higher psychological processes*. Cambridge, Mass.: Harvard University Press.

———. 1981. The genesis of higher mental functions. In *The concept of activity in Soviet psychology*, edited by J. V. Wertsch. Armonk, N.Y.: M. E. Sharpe.

Walker, R. 1978. Pine City. In *Case studies in science education*. Vol. 1. *The case reports*, edited by R. E. Stake and J. A. Easley. Urbana-Champaign: Univ. of Illinois, Center for Instructional Research and Curriculum Evaluation.

——— and C. Adelman. 1976. Strawberries. In *Explorations in classroom observation*, edited by M. Stubbs and S. Delamont. New York: John Wiley and Sons.

——— and I. Goodson. 1977. Humour in the classroom. In *School experience: Explorations in the sociology of education*, edited by P. Woods and M. Hammersley. London: Croom Helm.

Waller, W. 1932. *The sociology of teaching*. New York: John Wiley.

Watson, K., and R. Young. 1980. Teacher reformulations of pupil discourse. *Australian Review of Applied Linguistics* 3:37–47.

———. 1986. Discourse for learning in the classroom. *Language Arts* 63:126–133.

Watson, K. A. 1972. The rhetoric of narrative structure: A sociolinguistic analysis of stories told by part-Hawaiian children. Doctoral dissertation, University of Hawaii.

Watson-Gegeo, K. A., and S. T. Boggs. 1977. From verbal play to talk-story: The role of routines in speech events among Hawaiian children. In *Child discourse*, edited by S. Ervin-Tripp and C. Mitchell-Kernan. New York: Academic Press.

—— and D. W. Gegeo. 1985a. The social world of Kwara'ae children: Acquisition of language and values. In *Children's language and children's world*, edited by J. Cook-Gumperz and W. Corsaro.

—— and D. W. Gegeo. 1985b. Calling out and repeating: Two key routines in Kwara'ae children's language acquisition. In *Language acquisition and socialization across cultures*, edited by E. Ochs and B. B. Schieffelin. New York and Cambridge (England)-Cambridge University Press.

Watson, R. 1985. Toward a theory of definitions. *Journal of Child Language* 12: 181–197.

Wells, G. 1986. *The meaning makers: Children learning language and using language to learn*. Portsmouth, N.H.: Heinemann.

Wertsch, J. V. 1979. From social interaction to higher psychological processes: A clarification and application of Vygotsky's theory. *Human Development* 22: 1–22.

——. 1984. The zone of proximal development: Some conceptual issues. In Children's learning in the "zone of proximal development," edited by B. Rogoff and J. V. Wertsch. *New Directions for Child Development*, 23.

——. 1985. *Vygotsky and the social formation of mind*. Cambridge: Cambridge University Press.

—— and C. A. Stone. 1985. The concept of internalization in Vygotsky's account of the genesis of higher mental functions. In *Culture, communication and cognition: Vygotskian perspectives*, edited by J. V. Wertsch. Cambridge: Cambridge University Press.

White, M. A. 1974. Is recitation reinforcing? *Teachers College Record* 76:135–142.

Wilcox, K. 1982. Differential socialization in the classroom: Implications for equal opportunity. In *Doing the ethnography of schooling: Educational anthropology in action*, edited by G. Spindler. New York: Holt, Rinehart, and Winston.

Wilkinson, L. C., and C. B. Marrett. 1985. *Gender influences in classroom interaction*. New York: Academic Press.

Willes, M. J. 1983. *Children into pupils: A study of language in early schooling*. Boston: Routledge and Kegan Paul.

Willis, P. E. 1977. *Learning to labour: How working class kids get working class jobs*. Farnborough, England: Saxon House.

Wong, P. and S. McNaughton. 1980. The effects of prior provision of context on the oral reading proficiency of a low progress reader. *New Zealand Journal of Educational Studies* 15:169–175.

Woolfolk, A., and D. Brooks. 1983. Nonverbal communication in teaching. In *Review of research in education*. Vol. 10, edited by E. Gordan. Washington D.C.: American Educational Research Association.

—— and D. M. Brooks. 1985. Beyond words: The influence of teachers' nonverbal behaviors on students' perceptions and performance. *Elementary School Journal* 85:513–528.

Yanguas, M. J. 1980. The social parameters involved in language choice and preference among working-class Puerto Ricans in the Cambridge area. Unpublished honors thesis, Harvard/Radcliffe College.

Young, R. E. 1980. The controlling curriculum and the practical ideology of teachers. *Australia/New Zealand Journal of Sociology* 16:62–70.

Acknowledgments

(Continued from page iv.)

Chapter 7: Excerpts from Elise Forman, narratives of experimental sessions with Bruce and George, *The role of collaboration in problem solving with children*, doctoral dissertation, Harvard University, 1981. Reprinted by permission of the author.

Chapter 8: Excerpt from unpublished manuscript by J. L. Lemke, "The language of classroom science teaching." Reprinted by permission of the author.

Chapter 9: Excerpts from C. B. Cazden, "Language in education: variation in the teacher-talk register." In J. Alatis and R. Tucker (eds.), *Language in Public Life* (Washington, D.C.: Georgetown University Press, 1979), pp. 144–62. Reprinted by permission of the publisher.

Chapter 10: Excerpts from C. B. Cazden, "English for academic purposes: The student talk register," *English education* 19:1 (1987). © 1987 by the National Council of Teachers of English. Reprinted by permission of the publisher.

Subject Index

Affect, expressions of, 168
Appropriation, 26, 115
Attention
  of children, 19, 22, 50
  and event structure, 47–48
  in reading groups, 92
  in service-like events, 63
  of teacher, 19
Audience, of teacher and peers, 26, 188–89

Back-channels
  as metalinguistic comment, 66
  in peer groups, 144–46
  in writing conferences, 63–66
Bilingual discourse
  assessment, 93
  code switching, 178—79
  group work, 141–42
  reading instruction, 84
  teacher-talk register, 170–79

Changes in classroom discourse
  in children's communicative
    competence, 45–47
  in Heath's work, 69–71
  in KEEP, 71–72, 95
  limitations of research on, 69, 79 n. 35
  in sharing time, 27 n. 2, 94
  strategies for, 95–96
  in wait time, 60–61
  in writing conferences, 63–66
Chavrusa, 147
Classroom management, and discourse
    structure, 48–49, 52 n. 24, 160–61
Collaboration, discourse as, 14, 85–86,
    91–94, 146. See also Negotiation
Comembership, 169
Communicative competence
  of children, 45–47, 183–96 passim
  of teacher, 44–46, 159–81 passim
Computers
  computer-assisted instruction, 96–97
  diffusion of word processing skills,
    139–41

Author Index

227